Securing India's Maritime Neighbourhood:

Challenges and Opportunities

Securing India's Maritime Neighbourhood:
Challenges and Opportunities

Editors

Vice Admiral Pradeep Chauhan, AVSM & Bar, VSM, IN (Retd.)

Commodore R. Seshadri Vasan, IN (Retd.)

Rishi Athreya

Vij Books India Pvt Ltd

New Delhi

Published by

Vij Books India Pvt Ltd
(Publishers, Distributors & Importers)
2/19, Ansari Road
Delhi – 110 002
Phones: 91-11-43596460, 91-11-47340674
Mobile: 98110-94883
e-mail: contact@vijpublishing.com
web: www.vijbooks.com

First Published : 2020
ISBN: 978-93-89620-33- 7 (Paperback)
ISBN: 978-93-89620-64- 1 (ebook)

Contents

Foreword

With its extensive coastline of 7,516.6 kilometres, India lies at the junction of the busy International Shipping Lanes (ISLs) that criss-cross the Indian Ocean, and this fact shapes much of our maritime-security perspective. In terms of trade-flows, the Indian Ocean Region (IOR) contains three of the world's busiest and most critical choke-points (viz., the Strait of Hormuz, the Strait of Bab-el-Mandeb, and, the Strait of Malacca), through which about 80 per cent of the world's seaborne goods pass. It is, therefore, utterly unsurprising that India has a strong and abiding interest in ensuring that the freedom of navigation, underpinned by an internationally-accepted rules-based order at sea, is maintained in this part of the global 'maritime common'. India has an enormous stake in suppressing any and all threats to this internationally-accepted rules-based order at sea, and, consequently, in promoting stability and prosperity in its maritime neighbourhood. Towards these ends, a comprehensive understanding of India's maritime interests, a thorough knowledge of the United Nations Law of the Sea (UNCLOS) and allied legal instruments such as the Convention on Suppression of Unlawful Activities at Sea (SUA), and, the opportunities, risks and challenges that arise in the application of these instruments of international law to India's neighbourhood, are obvious necessities. The 39[1] littoral nations of the Indian Ocean Region (IOR) form India's 'Immediate' and 'Proximate' maritime neighbourhood constitute an intricate web of interlinked national and regional outlooks and national interests, whose inherent complexity is exacerbated by the moves and countermoves of major extra-regional maritime powers and multinational maritime groupings. These include, *inter alia*, the USA, the EU, and, most strikingly, China.

---

1 **West Asian Littoral: 11** (Bahrain, Iran, Iraq, Israel, Jordan, Kuwait, Oman, Qatar, Saudi Arabia, UAE Yemen); **East African Littoral: 14** (Comoros, Djibouti, Egypt, Eritrea, France, Kenya, Madagascar, Mauritius, Mozambique, Somalia, South Africa, Sudan, Tanzania); **South Asian Littoral: 7** (Bangladesh, India, Maldives, Pakistan, Seychelles, Sri Lanka, UK; **SE Asian and Australian Littoral: 7** (Australia, Indonesia, Malaysia, Myanmar, Singapore, Thailand, Timor Leste)

Whether or not China poses a direct threat to India, and, over what timeframe, are matters that are moot. However, the fact that China's geopolitical moves within the Indian Ocean constitute a risk that India must factor in the maritime manifestations of its own geopolitics is beyond argument. It is highly unlikely that China is actively seeking to surround India. However, the fact nevertheless remains that as China executes her geoeconomic strategies, — typified by her ambitious Belt-and-Road (BRI) formulation — India is most certainly *getting* surrounded. India's consequent geopolitical constriction is no small matter and is something against which it must develop a range of comprehensive and long-term strategies of its own. The centrality afforded by Beijing to the CPoKEC (China-'Pak-occupied-Kashmir' Economic Corridor) lends great urgency to this process.

In the prime-ministerial articulation of the concept of SAGAR — Security and Growth for All in the Region — India has the perfect foil to China's 'extractive' model of geoeconomic activity. However, Indian strategists are seldom able to recognise that SAGAR is a concept and is not, in and of itself, a 'strategy'. What SAGAR does is to spawn a number of maritime-strategies and it is these that need to be examined critically and holistically. Any serious examination of these strategies must necessarily rest on the foundational understanding that the term 'security' encompasses multiple dimensions that far exceed 'military security' alone and the term 'maritime' is far more than merely a navy-coast guard amalgam. To provide a structural-framework of context and content to this concept of SAGAR, India has been actively seeking to leverage the enormous potential of the Indian Ocean Rim Association (IORA). Any holistic-security structure must have at least three layers: a 'conceptual' layer (here represented by SAGAR), a 'political' layer (here represented by IORA), and, an 'Executive' layer that will actually do the doing (best represented by the Indian Ocean Rima Association [IONS]). The mechanisms by which the executive layer hones its skills so as to optimally execute the political imperatives, which themselves emanate from conceptual clarity about SAGAR, include the activities undertaken by sub-groupings of the IONS, as also the newly established MILAN multinational naval exercise — the inaugural edition of which was to be held off Visakhapatnam in March 2020.

While all these 'Track-1' formulations are underway, a continuous process of long-term analysis at the strategic and operational levels is critical if we are to avoid flash-in-the-pan judgements and the accompanying momentary expressions of either exultation of despair. This is squarely the job that 'Track-2' structures must perform — and perform well. In this regard, it is heartening to note that the National Maritime Foundation (NMF), in close cooperation with the Chennai Centre for China Studies (C3S) and with the willing-support of the Indian Navy and the Indian Coast Guard, had organised an excellently-conducted and well-attended symposium on the theme, ***"Securing India's Maritime Neighbourhood — Challenges and Opportunities"***, in Chennai, on March 28 2019. Participants included a whole galaxy of luminaries from the serving and veteran echelons of the Indian Armed Forces, the diplomatic community, maritime industry, doyens of Indian academia, and distinguished personalities from the Fourth Estate. A number of facets of seminal importance to national security were addressed in the conference. These included conceptual, geopolitical, economic, environmental and technological issues. At the helm of this initiative was Commodore R Seshadri Vasan, IN (Retd), who heads the C3S and is also the Regional Director (Tamil Nadu) of the NMF. He is deserving of high praise and much commendation for this highly successful endeavour, which is only the latest in a long string of excellent initiatives taken by him over the past several years.

I am delighted to find that the C3S and the NMF have compiled the papers into a compendium for wider dissemination of the excellent ideas and analyses that were on display during the conference. I am certain that the contents of this compendium will prove extremely useful to policy makers, practitioners and scholars alike.

Vice Admiral Pradeep Chauhan
AVSM & Bar, VSM, IN (Retd)
Director-General, NMF

Introduction

Since India is a peninsular country, maritime security is one of the core components of its national security. There are a number of traditional and non-traditional threats in this context. This book is a compilation of papers presented at a day-long conference organised in Chennai, on March 28 2019 by the Chennai Centre for China Studies (C3S) in partnership with the National Maritime Foundation (NMF) and the Department of Defence and Strategic Studies, University of Madras, on the theme, *"Securing India's Maritime Neighbourhood: Challenges and Opportunities"*.

The Concept Note provides a background of India's maritime neighbourhood and an outline of the issues addressed in the conference.

Chapter One contains the 'Keynote Address', by Vice Admiral Chauhan. It touches upon International Relations theory and offers a refreshingly different approach to the concept of geopolitics, applying this to India's maritime interests.   It goes on to provide a typology of India's maritime neighbourhood, before concluding with an overview of emerging issues relevant to India's maritime neighbourhood.

The next chapter reproduces the 'Theme Address', which was delivered by Mr CV Ranganathan, former ambassador of India. It provides a rich overview of India's regional alliances in the Indo-Pacific, assesses the threats and challenges that India may face, and explains how neighbours and partners can be of assistance.

The third chapter comprises the 'Inaugural Address' by Mr BS Raghavan, and sets the tone for the compendium as a whole. It dwells upon the Indian Ocean Rim and the various countries that constitute it. Inter-State linkages, based upon culture, trade, and security, are discussed at some length.

Chapter Four, by Mr Rishi Athreya, delves into the role of maritime diplomacy in furthering India's maritime aspirations. in the IOR. It examines the concept of maritime diplomacy, and provides an overview of

India's initiatives in this regard. The chapter concludes with a way-ahead summary.

This is followed by a chapter on "China's Rise and her Expanding Footprint in India's Neighbourhood". In this chapter, Commodore Sushant Dam of the Indian Navy examines the challenges facing China, addressing both, the structural strengths and the concerns of the government of President Xi Jinping, and touches upon the policy initiatives taken by China to address these concerns.

Chapter Six focusses upon the commercial and military applications of the Maritime Silk Road. In it, Lt Gen SL Narasimhan, Indian Army (Retd), discusses the major foreign policy initiatives of China. He outlines the increasing sphere of influence of China, and discusses how China's focus has shifted from one centred upon geoeconomics to one that is focussed upon a more comprehensive perception of geopolitics.

The next chapter, by Gp Capt AV Chandrasekaran, IAF (Retd), addresses integrated coastal-security management after the 2008 terror-attack in Mumbai, and discusses measures for the enhancement of security. Towards this end, it provides a useful outline of military coordination and new technology. The chapter reviews residual drawbacks and provides recommendations for the way ahead.

The following chapter, titled, "Kautilya's Prescription and Relevance for India's Neighbourhood Management", by Maj Gen G Murali (Retd), examines International Relations Theory from the perspective of the classical Indian writer, Kautilya, perhaps more famously known as Chanakya. The application of these ancient concepts to the contemporary maritime relations makes for absorbing reading, with the author concluding that greater cooperation at all levels is the optimum answer to the Sino-Indian relationship.

Chapter Nine concentrates upon sustainable fisheries and 'Best Management Practices' within the Bay of Bengal. In this chapter, Dr Yugraj Singh Yadava, studies ecological and economic issues relevant to fisheries in the Bay of Bengal large Marine Ecosystem, extending from India to Indonesia. Once again, the recommendation is for increased institutional cooperation.

The next chapter, penned by Mr SS Bangara, Master Mariner, examines the mercantile marine as a force-multiplier for prosperity and security. His conclusion is that contrary to the occasional gloom-and-doom perception held in some sections, Indian shipping does, in fact, meet global standards, and contributes very significantly to the economy.

In the following chapter, titled, "BIMSTEC and MAUSAM: India's Answers to China's Maritime Silk Route", Dr Binoda Kumar Mishra discusses India's relations with South East Asia. The author concludes that cultural ties with the region need to be systematically leveraged.

The penultimate chapter, authored by Mr Rahul Karan Reddy, focusses upon China's forays into the Indian Ocean, ostensibly to execute anti-piracy operations. He critically examines the role and deployment-pattern of the PLA Navy in the region, concluding that military diplomacy is giving China a presence in the IOR without apparently compromising sovereignty of smaller countries.

The final chapter contains the Valedictory Address by Mr S Paramesh, Inspector General, Indian Coast Guard. It provides an excellent overview of this very important armed maritime force, and its enormous contribution in ensuring that India's responses to the several maritime challenges that confront it are robust and that the policies formulated towards this end are comprehensive and coherent. Emphasising the criticality of a peaceful periphery, he highlights the roadmap and initiatives that India has adopted to very good effect.

Conference Concept Note

With the growing influence of regional and extra-regional powers in the littoral States within the Indian Ocean Region, there is an overarching imperative for India to re-evaluate its maritime policy-options. As a peninsular country, maritime security is one of the core components of India's national security. On the one hand, maritime prosperity, which is intrinsically linked to maritime security, includes developmental facets such as trade, shipbuilding, the exploration and sustainable harnessing of marine resources, law-enforcement, and the preservation of marine life. On the other, maritime prosperity is inextricably related to the politico-military-strategic dimension wherein the effort is to preserve the State's long-term strategic interests. Hence the term 'maritime security' in all its facets assumes enormous significance for all maritime nations.

The Indian Ocean Region is the third largest water body in the world, and is strategically crucial for India's security. More than 80 per cent of world's seaborne trade passes along the International Shipping Lanes (ISLs) that crisscross the Indian Ocean around India. The chokepoints located to the west and east of India provide access to and from the Indian Ocean for India and its surrounding countries to serve their respective economies.

India has an extensive coastline of 7,516 km and several hundred islands, largely but not exclusively concentrated upon the Lakshadweep island-group in the west, and the Andaman and Nicobar Islands in the east. India's Exclusive Economic Zone is 2.02 million square kilometres[1]. Over 95% by volume and 75% by value of India's external trade is transported by sea, along the ISLs, which are, indeed, the arteries or lifelines of the world.[2] India faces many challenges in its maritime neighbourhood and there is a pressing need to understand both the challenges and opportunities as India dreams of being a reckonable regional maritime power, thereby contributing to stability and security in the region.

The Indian Ocean Region is a rich source of minerals such as nickel, cobalt, iron, manganese, copper, iron, zinc, tin, silver, and gold, sizeable quantities of all of which are present in the seabed. Indian Ocean coastal sediments are also important sources of titanium, zirconium, etc.[3] This region also accounts for 15 per cent of the world's commercial fishing and aquaculture.[4] Living resources and untapped gas- and oil-resources are additional drivers of increasing competition in the IOR, leading to a series of power plays by State-actors as well as non-State ones.

The IOR is home to 39 nations and is a crucial source of income in their revenue generating capability. These 39 nations form India's adjacent-, proximate- and extended neighbourhood. Not only does the IOR contain numerous international shipping lanes that are essential for global trade but it is also home to three of the most critical chokepoints for trade, through which about 80 per cent of world's seaborne trade in oil passes.[5]

40 per cent of this trade in oil passes through the Strait of Hormuz, 35 per cent through the Strait of Malacca and eight per cent passes through the Strait of Bab el-Mandab. Given the criticality of safety of the region's ISLs and chokepoints, India, which is central to the IOR, needs to lead initiatives for a better framework to sustain connectivity, cooperation and security of the region[6].

This growing significance of the Indian Ocean Region has resulted in a regional power-play dynamic in the IOR, in which the two major players, India and China, are competing for greater influence. Traditionally, India, owing to its strategic geographical position, has been the major regional player in the IOR. The Mumbai terror attacks of November 2008, ('26/11') by LeT-trained terrorists, exposed the several chinks in the Indian armour and led to the adoption by India of a totally fresh approach to coastal and ocean security initiatives.

The maritime neighbourhood has historically remained friendly to India due to cultural and historical linkages that have persisted over centuries. India has, by and large, enjoyed a benevolent relationship with the neighbourhood States in the region and, despite occasional differences, has made sincere efforts to contribute to their development in a meaningful manner. These optimum relations are now being challenged by an expansive China that has its sights set on the Indian Ocean Region. China has, in the recent past, through massive investment spending, focussed port-development projects, and, collaborative naval equipment-transfers, managed to erode the traditional Indian influence. All these investments fall under China's larger economic and strategic designs in the Indian Ocean, and have been referred to by several US and Indian analysts as the "string of pearls". As the largest democracy in the world and the fastest growing economy, India has good reason to be concerned about the inroads that China is making through its ability to spend to serve its long term economic and strategic interests.

China considers that India's considerably large naval presence in the Indian Ocean poses a threat to its principal shipping lanes. In order to ensure its economic and energy security, China has embarked on an agenda to construct commercial support-bases in the littoral States that rim the Indian Ocean or lie within it as island-States, many of which are likely to be later leveraged as military ports. These projects include the building of Hambantota Port in Sri Lanka, which is now saddled with such enormous Chinese debt that the State has had to lease it out to Chinese State-controlled entities for a period of 99 years; and, the building of Gwadar port in Pakistan, as part of the China-Pakistan-Economic-Corridor (CPEC). Similar to the case in Sri Lanka, Pakistan has already handed over the operation of Gwadar port to China for a period of 40 years.

In Maldives, China is funding several mega infrastructure projects, including the Friendship Bridge linking Male to Hulhule Island, and the Ihavandhippolhu integrated project — also known as the iHavan project. In August 2017, in view of this increasing commercial relationship between the two countries, Maldives permitted three Chinese warships to dock in Male. Luckily for India, the recent election has resulted in an India-friendly government that is wary of Chinese investments and the possibility of being led into a debt trap.

In Myanmar, China is investing in several projects, one of the most prominent ones being the Kyaukpyu Deepwater Port and a railway line connecting Kunming, the capital of Yunnan province of China, to Ruili.

In Bangladesh, China has promised an investment of US$ 24 billion in infrastructure in Bangladesh, which will partially underwrite the Belt and Road Initiative. The recent elections in Bangladesh have brought back an India-friendly government, which eases the pressure on India in terms of managing its neighbourhood relations. Maldives, Pakistan and Myanmar have already established a Free Trade Area with China.

These economic measures, incorporating investments and trade, under the rubric of the Maritime Silk Road, provide China with future leverage as it increases its engagement in India's neighbourhood. China has been able to establish interdependencies between itself and various South Asian states, and has ultimately subjected some of these nations to a debt-trap. These projects have allowed China to increase its presence along the region's key ISLs, while guaranteeing China's access to developing markets and international trade.

These investments are not just part of China's economic strategy but are also an essential element of its 'chequebook diplomacy'. Through these financial investments, China seeks to ensure greater influence in India's neighbourhood. The investments have provided China with access into the political structures of these States, thereby giving Beijing a bigger say in their political decision-making. Such influence has been quite discernible in the elections of Sri Lanka, Pakistan, and now, increasingly, in Maldives — a country that is considered a natural extension of India's security perimeter. In India's favour, the internal dynamics of Maldives has led to a friendly government in Male that is sensitive to New Delhi's concerns.

This economic investment has great geopolitical implications for India. In the Indian strategic circle, China's aggressive maritime engagements impinge on India's interests in the IOR. The shape of things to unfold in the neighbourhood started to become visible when, in January of 2018, during a time of political turmoil in Maldives, a Chinese naval flotilla — a Type 52D destroyer, the *Changsha*; a Type 54 frigate, the *Hengyang*; a replenishment ship, the *Luomahu*, and, a large amphibious-support ship, the *Jinggangshan* appeared in the eastern reaches of the Indian Ocean, signalling a warning to India to desist from getting involved in the political process in the Maldives. In 2018 alone, fourteen Chinese submarines have been spotted in the Indian Ocean Region.

This is not the only concern for India in the IOR. India's maritime dispute with Pakistan, which involves the demarcation of the bilateral maritime boundary extending from the Sir Creek, is a persistent reminder of the several bones of contention between the two States. Although the creek has little military value, the angular alignment of its seaward extension holds immense economic significance. Much of the seabed in this area is rich in oil and gas, and control over the creek could have a huge bearing on the energy potential of each nation. Likewise, India has issues with Sri Lanka related to fishing activities in the Palk Bay, most especially on and off Kachchathivu Island.

The IOR faces certain other challenges as well. Rising levels of pollution increasingly threaten the Indian Ocean's fisheries. Coastal fisheries are particularly vulnerable to agricultural run-off, the dumping of sewage, and, construction activities. Deepwater fishing practices, such as bottom trawling, have seriously damaged the ecosystems of continental shelves and slopes by levelling the sea bed, kicking up clouds of sediment, destroying coral, and generating huge amounts of bycatch (species that are swept-up in fishing nets, but discarded because they lack commercial value). Meanwhile, fishing gear that has been jettisoned or lost at sea continues to attract and ensnare fish for years after it is discarded. Linked to this are the increased incidences of Illegal Unreported and Unregulated fishing (IUU), which will challenge those pursuing fishing as a means of livelihood, as also law-enforcement agencies, who will need to be extra vigilant to prevent IUU. Further, the shipping lanes in the Indian Ocean are a main artery of the global energy trade, heightening the risk of oil spills as the demand for fossil-fuels increases in emerging economies throughout the region. As if these were not challenge enough, territorial conflicts, piracy in the western IOR, the refugee-influx from the eastern IOR, natural disasters, smuggling, maritime terrorism, illegal fishing, and the trafficking of humans and narcotics throughout the IOR, offer additional and extremely serious challenges to safety and security in the region.

India is conscious of the need to engage its maritime neighbourhood more proactively and has initiated a slew of measures to contribute to collective prosperity. It has articulated its vision in terms of SAGAR — an acronym for 'Security and Growth for All in the Region' — by which the region can meet the aforementioned challenges. SAGAR aims to enhance regional capacities to safeguard land and maritime territories and other interests; deepen economic and security cooperation in the littoral; promote collective action to deal with natural disasters and maritime threats like piracy, terrorism and emergent non-state actors; work towards sustainable regional development through enhanced collaboration; and, engage with countries beyond India's own shores with the aim of building greater trust and promoting respect for maritime rules, norms and the peaceful resolution of disputes[7].

Looking at the scale, scope, and multinational nature of maritime activities and challenges in the region, India has launched several initiatives to institutionalise maritime cooperation under the rubric of Maritime Domain Awareness (MDA). A recent development in this regard is the launching of an *Information Fusion Centre – Indian Ocean Region* (IFC-IOR), co-located with the Indian Navy's *Information Management and Analysis Centre* (IMAC), at Gurugram, within the National Capital Region (NCR). The IFC-IOR seeks to engage with partner nations and multinational maritime constructs so as to develop comprehensive maritime domain awareness and share information on vessels of interest.

India has also been nurturing the Indian Ocean Naval Symposium (IONS) — a voluntary regional initiative that seeks to increase maritime cooperation among navies and principal maritime-security agencies of the littoral States of the Indian Ocean Region by providing an open and inclusive forum for discussion of regionally relevant maritime issues. Under this initiative, the navies of 24 States have become full members of the IONS, while another eight are Observers. India is also a member of the Indian Ocean Region Association (IORA), an intergovernmental organisation that aims to build and expand understanding and mutually beneficial cooperation through a consensus-based, evolutionary and non-intrusive approach in the rapidly changing environment in the Indian Ocean Region. In addition, India is also a founding member of the Contact Group on Piracy and has actively participated in anti-piracy patrols in the Gulf of Aden and off the Horn of Africa since 2008. Further, India has undertaken joint EEZ patrols off the waters of Maldives, Seychelles, and Mauritius and has also played a major role in Humanitarian Assistance and Disaster Relief (HADR) in the Indian Ocean Region. Recently, India has also joined the 30-member Trans Regional Maritime Network (T-RMN), a move that will give the country access to information about ships passing through the Indian Ocean Region. India has also organised various mega-naval exercises, such as the 'MILAN Exercise of 2019', with a view to enhance regional cooperation by proliferating maritime good order amongst the various navies operating in the region. *However, how effective these arrangements are in ensuring safety and stability in the IOR is a question that is yet to be answered.* This query gains significance especially after the failure of SAARC to bring about substantive maritime cooperation within the region gave way for BIMSTEC to provide a larger framework to ensure connectivity and cooperation in the Bay of Bengal region. How these organisations are performing is yet to be fully evaluated.

Against this backdrop, the Chennai Centre for China Studies (C3S) is organising a day-along conference in partnership with the National Maritime Foundation (NMF) and the Department of Defence and Strategic Studies, University of Madras, on the theme, *"Securing India's Maritime Neighbourhood: Challenges and Opportunities"*. The conference aims to answer the following questions:

1. What are the pressing threats to India's maritime security in the context of China's emerging influence in India's maritime neighbourhood?

2. How should India prepare to counter the traditional and non-traditional challenges in the region?

3. How can India engage its maritime neighbours to carve out a shared destiny in the century of the seas?

4. Given the emphasis laid upon improved Maritime Domain Awareness (MDA), how can regional synergy between India and the littoral States of its neighbourhood best be achieved?

5. How effective have these regional arrangements and different forums for maritime security proved to be in securing the Indian Ocean Region?

6. What are the options on the way ahead for India to retain its strategic space in the Indian Ocean in the backdrop of China's assertive initiatives in India's maritime neighbourhood?

Endnotes

1   Annual Report 2011-2012, Ministry of Home Affairs, Government of India, New Delhi, 2012, p. 57.

2   Indian Navy, (2016), Ensuring Secure Seas, India's Maritime Security Strategy, p.25

3   Indian Navy, (2015), Indian Maritime Doctrine 2009, updated online version 2015, Naval Strategic Publication NSP. 1.1, Pg. 58

4   FAO, (2018), State of the World's Fisheries, Pg. 45

5   Indian Navy, (2016), Ensuring Secure Seas, India's Maritime Security Strategy, Pg. 24

6   Indian Navy, (2016), Ensuring Secure Seas, India's Maritime Security Strategy, Pg. 32

7   Indian Navy, (2016), Ensuring Secure Seas, India's Maritime Security Strategy, Pg. 23

Keynote Address

VAdm Pradeep Chauhan, AVSM & Bar, VSM, IN (Retd.)

Over the next several decades, India will either succeed in positioning itself as a major global power or it will fail. Which one of these alternatives comes to pass is to very largely be a function of just how dextrously India is able to build and exercise its comprehensive maritime power, and, how astutely it is able to plan and execute its geopolitical game-moves within the maritime domain. Maritime power is the ability of a nation-state to use its maritime space (the seas) for its own purposes while dissuading or deterring or denying others the use of the seas in ways that are to its disadvantage. This ability manifests itself in three basic sets of cognitive and physical activities, namely, 'political', 'economic' and 'military' which, taken together, form the bulk of what is termed 'geopolitics'.

While considering geopolitics, it is a major conceptual error to place geopolitics, geoeconomics and geostrategy and the same hierarchical level. The following schematic offers a cogent depiction of the correct typology of geopolitics.

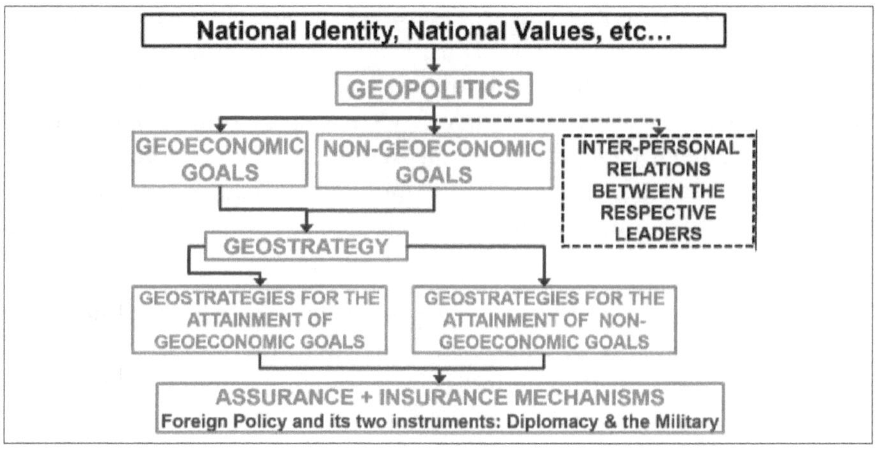

Like other countries, India's geopolitics, too, is a function of its pursuit of a set of 'geoeconomic goals' and a set of 'non-geoeconomic goals', all of which New Delhi seeks to attain. In both cases its efforts are either helped or hindered by the interpersonal relationships that exist between the Indian leadership and those of other nations with whom India interacts in competitive, collaborative or cooperative terms. It should be noted that the two instruments of foreign policy, namely, diplomacy and the military (as also logistic-support structures for the military such as overseas bases) are major components of the 'assurance and insurance mechanisms' depicted in the foregoing schematic.

It is very important to recognise that in geopolitics, the prefix 'geo' in 'geo-politics', 'geo-economics', 'geo-strategy', etc., refers to a country's *strategic geography*, i.e., the core spatial assumptions underpinning its grand strategy. The question is raised, on what actually is this relatively-unfamiliar animal: 'Strategic Geography'? How does it differ from 'real Geography'? If one were to take a chart or map that depicts 'real' geography and then place upon it a set of coordinates defined by specific latitudes and longitudes, and, within the area that has been so bounded or enclosed, if one were to then give special focus — at the national-level — in terms of the planning and execution of one's geopolitical strategies, this enclosed or bounded area would define one's 'strategic geography'. Obviously, the strategic geography of one country, say India for instance, can hardly be expected to be the same as that of, say, Maldives, or, for that matter, the USA. As such, every geopolitically defined 'region' is an artificial, manmade construct, whose defining-boundaries can be (and often are) different for different geopolitical players. This is as true of the 'Indo-Pacific' as it is of any other 'region'. (For sheer convenience, if for no other reason, it is necessary to give a name to the one's strategic geography — in the instant case, this is the 'Indo-Pacific'). Thus, it is perfectly natural for different states to have different strategic boundaries and it is imprudent to unduly obsess over why the limits of one country's conceptualisation of the 'Indo-Pacific' (its strategic geography) are not identical to that of another. Insofar as India is concerned, Prime Minister Modi has unequivocally described the Indo-Pacific as ranging *"from the shores of Africa to the shores of the Americas"*[1]

In discussing maritime challenges in India's 'neighbourhood', it is clearly necessary to provide some specificity to the term 'maritime neighbourhood' by identifying India's 'maritime neighbours' which, taken collectively, would define India's 'maritime neighbourhood' and whose 'stability' contributes to the maritime facets of India's core national interest.

A common but grossly-erroneous approach is to attempt to transpose to the maritime realm, 'continental' thinking in terms of what constitutes 'neighbours'. On the one hand, the provisions of the United Nation Law of the Seas, 1982, with the corresponding pieces of Indian domestic legislation[2], make at least two types of Indian 'maritime boundaries' relevant to this discussion. These are the maritime boundaries between Indian and adjacent 'Territorial Seas', and, the maritime boundaries between Indian and adjacent 'Exclusive Economic Zones (EEZs)'.

In discussing boundaries, it is, of course, important to be clear about the terms 'Delimitation', 'Demarcation' and 'Delineation' that are associated with establishing and identifying boundaries — whether maritime ones or land-specific ones.[3]

India's Immediate Maritime Neighbourhood

Thus, ***India's Immediate Maritime Neighbourhood*** comprises countries with which India shares either a common Territorial Sea boundary or a common Exclusive Economic Zone boundary — whether or not the afore-mentioned steps of delimitation, demarcation and delineation have been completed in their entirety:

Countries (alphabetically arranged) with which India Shares a Common Territorial Sea Boundary

1	Bangladesh	2	Myanmar	3	Pakistan	4	Sri Lanka

Countries (alphabetically arranged) with which India Shares a Common EEZ Boundary

1	Bangladesh	2	Indonesia	3	Maldives	4	Myanmar
5	Pakistan	6	Sri Lanka	7	Thailand		

India's 'Proximate Neighbourhood'

In addition to the foregoing there are a 'proximate' set of countries with whom India neither has a common 'Territorial Sea' border nor a common 'Exclusive Economic Zone' one, but whose politico-military stability nevertheless has an immediate and significant impact upon the preservation, pursuit, promotion, and protection of India's core national interest. Within a maritime context, India's 'Proximate Neighbourhood' would almost certainly include the following (alphabetically-arranged) listing:

1	Bahrain	2	Bangladesh	3	Comoros	4	France
5	Djibouti	6	Indonesia	7	Iran	8	Iraq
9	Kuwait	10	Madagascar	11	Malaysia	12	Maldives
13	Mauritius	14	Myanmar	15	Pakistan	16	Oman
17	Qatar	18	Saudi Arabia	19	Seychelles	20	Singapore
21	Sri Lanka	22	Thailand	23	UAE	24	Yemen

India's 'Extended Maritime Neighbourhood'

India's *'Extended Maritime Neighbourhood'* would comprise those countries whose geographic position within the 'Indo-Pacific' oceanic expanse directly impacts Indian overseas trade and hence the country's core national interest.

In *addition* to the three listings given above, this would include the countries of the Red Sea and East African littorals, as also the ten constituents of ASEAN, and the overall tabulation would now be as follows:

1	Bahrain	2	Bangladesh	3	Brunei	4	Cambodia
5	Comoros	6	Djibouti	7	Egypt	8	Eritrea
9	France	10	Indonesia	11	Iran	12	Iraq
13	Israel	14	Jordan	15	Kenya	16	Kuwait
17	Laos	18	Madagascar	19	Malaysia	20	Maldives
21	Mozambique	22	Myanmar	23	Pakistan	24	Philippines
25	Saudi Arabia	26	Singapore	27	Somalia	28	South Africa
29	Sri Lanka	30	Sudan	31	Tanzania	32	Thailand
33	Timor-Leste	34	Vietnam				

The criticality of Indonesia deserves special mention even though it needs little elaboration. This criticality stems from the geographic fact that Indonesia sits astride all the straits connecting the Indian and Pacific Oceans. Moreover, if Indonesia (the home to the world's largest Muslim population) and India (home to the third-largest Muslim population) can sing from the same sheet of music, any other state's ability to play the Islamic card against India anywhere will be severely limited.

India's Strategic Maritime Neighbourhood'

Finally, **'India's Strategic Maritime Neighbourhood'** would include, in addition to the foregoing listings, such coastal States that may or may not be geographically located within the Indo-Pacific littoral, but whose geostrategic 'game-plays' within the Indo-Pacific significantly impacts the economic, material, and societal well-being of the people of India. This criterion would bring in at least the following additional countries:

1	Australia	2	China	3	Japan	4	New Zealand
5	Russia	6	South Korea	7	UK	8	USA
9	14 x South Pacific Island nations						

In discussing the multifaceted nature of the several maritime challenges that India faces within its neighbourhood as just described, it is prudent to remember that the country's maritime policy is founded upon the 'core national interest' of India which, derived from the Constitution of India, is: *"to assure the material, economic and societal well-being of the people of India"*.

It is important to note that within this expression, the term 'societal' encompasses the various tangible and intangible forms, structures and processes (such as political systems, human development indices such as health, life-expectancy, eradication of poverty, education, as also more complex intangibles like the 'pursuit of happiness') that make-up India's body-politic. As such, the statement of India's core national interest does, indeed, encompass the human development of Indian 'society' at large.

Thus, even while retaining its moorings to the school of 'realism', this statement of India's core national interest adequately addresses the fact that economics is not the only factor in creating a high standard of living or the quality of life. Perhaps even more importantly, concentration upon the 'societal' well-being of India brings in a far more holistic understanding of 'security' than the traditionally accepted one.

Indeed, in times gone by, security used to be thought of only in terms of the defence of cartographic-territory within a state-system whose defining characteristic was an incessant competition for military superiority with other nation-states, all lying within a classic state of anarchy, largely devoid of superior or governing authority. Today, however, the world, including India, has swung around to a far more holistic approach. This changed approach finds its historical moorings in the famous "Common Security" report that had been authored as far back as 1980, by the "Independent Commission on Disarmament and Security Issues" chaired by the late Prime Minister of Sweden, Mr Olaf Palme. This report emphatically drew attention to alternative ways of thinking about peace and security by formally acknowledging that common security requires that people live in dignity and peace, that they have enough to eat and are able to find work and live in a world without poverty. While military security does, of course, continue to enjoy primacy for India, existing as it does in a world-system defined by Westphalian concepts of national sovereignty, new terms such as 'Non-Traditional Security' and 'Human Security', largely drawn from the 1994 Report of the UNDP, have made their way into maritime India's contemporary security-lexicon and lodged themselves within its collective security-consciousness. Maritime security is now firmly established within a new construct that incorporates military, political, economic societal and environmental dimensions, and recognises the many linkages between them.

Thus, challenges to human-security, such as religious extremism; international terrorism; drug and arms smuggling; demographic shifts — whether caused by migration or by other factors; human trafficking; environmental degradation; energy, food and water shortages; all now figure prominently as threats that are inseparable from military ones. These have led to the formulation of new concepts such as 'comprehensive security' and 'cooperative security'.

Contemporary India recognises that security issues need to be referenced more towards common interests rather than threats. At a regional level, it is these very 'human security' issues that have been mentioned above that constitute common 'interests'. It is a common regional interest to create and consolidate a region in which the comity of nations is both intrinsic and assured.... where every nation, big or small, is treated as an equal... where multiple options of governance are recognised as being functions of the independent choice of the people of each nation-state... where the people of every state of the region can live in dignity and peace... where poverty stands banished and prosperity sits in its place....

where the state protects the individual and the individual preserves the state in a symbiotic relationship designed to establish and spread stability across the region.... where malevolent non-state entities find neither spatial nor temporal room for manoeuvre.

India's 'holistic' security may be considered to be a function of two main features. The first comprises the policies, strategies, organisational-structures and the delivery-mechanisms that guide and shape her internal politics and determine her internal stability as a coherent geopolitical entity. The second feature consists of elements that define and shape India's interaction and interface with external structures — supranational and international organisations, nation-states, and, non-state entities, any of which may, at given points in time, be either supportive or inimical to India.

Narrowing down to 'maritime' security as a subset of national security as a whole, Shri Manmohan Singh, former Prime Minister of India, described the concept of 'maritime security' as a condition characterised by *"freedom from threats arising either in or from the sea."* Obviously, these threats might arise from natural causes or from manmade ones, or from the interplay of one with the other, as in the case of environmental degradation or global warming. The following figure depicts this typology.

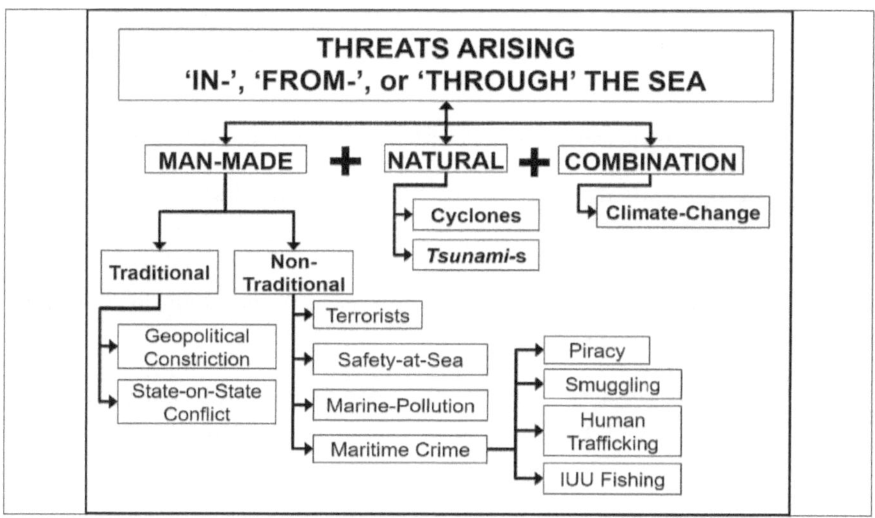

Figure 2

Source: Author

Insofar as the *targets* of such threats (arising from a *lack* of maritime-security) are concerned, these could be individuals themselves, or 'groupings' of individuals, such as societies and/or the nation-state as a whole. In some cases, such as the adverse security-impacts of climate-change, several states could be affected on a sub-regional, pan-regional, or even global level.

India's maritime security, in common with that of most other States, rests upon the foundational axiom that *'India wishes to use the seas for her own purposes — while dissuading, deterring and preventing others from using them in ways that are to India's disadvantage'.*

It is this very ability (to use the seas for her own purposes while dissuading, deterring and preventing others from using them in ways that are to her disadvantage) that denotes India's 'maritime power', which, of course, encompasses 'political', 'economic' and 'military' power, relevant to the use of the sea.

The military component of India's 'maritime power' is concentrated in an amalgam of the Indian Navy and Indian Coast Guard), as Naval Power. However, naval power should not be considered to be synonymous with maritime power. Indeed, maritime power includes a host of factors that are external to the navy and even the briefest mention only a few of these would be sufficiently indicative:

- The dependence of the nation upon the sea for its economic well-being.

- The maritime bent of mind of the government and of the people.

- The size and enterprise of the sea-faring population.

- The ship-building capability of the nation.

- The size, age, and condition of the nation's merchant fleet — both coastal, and foreign-going.

- The percentage of imports and exports being carried in national 'bottoms' (as opposed to being carried in foreign 'bottoms').

- The number, types, and functional efficiency of the nation's major and minor ports.

- The cargo-handling ability of the various major and minor ports, and the infrastructure for multi-modal transport of sea-borne goods.

- The state, size, and technological advancement of the coastal and deep-sea fishing fleets, and their geographic spread.

The nation's maritime canvas may thus be seen to be very large and fairly diffused in nature. Within this maritime canvas, *military* maritime power — largely embodied by the Navy (and to a lesser extent by the Coast Guard) — is the enabling instrument that allows all the other components of maritime power to be exercised— and, in some cases, even to exist. These are also the preventive instruments by which India dissuades, deters and prevents others from using the seas in ways that are to her disadvantage.

The 'reasons' for India desiring to use the seas in ways that are to her advantage while denying others the ability to use them in ways that are to her disadvantage collectively constitute India's 'Maritime Interests'. These flow from and also feed into the country's core national interest. The preservation, protection, pursuit and promotion of these maritime interests determine the contours of India's maritime strategy.

The consolidated plans by which each of India's maritime interests may best be preserved, promoted, pursued and protected — in times of peace, tension and or armed conflict — constitute India's maritime strategy.

In seeking to avoid the trap of *"defining vital interests too broadly"*, which has been accurately identified as *"the first step to strategic exhaustion"*,[4] it is necessary to be clear about India's maritime interests in order that that their preservation, promotion, pursuit and protection may logically lead to the enunciation of a coherent maritime strategy for India, particularly within the Indo-Pacific. The six principal maritime-interests of India, each of which simultaneously flows from and feeds-into the country's core national interest *(to assure the material, economic and societal wellbeing of the people of India)* are:

(1) Protection from sea-based threats to our territorial integrity.

(2) Ensuring stability in our maritime neighbourhood.

(3) Creation, development, and sustenance of a 'Blue' Ocean-Economy, incorporating:

(a) The preservation, promotion, pursuit and protection of offshore infrastructure and maritime resources within and beyond the Maritime Zones of India.

(b) The promotion, protection and safety of our Overseas and Coastal Seaborne Trade and our Sea Lines of Communication, including the ports that constitute the nodes of this trade.

(c) Support to Marine Scientific Research, including that in Antarctica and the Arctic.

(4) The provision of support — including succour and extrication-options — to our Diaspora.

(5) The provision of holistic maritime security ('human' security) — that is, freedom from threats arising 'in' or 'from' the sea.

(6) Obtaining and retaining a regionally favourable geopolitical maritime-position.

In positioning India's maritime strategy within the ambit of her grand strategy — whose very existence is a subject of some debate[5] — it is pertinent to note that India's maritime strategy as propounded here seeks to conform to the fundamental contours of India's grand strategy in that both adopt the classic *interests-based* approach as their foundation, without altogether discarding either the *international issues-based* approach or the *national values-based* approach.[6]

In contextualising the contemporary maritime strategy of India within a paradigm of Indian strategic thought, it is important to recognise Mr Kanti Bajpai's trifurcation of contemporary Indian strategic thinking into *"Nehruvians (followers of India's first prime minister), neoliberals and hyper-realists."*[7] In this formulation, the Nehruvian school affords centrality to inter-State communications — exemplified by diplomacy — as the principal determinant of geopolitical outcomes. The central tenet is that *"the greater the degree of communication and contact, the fewer the misunderstandings and misperceptions, and the greater the chances of stability, cooperation and peace."*[8]

Neoliberals, on the other hand, centre their geopolitical model upon the primacy of economics, holding that *"in an ever-globalizing world, trade, investment flows and technology are the keys to economic growth, internal social and political resilience, as well as relative national power."*[9] Hyper-realists view the world as an inherently competitive and dangerous place, *"in which power, force and war are the essence of international relations."* They hold that states exist in a state of anarchy and each state must necessarily engage in independent-, or collective-, or collaborative-geopolitics, in which it temporarily supports, or opposes, or allies, or aligns itself vis-à-vis other states so as to attain and sustain its national interests. Security, they aver, comes from strength — military strength, in particular — and the international order is nothing but a balance of power.

Obviously, these three schools of thought are not capable of being neatly stove-piped and a great deal of overlap exists between them. Interestingly, however, Lord Palmerston's views[10] — *"We have no eternal allies, and we have no perpetual enemies. Our interests are eternal and perpetual, and those interests it is our duty to follow"* —are as central to the hyper-realists' global construct as they are to that of the neoliberals. This is true of India's maritime strategy as well, which needs necessarily to be an amalgam of all three schools of Indian strategic thought, but with great importance — if not absolute centrality — being given to geo-economics and only a marginally lesser criticality being afforded to the attainment and retention of a favourable balance of power.

Since any strategy involves 'ends' and 'means' and 'ways',[11] and since the specific 'ends' (i.e., the objectives or goals) have been already determined to be the preservation, promotion, pursuit and protection of the maritime interests of India, it is necessary to undertake a time-sensitive analysis of the 'means' (i.e., resources that either are already available or must be generated in order to pursue the objectives) and the 'ways' (how these resources ought to be organised and applied).[12]

It is very important to recognise the *temporal* variable (i.e., time-sensitivity) in the development of this maritime strategy. There are two basic approaches that may be adopted.

- The first approach — one bedded in the present (the here and now) — is to assess the resources that are available to India and determine how these may best be utilised so that the degree or extent to which the desired ends can be achieved are deduced. This approach is typified by those who advocate that India must cut her coat according to her cloth, adjusting her ambitions (the desired ends) to the degree attainable by her available resources.

- The second approach — one bedded in the future — is to hold firm to the desired ends and then determine what resources are going to be required to achieve these ends — and to then create or obtain those resources, while multiplying the effect of those that are already available. In other words (and at the risk of seriously mangling the proverb/idiom), this second approach recommends that we bend all our efforts to obtain the cloth required to be cut so as to end up with the coat we desire.

The optimal approach to India's maritime strategy is, of course, an amalgam of both these, with their common bond being the 'ways' — i.e., the manner in which existing and future resources are prepared, honed and deployed. In identifying resources and determining their deployment, it would be a serious mistake to limit oneself to material wherewithal (capacity) alone. An unwavering concentration upon human resources that seeks to realise the enormous potential of intangibles such as determination, effort, ingenuity, innovation, efficiency, enthusiasm, competence, organisation, exemplarism, values, beliefs, empathy, synergy, professionalism, etc., would yield results far in excess of those resulting from capacity alone. This, then, is the approach that I would advocate.

India is acutely conscious of the symbiotic linkage between its geo-economic wellbeing and its maritime geostrategy. The globally renowned Chinese professor, Lexiong Ni, writing on "Sea Power and China's Development" in the April 17 2005 edition of the "People's Liberation Daily", offers a succinct and prescient summation: *"When a nation embarks upon a process of shifting from an 'inward-leaning economy' to an 'outward-leaning economy', the arena of national security concerns begins to move to the oceans. This is a phenomenon in history that occurs so frequently that it has almost become a rule rather than an exception."*

The geographical conformation of the Indo-Pacific maritime region obviously plays a major role in determining the geostrategies that India puts in play in seeking to attain its own geoeconomic and non-geoeconomic objectives. The manner in which these 'Indian' geostrategies interface with the geostrategies of other 'players' within the Indo-Pacific is, therefore, a matter of considerable import.

Defining the contours of India's grand strategy within this region, Prime Minister Modi has stated, *"India's... engagement in the Indo-Pacific Region... will be inclusive. We are inheritors of a Vedanta philosophy that believes in essential oneness of all, and celebrates unity in diversity... That is the foundation of our civilizational ethos — of pluralism, coexistence, openness and dialogue... We will engage with the world in peace, with respect, through dialogue and absolute commitment to international law. We will promote a democratic and rules-based international order, in which all nations, small and large, thrive as equal and sovereign. We will work with others to keep our seas, space and airways free and open; our nations secure from terrorism; and our cyber space free from disruption and conflict. We will keep our economy open and our engagement transparent. We will share our resources, markets and prosperity with our friends and partners."*

The Indian belief in an Indo-Pacific that is free, open and inclusive and one that is founded upon a cooperative and collaborative rules-based order, finds resonance across not just the region but the world at large. It finds its most eloquent yet succinct expression in the concept of SAGAR — which is not merely the Hindi word for 'ocean', but, far more meaningfully, is the acronym for "Security and Growth for All in the Region".

However, India is not the sole power within the Indo-Pacific and its geopolitics is impacted by the geopolitics of other regional and extra-regional powers that operate within the Indo-Pacific. This is, in fact, a region in which several Asian powers are once again rising, especially in geoeconomic terms. The more striking examples include India, Iran, Australia, China, Japan, South Korea, and the ten nations that constitute ASEAN. The 'geostrategies' that these rising powers are putting in place so as to attain their respective geoeconomic objectives, as also their non-geoeconomic ones, are grating against those of the world's established 'Grotian' powers. The resultant geopolitical friction is already of an order of magnitude that demands the most careful attention so as to be able to devise suitable pan-regional mitigating-geostrategies by all players within the Indo-Pacific. By virtue of the maritime dominance of this region, countries that demonstrate adroitness and adeptness in terms of competence within the maritime domain will tend to prosper more than others and will be better able to shoulder the multifarious responsibilities that are attendant upon regional leadership.

India's abiding belief in an inclusive, pluralistic, cooperative and collaborative rules-based order finds its most eloquent yet succinct expression in the Honourable Prime Minister, Shri Narendra Modi's concept of SAGAR, which is not merely the Hindi word for 'ocean', but, far more meaningfully, is the acronym for "Security And Growth for All in the Region[13].

In fleshing out the concept of SAGAR, it is important to differentiate between the terms: 'capacity' and 'capability'. 'Capacity' connotes material wherewithal (the provision of ships, aircraft, submarines, etc.), while 'capability' denotes conceptual, organisational, operational, training, and legal acumen. While capacity shortfalls (by way of material wherewithal) are not to be glossed-over, infirmities in capability (lack of cohesion, incoherent formulation and execution of policy, and, poor development of intangible factors such as inspirational leadership, aspirational-sensitivity and morale) are far more grave; and if at all priorities have to be assigned in addressing such shortcomings, 'capability-enhancement' must almost invariably take precedence over 'capacity-building'.

The mechanism that India has adopted to advance her maritime geopolitics is *'Constructive Engagement'*, guided by her 'Look-East/Act-East' and 'Look West' policies.[14] However, India's commitment to the provision of net security to the island States of the IOR remains an ongoing challenge of significant proportions. Amongst the several mitigating measures that have been put in place, revitalising and rejuvenating the IONS construct so as to leverage its very substantial potential, is one of the more important ones. It is most encouraging to see the current leadership buckling down to this critical requirement in all earnest.

There is little doubt that the Indo-Pacific is a contested region, with the principal contemporary protagonists being the USA and China. However, as the engine of China's economic growth demands ever greater resources of raw materials and petroleum-based energy, the bulk of China's imports of these resources are being drawn from increasingly distant areas that are either accessible only by sea or where seaborne transit offers the most cost-effective movement in terms of volume, time and space. China's geoeconomic imperatives are driving Beijing into the Indian Ocean, where India's own imperatives — both geoeconomic and non-geoeconomic — will create a competitive and possibly confrontationist dynamic between Beijing and New Delhi. With almost any other country, a collaborative dynamic, too, would have been a possibility — and one well-worth working towards, at that! In the case of China, however, there is a deep-rooted historical belief that China is the Middle Kingdom surrounded by barbarian States whose sole raison d'être is to offer tribute to China. As a result, accommodative- or cooperative-behaviour by other States (India, for instance) is likely to generate only disdain in the Chinese mind, because that is the behaviour that is expected of vassals.

New Delhi is highly unlikely to wish to play the role of a vassal State to Beijing. For one thing, it has its own axes to grind in terms of maritime trade. India, which had a closed economy until the beginning of the 1990s, has now seen two-and-a-half decades of acceleration in its economic opening-up and integration with the global economy. The contemporary economy is nurturing competitive forces in order to boost efficiency. It is characterised by a sharp relaxation of government controls and a very substantial role for the private sector as the engine of growth in a free market framework. While globalisation means many things to many people, increasing dependence upon international trade is amongst its most ubiquitous feature. India is no exception to this trend. India's 'Openness Index' (its 'Trade to GDP Ratio') has jumped from a paltry 11% in the 1990s to the present decadal percentage value of over 0.55 (i.e., over 55%). India's merchandise trade, as a percentage of its GDP, too, has been rising steadily and from a meagre 12.4% in 1980s, the present decadal average is as high as 37%. With 90% by volume and some 77% by value of the country's merchandise trade flowing over the seas, India is, to all intents and purposes, an island nation, and the preservation, promotion, pursuit and protection of her external trade is a major maritime security challenge. Over the last 25 years, there have been significant changes in the direction of India's external trade and the EXIM Bank confirms that the direction of both, imports and exports is decidedly shifting away from Europe and towards Africa, Latin America and Asia.

This change in direction of Indian trade, as also the centrality of petroleum-based energy within India's external trade-matrix has profound linkages with the choke-points of the Indian Ocean. India's imports and exports are both dominated by petroleum-based energy. Crude oil is the largest import item, while refined petroleum-products were until a year ago, the country's largest export. The only reason for their having slipped to second-place is the sharp rise in domestic demand for products.

In fact, an ever-increasing demand for energy fuels both, China's and India's economic growth. Although the share of coal is still the largest in the energy-basket of both countries, oil consumption is growing so rapidly that it is driving the foreign policy and security perspectives of both China and India. In 1985, China was East Asia's largest exporter of oil. In 1993, China became a net importer and, in 2015, she became the largest importer of crude oil on the planet. China is currently importing a staggering 8.7 million barrels per day (bbd) and as per energy-market researchers Wood Mackenzie, by 2020, China will be importing something like 10 million bbd of crude-oil! In recent months, there has been much brouhaha regarding China's oil pipelines. However, these are not particularly effective mitigating options for China's burgeoning dependence upon the seaborne-import of energy. There are currently three major pipelines feeding crude-oil into China, viz., the ESPO, the Kazakhstan-China Pipeline, and, the Myanmar-China Pipeline. Impressive as they may be in engineering terms, these pipelines can cater for only 15% of China's crude-oil imports. The remaining 85% of her crude-oil imports must still come by sea, from sources that lie either in — or must travel across — the Indian Ocean. This means that China's oil-imports must transit one or more of the choke-points that connect the Indian and the Pacific oceans. Of these, the Malacca Strait and the Lombok Strait of are particular importance to China and, considered generically, constitute what China leaders terms the 'Malacca Dilemma'. In seeking to solve this dilemma, the People's Republic seems to draw strategic inspiration from the famous Chinese game of 'Go', and is putting in place the pieces that will shape her desired geopolitical space.

With the external merchandise trade of both, India and China, being almost entirely sea-borne, nurturing the symbiotic relationship between 'Flag' and 'Trade' is a crucial facet of the maritime security of both countries. Commercial relations between importers in the home-nation and exporters in nations located abroad (or vice-versa) cannot be stove-piped and made distinct from the international relations that govern the nation-states to which the importer and exporter respectively belong. In addition to the price and quantity of goods and services, importers and exporters must necessarily take account of the place of origin of these products and the political relationship between the importing and the exporting nation. This because both are motivated to manage their trade relations in ways that minimise risks of disruption of supply or the possibility of hurting friends or aiding foes. Taking a leaf from the much more vigorous maritime-moves of the Chinese 'flag', India, too, is beginning to once again acknowledge the symbiosis between 'flag' and 'trade', which was in such strong evidence in the ancient and medieval kingdoms of the Indian peninsula.

China's aggressive maritime geostrategy in pursuit of her geoeconomic objectives is what then-Lt. Col. Christopher J. Pehrson, USAF, had termed the 'String of Pearls', in his 2006 paper written at the US Army War College.[15] The phrase was catchy enough to captivate the imagination of academics and the global media alike.

Consequently, for over a decade, China has chafed under the opprobrium heaped upon it for a concept that, to be fair, it never once articulated. However, in a brilliant re-branding exercise by Beijing in 2014, the world's attention is being increasingly drawn away from the negative connotations associated with the phrase 'String of Pearls' and towards the much more economically-seductive 'Belt and Road Initiative' (BRI). The BRI-narrative emphasises trans-regional inclusiveness and evokes the romance of a shared pan-Asian history with the implied promise of a reestablishment of the economic prosperity that the Asian continent's major civilizational and socio-cultural entities, namely China and India, enjoyed until Prince Henry of Portugal launched the 'Age of Discovery', which was quintessentially a maritime concept.

Each 'pearl' in the 'String of Pearls' construct — or in more contemporary parlance, each 'node' along the 'Maritime Silk Route', which is a major component of the BRI — is a link in a chain of Chinese geo-political and geo-strategic influence. It is by no means necessary for a line joining these pearls/nodes to encompass China in one of the concentric circles typified by the Island Chains strategy. In fact, since the 'String of Pearls' (or the 'Maritime Silk Route') is a true maritime construct, it is highly unlikely that they would do so. Thus, for example, Hainan Island, with its recently upgraded military facilities and sheltered submarine base, is a pearl/node. Other pearls/nodes include the recent creation of artificial islands in the Paracel and Spratly islands incorporating, inter alia, the construction/upgrade of airstrips and missile-batteries. Additional pearls/ nodes are obtained through Chinese investments being made in Cambodia and China's continuing interest in the Thailand's Isthmus of Kra. China's development of major maritime infrastructure abroad — the container-terminal in Chittagong, Bangladesh, the Maday crude-oil terminal in Myanmar's Kyakpyu port; the development of ports such as Hambantota in Sri Lanka, Gwadar and Jiwani in Pakistan, Bagamoyo in Tanzania, Beira in Mozambique, Walvis Bay in Namibia, Kribi in Cameroon, and, of course, the overt Chinese base in Djibouti along with the Doraleh Multipurpose Port — all constitute yet more pearls/nodes. The development of an atoll in Maldives, oil-infrastructure projects in Sudan and Angola, and the financing of newly discovered massive gas-finds in offshore areas of Mozambique, Tanzania and the Comoros, are similarly recently acquired pearls/nodes.

From an Indian perspective, China's new strategic maritime-constructs (by whatever name) are simultaneously operative on a number of levels. While several are predominantly economic in nature and portend nothing more than fierce competition. However, as the geographical competition-space between India and China coincide in the Indian Ocean, coincide, there is a very real possibility of competition transforming into conflict, particularly as the adverse impact of climate-change upon resources and available land-area becomes increasingly more evident.

All that I have mentioned is but a small sampling of the challenges that confront contemporary India. I have no doubt that the deliberations that are to follow, in this and subsequent seminars, will substantially and substantively address them.

Jai Hind.

Endnotes

1 Prime Minister's Keynote Address at Shangri La Dialogue (June 01, 2018). Ministry of External Affairs, Government of India, Media Centre, Speeches and Statements. https://www.mea.gov.in/Speeches-Statements.htm?dtl/29943/Prime+Ministers+Keynote+Address+at+Shangri+La+Dialogue+June+01+2018

2 **(a)** The Territorial Waters, Continental Shelf, Exclusive Economic Zone and Other Maritime Zones Act, 1976; **(b)** The Maritime Zones of India (Regulation of Fishing by Foreign Vessels) Act, 1981

3 **Delimitation** *is the legal process by which two sovereign nations establish and describe in writing the location of their common boundary. This is the task of diplomats and treaty negotiators, and it may require more than a single agreement... care must be taken to ensure that the words are unambiguous and will not be susceptible to later controversy.* **Delineation** *is the graphical or mathematical representation of the boundary. It often coincides with a line on a specifically identified map.* **Demarcation** *is a field operation; its purpose is to mark the position of the boundary on the ground for all to see. A joint commission, composed of an equal number of members from each country, normally undertakes demarcation* — Dr Alec McEwen, Professor Emeritus of Geomatics Engineering, University of Calgary, Canada. "The Demarcation and Maintenance of International Boundaries". Paper presented at the University of Durham, 8-10 July 2002; available at url: http://www.ucalgary.ca/~amcewen/IBCdem.pdf

4 Worley. *Ibid*

5 Frank O'Donnell and Harsh V. Pant, "Managing Indian Defence Policy: The Missing Grand Strategy Connection", Foreign Policy research Institute, Philadelphia, Pennsylvania, USA, February 14, 2015. https://www.kcl.ac.uk/sspp/sga/kii/documents/Managing-Indian-Defence-Policy-The-Missing-Grand-Strategy-Connection-FrankODonnell-HarshVPant.pdf (accessed on 01 June 2016)

6   The 'International Issues' school *"focusses on global problems that impede the achievement of a fair international system based on the improvement of the quality of life of the world's population. Resolving these issues, its advocates maintain, will address the most obvious sources of human conflict and suffering."* The "Principles-based' approach is that a State's geopolitics should be in accordance with specific principles — these may emanate from political, economic, or religious ideology — rather than calculating outcomes based on interests. The goodness of policy action is determined by how it adheres to or diverges from the chosen guiding principles rather than on the consequences obtained. Spreading free market capitalism, spreading democracy, supporting Israel, intervention against genocide, intervention for humanitarian assistance and disaster relief, and non-intervention are examples of principles to be followed.

See: Stephen A Cambone. "A New Structure for National Security Policy Planning", Centre for National and International Studies, Barnes & Noble, October 1988, p. viii and Dr D Robert Worley. "Grand Strategy — Orchestrating Instruments of Power: A Critical Examination of the US National Security System", Chapter 4 (Part 2), Potomac Books, University of Nebraska Press, USA, 2005. www.drworley.org/Pubs/Orchestrating/2b-GrandStrategy.doc (accessed on 01 June 2016)

7   Kanti Bajpai, "India Does Do Grand Strategy", Global Brief - World Affairs in the 21st Century, 05 Mar 2013. http://globalbrief.ca/blog/2013/03/05/india-does-go-grand-strategy/ (accessed on 31 May 2016)

8   *Ibid*

9   *Ibid*

10 Henry John Temple, 3rd Viscount Palmerston, KG, GCB, PC. Speech to the House of Commons (01 March 1848). http://hansard.millbanksystems.com/commons/1848/mar/01/treaty-of-adrianople-charges-against (accessed on 27 May 2016)

11 Dr Robert T Foley, "Can Strategy Be Reduced to a Formula of S = E + W + M?", Defence Studies Department, King's College London, 03 November 2014. https://defenceindepth.co/2014/11/03/can-strategy-be-reduced-to-a-formula-of-s-e-w-m/ (accessed on 01 June 2016)

12 Joseph R. Cerami and James F. Holcomb, Jr, (Editors), "Guide to Strategy", US Army War College, February 2001. www.comw.org/qdr/fulltext/01cerami.pdf (accessed on 01 June 2016)

13 Indian Navy, (2016), Ensuring Secure Seas, India's Maritime Security Strategy, Pg. 23

14 Indian Navy, (2016), Ensuring Secure Seas, India's Maritime Security Strategy, Pg. 47

15 Pehrson, C.J., (2006), String of Pearls: Meeting the Challenge of China's Rising Power Across the Asian Littoral, US Army War College

Theme Address: India's Regional Alliances in the Indo-Pacific

CV Ranagnathan, IFS [Retd.]

(*Former Ambassador of India*)

The concept note circulated to the speakers at this Conference has been diligently prepared and is comprehensive. India has a vast maritime neighbourhood and an expansive sphere of political and economic interest.[1] China's increased presence, through massive assistance in India's neighbourhood, is denting India's influence in this area.[2] In recent years, the China factor has become even more important, largely due to the 'Belt and Road Initiative' (BRI).[3] A major challenge is the preservation of security in the area, with an awareness of the conventional and other possible threats, as also the environmental challenges in safeguarding the rich fisheries stocks.[4] There is a need for improving relations with other powers in the vast Indo-Pacific region, with a view to achieving close cooperation and coordination in the strict observance of norms that have been laid down by the UNCLOS.[5]

India-Japan Relations

On this last point, India and Japan have evolved the *India-Japan Special Strategic and Global Partnership.*[6] They share common values and enjoy friction-free and good relations covering politics, and economics. Trade and investments have made rapid strides. Japan has emerged as an important ally of India.[7] This has been the case for over a decade now. In his address to the Parliament of India, in August 2007, Prime Minister Shinzo Abe (hereinafter referred-to as Abe) laid his conceptualisation of the *Confluence of the Two Seas.*[8] This was seen by him as being based on the principles of universal values and norms and has created space for India in Japan's grand strategy.

For the past few years there have been annual summits at the Prime Ministerial level. India and Japan are in the process of developing an *Action Oriented Partnership* for their common Indo-Pacific Vision 2025.[9] In 2017, the Prime Minister of India, Shri Narendra Modi (hereinafter referred-to as Modi) and Abe have articulated a common vision of a *Free and Open Indo Pacific* that is "inclusive" of all countries within this geography as also others beyond who have a stake in it.[10]

The latest summit identified certain common areas of cooperation for both countries. A few common elements define the India-Japan combination in the Indo-Pacific. These are: a rules-based and inclusive world order, with respect for international law, to solve disputes, ensure peaceful overflight and freedom of maritime navigation, unimpeded trade and flow of people technology and ideas, infrastructure development, and, enhance communication and connectivity.[11]

The two regional powers enjoy an agreement on the centrality of ASEAN, as also cooperation in smaller countries like Sri Lanka, Myanmar and Bangladesh. There is also an agreement to cooperate in Africa and concurrence on the need for cooperation in counterterrorism. Both countries are also aligned at multilateral fora. At the operational level, too, there is agreement on continued maritime military cooperation.[12]

Japan is also an important bilateral economic partner for India, with major technological agreements existing across a whole range of sectors. India is even willing for Japan to cooperate in its politically sensitive North East region[13].

Group Alliance

In the context of tensions with Pakistan and China, there have also been suggestions for India and Japan to form group alliances with each other and with other compatible countries, particularly the USA and Australia. As part of this, there are recommendations that India increase maritime military engagement with these countries.[14] This is sometimes described as the *Quad*. Other cooperative dialogue structures include 'Japan-US-India' (JAI) and 'India-Australia-Japan'. There is increased cooperation between the Indian and US navies in the western Pacific Ocean.[15] This, too, is aimed at containing Chinese influence.[16, 17] India's official position is to be a net provider of security in the Indo-Pacific Region.[18] This is apparently based on US support.[19] While the US would be keen to push its own agenda, it sees India as a reliable partner.[20] However, there are concerns about a US withdrawal and India's ability and willingness to fill the gap.[21]

At a political level, the Quad was first experimented-with in 2007. Since 1992, the Indian and US navies have carried out various editions of the MALABAR series of exercises.[22] Australia had participated in this exercise in 2007. However, Australia withdrew under Chinese pressure. Australia is reportedly keen to re-join the exercise. This is being resisted by India due to the perceived closeness of Australian to China.[23] The issue of whether Australia should participate or not continues to be an open one. The current dispensation in Australia is favourable towards the Quad.[24] Australia is keen to support US presence in the Indo-Pacific.[25] There has also been increased bilateral engagement with Japan,[26] and there is a Trilateral Security Dialogue In place between the three countries.[27]

Given the existing close ties of India with Japan and the USA, there is a natural logic for Australia to also align with India. However, Indo-Australian ties remain the weakest of all bilateral relationships.[28] It is not clear if India is keen to formalise the Quad as an alliance given that there is a historic aversion in India to join alliances. This remains the case, India's movement from its old position of non-alignment to a more realist position notwithstanding.[29] India prefers 'strategic autonomy'. Thus, it is more likely that India would want 'coordinated' rather than 'combined' operations with a unified command[30].

ADMM Plus

The Association of South East Asian Nations (ASEAN) is the main regional body in South East Asia and has emerges as a major cooperation forum for all its ten constituent countries. ASEAN itself has a security apparatus, viz., the ASEAN Defence Ministers Meeting-Plus (ADMM Plus), which consists of the ten ASEAN Member States, and eight 'Plus' countries — Australia, China, India, Japan, New Zealand, South Korea, the Russian Federation and the United States of America[31] — all countries of significance. The ADMM Plus grouping also holds maritime exercises in which India, too, participates.[32]

ASEAN may not necessarily welcome the creation of a new military alliance in its region. Further, China is yet to militarise the South China Sea. Thus, Australia may prefer the Quad to remain an informal grouping.[33] Australia does, however, believe that it will play a positive role in the East Asia Summit (EAS), and that it will encourage India's strategic engagement with East Asia and the United States. The intention expressed is to work with India in the EAS and build upon the growing strategic collaboration between Australia, India and Japan.[34] Australia, in its latest Foreign Policy White Paper, specifically mentions supporting a US-led global order.[35] In the maritime sphere, Australia is keen for combined exercises and building maritime domain awareness with India.[36] It is, however, worth noting that even in the EAS, Australia gives primacy to Japan, and the USA, even while it wants to integrate India with these countries.

The China Factor

There seems to be a general sense of awe about China, which is not actually warranted. While there is no denying that China's achievements in the economic, military, technological, space and social areas attract the envy of the world, there are flaws in the visions outlined in the speech made at the 19th CPC Conference.[37] A few of the more significant ones are outlined in the succeeding paragraphs.

Economic Model. To expect that the Chinese model of development would be emulated across the globe is unrealistic. China's role is restricted to 'economic globalisation' but does not include the upholding of established values that underpin international modernity, such as respect for social, cultural and political pluralism, an exclusive attitude to foreign influence, freedom of expression, and a domestic autonomous rule of law.

South China Sea. The building of infrastructure on islands and reefs in South China Seas is seen within China as a laudable achievement. However, these actions find no supporters from other littoral States. The rejection by China of the decision by the Permanent Court of Arbitration[38] is seen as a defiance of the rule of law as laid down by the UN Convention on the Law of the Sea.[39] Australia has even made a formal declaration of such a position about China.[40] Amongst the important global powers, the UK, too, is concerned about China's expansion in this region.[41] While India has supported the PCA decision, this creates an added challenge for India itself to scrupulously respect global norms.[42]

Military. Equally unrealistic are the expectations that PLA would be transformed to a world class military by 2050. Such a vision attracts counter-strategies and inevitably engenders a realignment of forces against it, thus making it difficult for China to increase its military strength, as also its diplomatic and political influence, beyond a point. China continues to face strong global military opposition.[43] Australia, for instance, is concerned about the expansionist nature of China, and its potential rivalry with USA.[44] The Quad is seen as a counterweight to China. This is despite some scholars doubting that it will achieve a hard containment of China.[45]

Conclusion

The main priority for India is regional production networks and value chains, and, securing the global commons by strengthening security cooperation with likeminded partners. Thus, India's approach towards geopolitical realities is guided by a balance between engagement and autonomy.

As can be seen, China and Japan are both major East Asian players. However, there are also other players, such as Australia, and other East and South East Asian countries. The United States of America, too, is an active player in the Indo-Pacific. At a political level, India has done well to engage with these countries. The Quad continues to be a major element of India's maritime policy.

Over the past few years Japan has emerged as a reliable partner, and one with whom India has a special relationship. There is cooperation at the multilateral diplomatic level. Further, military cooperation continues to be an important element. Japan is also an extra regional partner, with a strong involvement in Africa. Another important element is Japan's engagement with Andaman Islands and India's North East.

At a military level, the Indian Navy has done well to build its credibility as a possible counterweight to the PLA-N. There is even talk of India being a net provider in of security in the Indo-Pacific region. This, too, is worthy of pursuing. India must have and display the confidence that its navy is viewed by its maritime neighbours as a major asset in the region, which is vigilant against conventional and unconventional threats, is geared to be helpful with humanitarian assistance when needed, and, has shown that it can be a dependable partner of countries to uphold norms and laws as applied to the maritime common.

China is almost certainly being overrated as a threat. There are underlying weaknesses that may cause it to decline. Further, China is seen as belligerent and, as such, does not have many allies in the Indo-Pacific Region. The US, too, considers China to be a major threat. India would do well to continue the current policy of cooperation with the US, and continue building other regional alliances.

Australia remains an enigmatic and uncertain factor in the Indo-Pacific. As can be seen, it has been oscillating between a Sino-centric and a US-centric position. However, in more recent times, Australia can be said to have firmly aligned itself with the US. Moreover, Australia is keen to engage with India more intensively and considers India an important potential ally. At the diplomatic level, given the historical Commonwealth connection, India should enhance cooperation with Australia. There is also support for India and Australia from the UK. Engagement with the UK, too, needs to be built up at the diplomatic and military levels.

India, quite rightly, has not totally shed its old position of non-alignment, as witness its current emphasis upon 'strategic autonomy'. Hence, it is right to maintain a position of not actively formalising the Quad, especially at a military level. Given that there are already institutions for regional security operating in the Indo-Pacific, it is not clear if India would like to join an alliance within these bodies.

Endnotes

1   Indian Navy, (2016), Ensuring Secure Seas, India's Maritime Security Strategy, Pg. 6, Pg. 33-35

2   Singh, A., (2018), China's strategic ambitions seen in the Hambantota port in Sri Lanka https://www.orfonline.org/research/chinas-strategic-ambitions-seen-in-the-hambantota-port-in-sri-lanka/Shrikhande, S., (2018), Making India's Sea Power Formidable and Future-Ready, ORF Occasional Paper 152

3   Singh, A.K., (2018): Emerging Contours of Maritime Security Architecture under the Belt and Road Initiative, Journal of Defence Studies, Vol. 12, No. 4, October-December 2018, pp. 35-55

    Singh, A.K., (2017), Unpacking China's White Paper on Maritime Cooperation under BRI, Issue Brief, IDSA

4   Indian Navy, (2016), Ibid., Pg. 5

5   United Nations Convention on the Law of the Sea of 10 December 1982

6   Government of India, Prime Minister's Office, India-Japan Vision Statement, 29 October 2018. http://pib.nic.in/newsite/PrintRelease.aspx?relid=184458

7   Mukerji, A.K., India-Japan Collaboration in the Indo-Pacific, Journal of the United Service Institution of India, Vol. CXLVIII, No. 614, October-

December 2018. https://usiofindia.org/publication/usi-journal/india-japan-collaboration-in-the-indo-pacific/

8   Abe, S., ***Confluence of the Two Seas***, Speech by Prime Minister of Japan at the Parliament of the Republic of India, 22 August 2007. https://www.mofa.go.jp/region/asia-paci/pmv0708/speech-2.html

9   Ministry of External Affairs, Joint Statement on India and Japan Vision 2025: ***Special Strategic and Global Partnership Working Together for Peace and Prosperity of the Indo-Pacific Region and the World*** (December 12, 2015), https://www.mea.gov.in/bilateral-documents.htm?dtl/26176/Joint_Statement_on_India_and_Japan_Vision_2025_Special_Strategic_and_Global_Partnership_Working_Together_for_Peace_and_Prosperity_of_the_IndoPacific_R

10 Ministry of External Affairs, ***Toward a Free, Open and Prosperous Indo-Pacific***,India-Japan Joint Statement during visit of Prime Minister of Japan to India (September 14, 2017) https://www.mea.gov.in/bilateral-documents.htm?dtl/28946/IndiaJapan

11 Government of India, Prime Minister's Office, India-Japan Vision Statement, 29 October 2018. http://pib.nic.in/newsite/PrintRelease.aspx?relid=184458

12 Government of India, Prime Minister's Office, India-Japan Vision Statement, 29 October 2018. http://pib.nic.in/newsite/PrintRelease.aspx?relid=184458

13 Government of India, Prime Minister's Office, India-Japan Vision Statement, 29 October 2018. http://pib.nic.in/newsite/PrintRelease.aspx?relid=184458

14 Singh, A., (2018a), Decoding Chinese submarine 'sightings' in South Asia, ORF Commentaries, https://www.orfonline.org/research/decoding-chinese-submarine-sightings-in-south-asia/

15 Khurana, G.S., (2017): High End in the Pacific: Envisioning the Upper Limits of India-US Naval Cooperation in Pacific-Asia, Journal of Defence Studies, Vol. 11, No. 4, October-December 2017, pp. 51-71

16 Yadav, D., (2017), Revival of Quadrilateral: A shift in India's Policy towards China? NMF

17 Pant, H.V., and Bommakanti, K., (2018), Can the Quad deal with China?, ORF Website https://www.orfonline.org/research/can-the-quad-deal-with-china-45750/

18 Indian Navy, (2016), Pg. 8

19 Khurana, G.S., (2017): High End in the Pacific: Envisioning the Upper Limits of India-US Naval Cooperation in Pacific-Asia, Journal of Defence Studies, Vol. 11, No. 4, October-December 2017, pp. 57

20 Khurana, (2017), Ibid., Pg. 57-58

21 Khurana, (2017), Ibid., Pg. 60

22 U.S. Embassy Website, (2018), U.S., JMSDF and Indian Naval Forces Conclude Malabar 2018 Release #032-18, https://in.usembassy.gov/u-s-jmsdf-and-indian-naval-forces-conclude-malabar-2018/

23 Singh, A., (2017a), India remains cautious about the 'quad', https://www.lowyinstitute.org/the-interpreter/india-remains-cautious-about-quad

24 Lee, L., Abe's Democratic Security Diamond and New Quadrilateral Initiative: An Australian Perspective, The Journal of East Asian Affairs, Vol. 30, No. 2 (Fall/Winter 2016), pp. 1-41

25 Lee, L., Ibid., Pg. 18

26 Lee, L., Ibid., Pg. 20

27 Lee, L., Ibid., Pg. 22

28 Lee, L., Ibid., Pg. 25

29 Brewster, D., (2016), Australia, India and the United States: The Challenge of Forging New Alignments in The Indo–Pacific, United State Studies Centre, Pg. 5

30 Khurana, Gurpreet S. (2016), America's Expectation versus India's Expediency: India as a Regional 'Net Security Provider. National Maritime Foundation

31 ASEAN Website, About the ASEAN Defence Ministers' Meeting (ADMM-Plus) https://admm.asean.org/index.php/about-admm/about-admm-plus/2013-01-22-11-01-22.html

32 ASEAN Website, About the ASEAN Defence Ministers' Meeting (ADMM-Plus) https://admm.asean.org/index.php/about-admm/about-admm-plus/2013-01-22-11-01-22.html

33 Lee, L., Ibid., Pg. 30-32

34 Australian Department of Foreign Affairs and Trade, (2017), Foreign Policy White Paper, Pg. 42

35 Australian Department of Foreign Affairs and Trade, (2017), Ibid., Pg. 7

36 Australian Department of Foreign Affairs and Trade, (2017), Ibid., Pg. 46

37 Xi Jinping, Secure a Decisive Victory in Building a Moderately Prosperous Society in All Respects and Strive for the Great Success of Socialism with Chinese Characteristics for a New Era, Delivered at the 19th National Congress of the Communist Party of China October 18, 2017

38   UN Permanent Court of Arbitration. 2016. Award PCA Case No. 2013-19: In the Matter of the South China Sea Arbitration before an Arbitral Tribunal Constituted Under Annex VII to the 1982 United Nations Convention on the Law of the Sea between The Republic of the Philippines and The People's Republic of China. 12 July Available https://pca-cpa.org/wp-content/uploads/sites/175/2016/07/PH-CN-20160712-Award.pdf

39   Dutton, P.A., A Dispute about Legality, or a Political Onslaught? China's Response to the Arbitration Decision on the South China Sea Issue, RUSI *Commentary*, 8 August 2016 https://www.rusi.org/commentary/south-china-sea-dispute-legality

40   Australian Department of Defence, (2016), Defence White Paper, Pg. 42, 58

41   Hemings, J., Charting Britain's Moves in the South China Sea, RUSI Commentary, 6 February 2019   https://rusi.org/commentary/charting-britain%E2%80%99s-moves-south-china-sea

42   Roy-Chaudhary, R., India and shared maritime values in the Indo-Pacific, Analysis, 30 January 2019,

43   https://www.iiss.org/blogs/analysis/2019/01/india-shared-values-indo-pacific Nouwens, V., Collision Course in the South China Sea? RUSI Commentary, 3 October 2018 https://rusi.org/commentary/collision-course-south-china-sea

44   Australian Department of Defence, (2016), Ibid., Pg. 41-45 Lee, L., Ibid., Pg. 10-12

45   Choong, W., The revived 'Quad' – and an opportunity for the US, Analysis, 10 January 2018, https://www.iiss.org/blogs/analysis/2018/01/revived-quad

Inaugural Address

Shri BS Raghavan, IAS (Retd)

Opinion leaders, strategic thinkers, and policymakers of Asian countries have long shied away from examining — boldly and with a fresh mind — the new and exciting vistas of social, cultural and economic partnership that exist right under their collective nose. There is scant evidence of discussion or even awareness amongst scholars of the Asian region of the dynamics of one such compelling vision, namely, the Indian Ocean Community (IOC).

The time has come to give a new thrust, suited to the genius of the Asian region, to new paradigms of collaboration and synergy, which would put these countries on the fast track, if not actually ahead-of several so-called advanced countries. The combined strengths of 59 countries of the Indian Ocean Region, which together constitute a six-trillion-dollar powerhouse, are capable of setting in motion hitherto undreamt-of avenues of cooperation for making the most of their abundant human and natural resources.

If only the countries of the Indian Ocean Region were to constitute themselves into a collective entity, the tremendous financial and economic leverage that such a collective would exercise could easily redress the imbalance of the present world economic order and resolve many of the perceived threats confronting the region.

We already have a replicable model, in terms of the supra-national European Union, which was initially conceived as a mechanism for joint policymaking with reference to production and marketing of coal and steel, but rapidly expanded into a full-fledged and integrated economic organisation with the Euro as a common currency and a European Central Bank as a provider of banking-services to all its members, based on homogenous norms and criteria. This happened as an economic imperative despite the two World Wars having been fought amongst European nations.

Similarly, the IOC, too, can transform itself into a Free Trade Zone, to start with, so as to provide for free movement of goods and services, which can, at some later stage, even adopt a common currency. Such a zone would, of course, stretch from South Africa to Tasmania along the 63,000 km of the Indian Ocean Rim, but this spatial expansiveness need not, in and of itself, be regarded as an argument against it.

The Indian Ocean Rim Association for Regional Cooperation (IOR-ARC) was set up as a forum for diplomats of the States of the region to meet annually to exchange views in the common interest of the region. Formally launched in 1997 with a very limited membership of some 20 States of the Indian Ocean littoral, it was supposed to focus on prospects for trade and tourism through joint ventures and the like, but it is still in a state of flux, and very little is known of its efforts to give economic content through Free Trade Agreements and MOUs for bilateral and multi-lateral cooperation in infrastructure projects.

There is also the Southern African Development Community (SADC), of which some Indian Ocean Islands are members. Again, few are aware of the extent to which it has been able to achieve its objectives.

Likewise, the expectation that the Association of South East Asian Nations (ASEAN) and the South Asian Association for Regional Cooperation (SAARC) would take the lead in forging linkages with the Indian Ocean community, has not been realised. Each of these groupings are, instead, pursuing their own variegated agendas with little or no synchronisation or mutual reinforcement of their policies.

The projects for the construction of a Trans-Asian Highway and a Trans-Asian Railway from Bangkok to Vladivostok, and the extension of the Exclusive Economic Zones of the Indian Ocean Rim States to 200 nautical miles under the UN Convention on the Law of the Sea (UNCLOS) were all meant to bring about unlimited economic opportunities for mutual cooperation and the sustainable harnessing of the riches of the oceans. Full and comprehensive information is not available on the extent of progress made by them and the extent to which they have served the purpose intended.

The IOC has socio-cultural interaction bonds that have been matured over thousands of years, essentially signifying a *dharma-dhamma* continuum, evidenced by thousands of Hindu-Buddhist temples in Malaysia, Indonesia, Thailand, Cambodia, Vietnam, Laos, Myanmar and other States and the historical presence of Hindu kings in the region for over a millennium.

The IOC can be the first example of weaving these socio-cultural bonds into socio-economic spheres of cooperation. These can be further buttressed by exchanges in the fields of higher technical education, the use of satellite and IT technologies, oceanography, and so on.

Unfortunately, since most of these social and cultural influences have had their origins in South India, policymakers at the Centre in New Delhi take minimal interest in the opportunities and possibilities that exist in the region. In that sense, The International Conference organised jointly by the Chennai Centre for China Studies, the National Maritime Foundation, and the Department of Defence and Strategic Studies, University of Madras, at Chennai, is of great help in making the academic community and persons prominent in public and political life in India's southern states aware of the significance of the country's maritime neighbourhood and hopefully stands as the precursor to further steps that can set India on a course that would bring about a revolutionary change in the complexion of world affairs.

There has been no serious study undertaken so far of the implications and ramifications of issues relating to the security, stability and sustainability of the Indian Ocean Region, within a 21st Century perspective. Five years ago, the Australia-India Institute had brought out a critically and clinically analytical, and at the same time lucidly-written report, setting out the various factors contributing to the changing significance of the geopolitics and security challenges of the Indian Ocean Region (IOR). The multifarious aspects covered by the report are of extreme sensitivity and vital importance and provide the basis of a viable framework of willing and active cooperation among the IOR nations. Amongst the several noteworthy features of the report, the foremost is its stress on security as a multi-dimensional rather than the traditional military or power-play concept, bringing within its purview the inter-dependence of human security, economic and resources security, maritime security and environmental security. It is not merely a question of the stability and sustainability of the IOR; a stable global world order itself is predicated upon a holistic approach to security. Expectedly, the report goes in some detail into the role that India and Australia can jointly play in binding the IOR nations — as the driving force of efforts towards the realisation of the immense potential of a region that had long been bypassed and ignored by Western colonial powers which sucked its resources dry.

The short point is that the Indian Ocean has to be regarded as part of a wider Indo-Pacific system that embraces the trade routes and sea lanes that cross the oceans and extends past the Straits of Malacca-and-Singapore, into the South China Sea, and north to China, Taiwan, Korea and Japan and, thence, on to the west coast of the Americas. Transforming the Indian Ocean Rim as a vibrant economic and cultural entity by mobilising the collective energies and resources, and exploiting the commonalities, of the countries of the region can be taken up by India as a mission of vital importance in its own right that will define the character and complexion of the new world order. It stands on its own footing without needing to be guided by, or without relating it to, what China or any other country does. The many-splendored benefits flowing from it will automatically invest the region — and India's maritime neighbourhood — with the strength and the confidence to stand up and assert its rights and entitlements.

Maritime Diplomacy furthering India's Maritime Aspirations in the IOR

Rishi Athreya

India's Maritime Domain

India's primary area of maritime interest includes India's coastal areas and the Indian Navy and Coast Guard patrol areas falling within the Maritime Zones of India;[1] the Arabian Sea, the Bay of Bengal, the Andaman Sea, the Persian Gulf, the Gulf of Oman, the Gulf of Aden, the Red Sea, the Mozambique Channel, and South-West Indian Ocean (SWIO); and, the littoral regions of each of these fringing-seas of the Indian Ocean, as also the several island nations contained within this oceanic expanse.[2,3] Within these loose spatial bounds, India aims to secure the maritime commons.[4] Historically, India has had an active maritime presence in the Indian Ocean littoral, particularly with countries that have had close cultural ties to India.[5,6] Sri Lanka and Maldives are India's proximate southern neighbours, while Mauritius and Seychelles are in the larger Indian Ocean littoral. The main chokepoints within India's maritime domain are those leading to, -from, and -across the Indian Ocean, including the Six-Degree Channel; the Eight/Nine-Degree Channels; the straits of Hormuz, Bab-el-Mandeb, Malacca, Singapore, Sunda, and Lombok; the Mozambique Channel, and, the Cape of Good Hope.[7] Given its access to the major chokepoints leading to the South China Sea, especially the Malacca Strait, and including the Andaman and Nicobar Islands, India enjoys a geographically advantageous position in the eastern Indo-Pacific. An important regional grouping that India is pushing is the Bay of Bengal Initiative for Multi-Sectoral Technical and Economic Cooperation (BIMSTEC).[8]

This paper focusses on the immediate maritime neighbourhood as defined by the following areas[9]:

- The Strait of Hormuz to the West: countries of the Persian Gulf and North Arabian Sea.

- The Mozambique Channel to the South West: Seychelles, Mauritius and Reunion Island.

- The Malacca Strait and the Andaman Sea to the East: Singapore, and the Banda Aceh port on the Indonesian Island of Sumatra.

Determinants of Maritime Security

The key determinants for shaping the maritime security strategy cover broader maritime strategic imperatives and more specific maritime security drivers[10].

Broader maritime strategic imperatives.[11] India is centrally located within the Indian Ocean, with unfettered access across the IOR. The country has cooperative relations with neighbours, based on adherence to international norms. India depends on the seas for its national development. Maritime economic activities include energy, trade, and fisheries. Non-Resident Indians and Overseas Citizens of India are another important interest. There are major foreign investments by Indian businesses. Many of India's activities are dependent upon the 'International Shipping Lanes' (ISLs) that crisscross the Indian Ocean. Consequently, ensuring Freedom of Navigation (FoN) along these ISLs (and, in times of tension or conflict, ensuring these freedoms along the country's 'Sea Lines of Communication' [SLOCs]), is an important national maritime interest. In pursuance of these imperatives, India faces both, traditional and non-traditional maritime threats. These are continuously being assessed.[12] There is considerable scope and value in undertaking cooperation and coordination between various navies to counter common threats at sea. Table 1 provides a summary of India's main maritime interests.

Traditional Threats and Sources. These are threats from States holding an inimical posture vis-à-vis India. Hostile actions on the part of these States would be high in terms of scale and scope. Sudden politico-economic and/or military events may also affect the regional security scenario. Historical alliances are increasingly becoming indistinct. Moreover, there are multiple players in the global scenario and it is not uncommon to find that economic ties and imperatives are not perfectly aligned with a country's traditional political agenda.

According to some analysts, an important aim for India's maritime policy is to reduce the influence of China.[13] India has longstanding challenges in its relations with China and Pakistan,[14] but in recent years, the China factor has become more important due to that country's 'Belt and Road Initiative' (BRI).[15] There is Chinese presence across the board, which India is forced to factor into its own security calculus. For instance, the sharply increased presence of Chinese submarines in the Indian Ocean can definitely be perceived to be an expansionist tactic. It is suggested that India increase maritime military engagement with the major littoral States of Australia, Japan, USA and Indonesia.[16] Of these, the first three form part of the *Quad*.

Although Pakistan's naval expansion not as often noticed as it might have been before the military rise of China, the latter has been providing maritime assistance to the former[17] and, as a consequence, Pakistan, too, has been able to upgrade its naval infrastructure[18] and has developed sea-denial capabilities.[19] Pakistan undertakes the biennial exercise, AMAN,[20] whose latest edition was attended by a large number of navies.[21] Moreover, tensions on land often spill over into the maritime domain.[22]

Non-Traditional Threats and Sources. There has been an increase in non-traditional security threats, e.g., piracy, and terrorism, in recent years. There are often State-sponsors of such activities. Changes in the nature of non-traditional threats and challenges necessitate corresponding changes in strategies, force structures, operating methodology, training and coordination mechanisms. In the specific case of India, the events of 26/11 are a prime example of non-traditional threats.

Table 1: National Maritime Interests[23]

India's *maritime interests* that are addressed by the country's maritime-security strategy are summarised as follows: -

- Protect India's sovereignty and territorial integrity against threats in the maritime environment.

- Promote safety and security of Indian citizens, shipping, fishing, trade, energy supply, assets and resources in the maritime domain.

- Pursue peace, stability and security in India's maritime zones, maritime neighbourhood and other areas of maritime interest.

- Preserve and project other national interests in the maritime dimension.

Maritime Engagement

India takes a realist approach to the global maritime domain, viewing it as essentially anarchic and characterised by intense competition. It consequently concludes that nation-states need to adopt hard-power and/or soft-power measures.[24] The main roles for the Indian Navy are Military, Diplomatic, Constabulary, and Benign.[25] Navies are good at the diplomatic role on account of the inherent characteristics of warships and the sovereign power that they represent, which is easy to deploy in distant areas.[26] Shaping the broader maritime environment to counter threats across regions requires cooperation between concerned nations and their navies. Maritime engagements are the principal means of maritime diplomacy. Maritime diplomacy is in frequent evidence at the conceptual, political and executive levels and there needs to be cooperation at each of these levels.[27] Table 2 gives an overview of India's Maritime Security Aims and Objectives.

Maritime Security Objective: To shape a favourable and positive maritime environment, for enhancing net security in India's areas of maritime interest[28].

Defence Diplomacy. Defence Diplomacy could be defined as the peaceful use of the military as a tool of national foreign policy. Obviously, it has to be synergised with other forms and uses of diplomacy.[29] It does not replace but, instead, supplements the overall foreign and security policy, under a given political leadership.[30] All military diplomacy has the objectives of strengthening diplomatic ties with other countries, training the nation's armed forces, acquiring better weapon-technologies, and, acquiring a sphere of influence.[31] The basic aim of India's defence diplomacy is to promote goodwill towards India overseas.[32,33] Each of the three Defence Forces has a role in the conduct of defence diplomacy. India has, in the past few years, embarked on a policy of maritime or naval diplomacy, but an oft-voiced concern of some scholars has been that India is not effectively engaging in military diplomacy.[34]

Table 2: India's Maritime Security- Aim and Objectives[35]

> *India's maritime security aim is to safeguard its national maritime interests at all times.*
>
> India's maritime security objectives, flowing from the above aim, are:
>
> - To deter conflict and coercion against India.
>
> - To conduct maritime military operations in a manner that enables early termination
>
>   of conflict on terms favourable to India.
>
> - To shape a favourable and positive maritime environment, for enhancing net
>
>   security in India's areas of maritime interest.
>
> - To protect Indian coastal and offshore assets against attacks and threats emanating from or at sea.
>
> - To develop requisite maritime force levels and maintain the capability for meeting India's maritime security requirements.

Actions for Net Maritime Security.[36] The main actions to achieve peace, with stability and security within the maritime domain are: 'presence', 'rapid response', 'maritime engagement', 'capacity-building', 'capability-enhancement', 'regional maritime domain awareness (MDA)', 'maritime security operations', and, 'strategic communications and signalling'.

SAGAR.[37] In terms of shaping the global maritime environment, India has embarked on a pan-IOR concept of Security and Growth for All in the Region (SAGAR). While translating this vision into reality, India would do everything to safeguard its mainland and islands and defend its interests. Further, India will also work to ensure a safe, secure and stable IOR. It aims to augment economic and security cooperation with its maritime neighbours, and provide support by way of capacity-building and capability-enhancement aimed at promoting 'holistic' maritime security. SAGAR is a natural progression of India's pre-existing maritime diplomacy in the region.[38] It highlights India's role as 'a net provider of maritime security'.[39] SAGAR may not necessarily be a counterforce structure vis-à-vis China, [40] but it is seen as a way to counter China's 'Maritime Silk Route'. Although there are suggestions for increased economic cooperation between India and China,[41] there are deep and probably irreconcilable political differences between the two countries.

A number of India-led initiatives could be considered under the rubric of SAGAR. For instance, the Indian Ocean Naval Symposium (IONS), and the DOSTI series of Coast Guard exercises could be said to be part of SAGAR. The Indian Ocean Rim Association (IORA) is also important in this context.[42]

Indian Navy Activities. Naval diplomacy entails the use of naval forces in support of foreign policy objectives to build 'bridges of friendship' and strengthen international cooperation, on the one hand, and, to signal capability and intent to deter potential adversaries, on the other. The larger purpose of a navy's diplomatic role is to favourably shape the maritime environment in the furtherance of national interests, in consonance with the foreign policy and national security objectives.[43] India's Maritime Security Strategy, as enunciated by the Indian Navy, provides a strategy for shaping a favourable and positive maritime environment. It covers the wide range of activities undertaken by the Navy in peace time, across all doctrinal roles. The main activities of the Indian Navy towards this end include port-visits, personnel exchanges, staff-talks and professional interaction, exercises with foreign navies, the provision of maritime assistance, operational interaction, and, high-level maritime strategic interaction. In this context, the Indian Navy has undertaken several initiatives,[44] utilising its own soft power. Two major tasks undertaken by the Indian Navy in terms of maritime diplomacy are 'technical cooperation' and 'combined exercises'.

Constabulary Role

An important aspect of maritime security is coastal security. The '26/11' terrorist attack in Mumbai was a watershed in terms of coastal security. Subsequent to this tragic event, several measures were taken to enhance coastal security. These include the installation of a three-tier security arrangement (with the Indian Navy [IN], the Coast Guard [ICG], and the marine police, jointly safeguarding India's maritime zones), the creation of coastal police stations and surveillance infrastructure under a Coastal Security Scheme (CSS), the commissioning of radar stations along the coastline, and the installation of Automatic Identification Systems (AIS) and Joint Operation Centres (JOCs). Each undertaking is aided by intelligence networks so as to ensure effective monitoring of maritime activity in India's 'near-seas'.[45] The Indian Coast Guard plays an important role in this sphere.[46]

Although the Coastal Security Scheme had been instituted in 2005, it was enhanced only after 26/11. There are, however, systemic flaws in its practical implementation. In the context of India's federal polity, state governments and police forces are unwilling to assume responsibility. There are insufficient marine police stations, and lack of infrastructure and personnel for these tasks.[47] The SAGAR KAVACH series of coastal security exercises are held several times a year across several littoral states of the Indian Union.[48] These involve the Indian Navy, the Indian Coast Guard and the coastal police, and, are intended to enhance *esprit de corps* amongst these organisations. All this notwithstanding, significant lacunae in the coastal policing apparatus persist.[49]

Amongst the recommendations for improvement are legislative reforms and the adoption of new technologies. There is a pressing need to promulgate a multiagency policy for coastal security, which would include representatives from the Ministry of Shipping, the Directorate General of Shipping, the Ministry of Home Affairs, the Department of Fisheries (presently nested within the Ministry of Animal Husbandry and Dairying), the Intelligence Bureau, the Ministry of Defence, the Indian Navy, the Indian Coast Guard, State Police forces, port authorities, and, civilian agencies. The involvement of the State Police is vital since they enjoy credibility and trust amongst fishermen and the local population in littoral areas.[50] In January of 2019, the Indian Navy, along with the Indian Coast Guard and other security agencies, held the first ever SEA VIGIL exercise, spanning the entire coastline of India. This exercise is intended to be an extension of the tri-Service 'Theatre-level Readiness Operational Exercise' (TROPEX),[51] which is held every two years.[52] This is certainly a significant step towards addressing the security-concerns through inter-agency cooperation.

Neighbourhood Combined Exercises

The Indian Navy and Coast Guard undertake combined exercises with countries in the neighbourhood. The main ones are:

Sri Lanka and Maldives. The immediate South Asian region is part of the primary maritime neighbourhood of India. Sri Lanka and Maldives are the two significant maritime partners of India in South Asia. There was, at one point in time, a trilateral alliance of India and these two countries.[53] India and Sri Lanka are close maritime neighbours with strong and cordial defence and diplomatic relations. The two navies regularly interact during the biennial Exercise SLINEX. The Indian Navy hosts large numbers of trainees from the Sri Lankan Navy in its professional schools. At a more operational level, however, the issue of fisheries is proving to be a bone of contention between India and Sri Lanka.[54]

A major concern of India with regard to Sri Lanka is the influence of China. The Hambantota Port has been leased for 99 years to China Merchant Ports Holdings Ltd, a Chinese commercial company. Further, the Sri Lanka Navy has moved a unit to this location. China, in turn, is reported to have gifted a frigate to Sri Lanka. While Sri Lanka would like to claim that the relationship with China is entirely economic, this does not seem plausible.[55] Nevertheless, India is doing well to maintain strong maritime military diplomatic ties with Sri Lanka.

India and the Maldives have a long-term maritime defence agreement with India.[56] In 1988, India sent its warships to avert a military coup in the Maldives.[57] In 2018, however, Male decided not to extend its military ties with India and even returned a Naval helicopter.[58] This is believed to be largely due to the influence of China.[59] Given the larger economic power of China, and the high level of indebtedness of Maldives, it will prove difficult to counter the former's influence. Towards this end, there are suggestions for India to call on its larger partners.[60]

The Indian Coast Guard has been conducting an annual exercise, called DOSTI, with the Maldives National Defence Force, since 1991. Since 2012, DOSTI has been upgraded to a trilateral exercise with the addition of the Sri Lanka Coast Guard. The Indian Navy's CENDEP patrols are undertaken in these seas.[61]

Bangladesh. In early September of 2018, Bangladesh Naval ships made a four-day visit to the Eastern Naval Command.[62] This visit was significant in enhancing maritime cooperation with a friendly neighbouring country. The Indian Navy's NORDEP patrols are undertaken in the seas of the northern Bay of Bengal and the Andaman Sea.[63] Given the border issues of Rohingya refugees and infiltration, this is a positive development in terms of maritime military diplomacy.[64]

Andaman Sea. A little understood but vital part of India's maritime domain is the Andaman and Nicobar Islands archipelago. The Indian Navy undertakes ANDEP and MALDEP maritime patrols to cover the Andaman Sea and the approaches to the Strait of Malacca.[65] The 32nd edition of the India-Indonesia Coordinated Patrol (INDINDOCORPAT) was held from 11 to 27 October 2018. Shore-based interaction was held in Belawan, Indonesia, and Port Blair in the Andaman and Nicobar Islands. Likewise, the Eastern Fleet of the Indian Navy and the Republic of Singapore Navy held the 25th edition of SIMBEX — Singapore India Maritime Bilateral Exercise — in November of 2018.

Persian Gulf. India's 'Look West' policy is premised upon the facts that countries of the Persian Gulf region are major economic partners, host over four million Indian expatriates, and, are a vital source of India's energy security.[66] On the other hand, the challenges of this region are formidable and, apart from terrorism, include a number of emerging non-traditional challenges. This has led to greater capacity-building assistance, allowing regional maritime forces to combat piracy and other criminal activities in the North Western Arabian Sea.[67] GULFDEP maritime patrols are undertaken in this area by the Indian Navy.[68]

The Royal Oman Navy, and Indian Navy have held the exercise *THAMMAR-AL-TAYYIB*, since 1993. The exercise was renamed *NASEEM-AL-BAHR* in 2007. Oman has recently permitted India to use Duqm port.

For New Delhi, balancing relations between the various countries in West Asia, especially major actors such as Saudi Arabia, Iran, UAE, Qatar and Israel, continues to be a significant challenge.[69] The rivalry between Qatar and remaining members of the Gulf Cooperation Council (GCC) exacerbates India's efforts to maintain neutrality in its own dealing with these nation-states, especially as India progresses defence cooperation with Iran and Israel.[70] Increased ties with Israel also affect India's involvement with Gulf States.[71]

India has been involved in building the Iranian port of Chabahar. However, Iran is not keen to have a permanent Indian naval presence.[72] India is also involved in the International North South Transit Corridor (INSTC). The Chabahar port plays an important role in this mega connectivity project.[73]

There is no gainsaying the fact that China is making inroads into the IOR and that India urgently needs to address regional imperatives. Moreover, Pakistan has common religious ties with countries of the Persian Gulf and conducts combined exercises with their navies. Thus, maintaining links with navies of the Persian Gulf is essential if India is to retain its influence in the IOR.[74] Were the United States, currently the major regional security provider, to withdraw from this area, there would be countries other than India that may want to fill the void.[75]

Mauritius and the Seychelles. The population of Mauritius predominantly comprises descendants of indentured labourers from India and it is unsurprising that the country has close naval ties with India. Mauritius does not have a military as such. There is a Mauritius National Police Force (MPF) which controls air, sea and land security forces. It has close training links with India since 1978. Many elements of the Mauritian security establishment are commanded by officers of the Indian armed forces attached to the MPF. In 1986, India undertook a maritime intervention to avert a coup.[76] Likewise, India has long had defence links with the Republic of Seychelles. In January 2018, the Governments of India and Seychelles signed a 20-year agreement enable the construction of Indian naval/ military infrastructure on Assumption Island. Subsequently, the Prime Minister of India visited the Seychelles, and gifted that country a Dornier aircraft.[77] The Indian Navy undertakes IODEP patrols in this area.[78]

Southern and South-western Indian Ocean. Since 2001, the Indian and French Navies have conducted successive annual editions of Exercise *VARUNA*. In March 2018, this exercise was held across the Arabian Sea, the Bay of Bengal, and the South West Indian Ocean,[79] ending with a debrief in Reunion Island.[80] France is the only NATO country that continues to have a permanent presence in the Indian Ocean. There is an expectation that India and France will sign an agreement akin to the LEMOA Agreement with USA. Access to French naval bases would augment India's ability to be a "net provider of security" and protect the ISLs as also her own SLOCs and those of France. Given that France has maritime territories in the Pacific Ocean, the Andaman Islands, too, could be a useful base for maritime cooperation.[81] India is also seen as a possible mediator between Iran and France. This is of considerable importance, given the strained ties between Paris and Tehran due to issues relevant to the Joint Comprehensive Plan of Action. Given the proximity of Iran to the Strait of Hormuz, its role in anti-piracy operations in the western IOR is critical.[82]

The Indian Ocean Commission (IOC) is an international organisation established in 1982.[83] Its member States are the Indian Ocean islands States of Comoros, Madagascar, Mauritius, Reunion, and Seychelles. The goals of the IOC are mainly developmental, with little political activity. Of the member states, two are maritime allies of India. France, too, is part of this body. There are suggestions for India to be granted observer status.[84]

Other Combined Exercises

The Indian Navy undertakes exercises with several other foreign navies. Many of these engagements are institutionalised and conducted regularly.[85] Although they do not incorporate navies of India's immediate neighbourhood, these exercises are noteworthy in themselves. The main ones are:

MALABAR Series. This series of exercises has been undertaken along with USA since 1992.[86] Japan participated in the 2007 edition of MALABAR and has been a regular since 2015. There has been Australian participation too.

AUSINDEX. The Royal Australian Navy and Indian Navy have held the biennial Australia-India Maritime Bilateral Exercise AUSINDEX, since 2015.

JIMEX. The Indian Navy and the Japanese Maritime Self Defence Force have been holding the Japan-India Maritime Exercise (JIMEX), since 2012.

INDRA Series. The Russian and Indian Navies have conducted the INDRA series of biennial exercises since 2003. In 2018 it was held off Vishakhapatnam, with participation of both, ships and submarines, with a particular focus upon the exchange of best practices.[87, 88]

KONKAN Series. KONKAN is the generic name of a series of exercise between the Indian Navy and the British Royal Navy, which has, since its inception in 2004, grown in complexity and scale.[89] Both navies have, over the years, also undertaken bilateral activities such as training exchanges and technical cooperation. KONKAN is usually held off Goa. The 2019 edition, however, was held in the English Channel.[90]

Op ATALANTA. This is not an exercise, but a joint-and-combined operation by a European Union Naval Force (EU NAVFOR) in and off the Gulf of Aden. The primary aim is counter-piracy. There has been participation by Indian Navy units.[91]

ADMM Plus.[92] India is part of the Association of South East Asian Nations (ASEAN) Defence Ministers Meeting-Plus (ADMM Plus), and has participated in the ADMM PLUS maritime exercises. The ADMM-Plus consists of ten ASEAN Member States, and eight 'Plus' countries, viz., Australia, China, India, Japan, New Zealand, South Korea, the Russian Federation, and, the United States.[93] The Indian Navy participated in the latest exercise that was held in Busan, South Korea, from 28 April to 01 May

2019. There was a 'GROUP SAIL' from Busan to Singapore, in which the Indian Navy, along with the US and Philippine navies, participated.[94] The ADMM PLUS is considered to be a major security exercise in the Indo-Pacific.[95, 96] Given that the membership of ADMM mirrors that of the East Asian Summit (EAS), it is perceived to be a good forum for cooperation.[97]

Operational Interaction

The Indian Navy also interacts with friendly maritime forces in specific professional mechanisms, so as to enhance mutual understanding, operational coordination and maritime security cooperation.[98]

MILAN. This is a biennial congregation of mid-level officers and ships of littoral navies of the Indian Ocean, conducted by the Indian Navy in the Andaman and Nicobar Islands, facilitating cooperation.[99] It has now grown into a prestigious international event and encompasses participation by maritime forces from not just the Bay of Bengal and South East Asia but the larger IOR. MILAN 2018 was held at Port Blair from 06 March to 13 March 2018.[100] The participating navies cover the better part of the Indian Ocean and South Pacific. Due to internal politics and external factors, Maldives did not join MILAN 2018.[101]

IONS.[102] The Indian Ocean Naval Symposium (IONS), an Indian initiative established in 2008, brings together 35 navies and coast-guard organisations. It seeks to increase maritime cooperation among navies of the littoral countries of the Indian Ocean Region.[103] The 3rd Meeting of the IONS Working Group on Humanitarian Assistance and Disaster Relief (HADR) was held from 27-29 September 2018. Members deliberated upon lessons learnt during HADR operations, and best practices that can be proliferated.[104]

The tenth anniversary commemorative events of the IONS were held on 13 and 14 November 2018. The theme was *"IONS as a Catalyst for SAGAR"*. SAGAR is in consonance with India's Act East policy and reflects the nation's diplomatic, economic and military outreach in the region.

IORA: The Indian Ocean Rim Association[105] could be said to be the closest to a multilateral body for Indian's maritime neighbourhood.[106] The Jakarta Concord, signed in 2017, has provisions for the honouring of international treaties, as also for the avoidance of maritime incidents. In many ways, this can be seen as an acknowledgement of major power rivalry.[107] There is a disjoint between the IONS and IORA. There are some countries that participate in IONS but are not signatories to IORA.[108] Thus, while IORA is necessary at a political level, at the executive level, IONS has a major role to play in increasing cooperation. There is also a need for bilateral level cooperation.[109] In this context, it can be said that the Indian Navy and Coast Guard are effective in promoting bilateral cooperation.

Goa Maritime Conclave 2018.[110] The second edition of the Goa Maritime Conclave (GMC) — a forum designed to foster friendly relations with India's maritime neighbours — was held on 16th October 2018. The theme was *Building Stronger Maritime Partnerships in the IOR.* This international seminar was attended by delegates from Bangladesh, Myanmar, Mauritius, Sri Lanka, Singapore and Thailand. The GMC, which was conceptualised and first held in November of 2016, aimed at establishing academic excellence as well as the sharing of ideas among India's maritime neighbours by facilitating interaction between senior representatives of navies and maritime agencies in the IOR. As such, it plays a constructive role in bringing together stakeholders involved in evolving strategies, policies and implementation mechanisms in the maritime domain.

INS *Tarangini.*[111] The *Tarangini*, one of the Indian Navy's two sail training ships, made a goodwill voyage named *Lokayan 18* commencing 10 April 2018 and ending on 30 October 2018. During the voyage, the ship proudly 'showed the flag' and highlighted the diverse culture of India across 15 ports in 13 countries. The ship sailed across the Arabian Sea, the Red Sea, negotiated the Suez Canal to enter the Mediterranean Sea, then through the Strait of Gibraltar into the North Atlantic Ocean, the Bay of Biscay, the English Channel and the North Sea, right up to Norway.

Technical Cooperation and Training

India has naval cooperation agreements with UAE, Qatar, Oman and Iran.[112] The main features of these agreements are joint military exercises, information sharing, exchange of goodwill visits, exploring the possibility of joint production of military equipment, and, training and education courses for military personnel[113].

In the past year there has been significant maritime military cooperation with Oman[114] and the UAE[115]. Royal Navy of Oman (RNO) officers being trained in India[116]. Likewise, India has upped its military maritime cooperation with the United Arab Emirates (UAE), including visits and agreements[117]. The India-UAE Joint Defence Cooperation Committee has been meeting consistently. However, active exercises between the two navies, although suggested in December 2017 are yet to materialise.[118]

Although Japan is not part of India's immediate neighbourhood, it is nevertheless emerging as an important player in the region. In response to China's Belt and Road Initiative, Japan has pursued has pursued the Partnership for Quality Infrastructure (PQI) and a 'Free and Open Indo-Pacific Strategy'. India, USA and Australia are considered important partners[119] and Japan is taking an active interest in the Pacific littoral, including South Asia.[120] Japan, has been involved in port-development in the Indian Ocean littoral. Examples include the port of Matarbari in Bangladesh, and Galle in Sri Lanka. There is also technological cooperation with Maldives. There are suggestions for India-Japan cooperation in Sri Lanka.[121] Given its pacifist doctrine, Japan has hitherto mainly deployed its coast guard to counter piracy and there is a great deal of cooperation with the Indian Coast Guard including joint exercises.[122] An important element of India's cooperation with Japan is the willingness of India to invite Japan to undertake infrastructure development in the Andaman Islands. Japan has also been invited to undertake socio-economic development in India's North East.[123] Further, there is talk of the Japan Self Defence Force (JSDF) having access to the Andaman and Nicobar Islands.[124]

The Asia Africa Growth Corridor (AAGC) is a joint effort by Japan and India to extend their influence.[125] There is lack of clarity among scholars as to whether the AAGC is meant to be a counterweight to the BRI and MSR[126,127,128]. This notwithstanding, the AAGC is certainly seen as being conceptually linked to SAGAR. There are even suggestions that the AAGC should be integrated into IORA.[129] Japan is understood to be keen to be part of the International North-South Transport Corridor (INSTC) and this is yet another driver for Japan's strong maritime relationship with India.

On 19 January 2018, the Australian Navy Chief and his delegation visited the Indian Naval Academy.[130] The AUSINDEX was followed by the visit of Royal Australian Navy (RAN) ship, HMAS Newcastle to Kochi, Kerala from 04 to 07 July 17. In the past year, there have been maritime military discussions with USA and Australia and also a number of high-level visits.[131,132]

India is not only a provider of maritime expertise and technology, but also a recipient of the same. As a carryover from the Soviet era, Russia continues to be a major defence supplier.[133] A major challenge for India is maintaining equidistance from the USA and Russia.[134]

Way Ahead

India's maritime area of interest ranges right across the Indian Ocean and extends into the western and southern Pacific Ocean. In pursuit of its maritime strategic imperatives, Indian confronts a variety of traditional and non-traditional threats. India has embarked on maritime diplomacy, informed by the conceptual principle of SAGAR. The past year has seen an upsurge in India's maritime defence diplomacy. Based on the current scenario the following options are suggested:

1. Military exercises and exchanges should continue as instruments-of-choice in India's maritime military diplomacy.

2. China remains India's principal maritime rival. Thus, India's signalling of intent is directed at this country. India has been able to effect its strategic signalling reasonably well, and to hence maintain a semblance of balance-of-power. India's engagement with South Asia does much to counterbalance China. However, an often-ignored maritime rival of India is Pakistan.

3. India should continue its proactive maritime engagement of Persian Gulf States, while maintaining neutrality. Previously planned combined exercises need to be implemented.

4. India is doing well to engage with its Diaspora in Mauritius and the Seychelles.

5. There has been good cooperation between India and France in the western IOR and India is extending its influence to France's Reunion Island. India has aspirations to be a net provider of security. Entering into a LEMOA Agreement with France will facilitate this process in the Gulf Sea and Indian Ocean. The Andaman Islands could also be made accessible to France.

6. Given the ties with Middle East Navies, India is also seen as a possible mediator between Iran and NATO and this role needs to be explored vigorously.

7. On its eastern flank, India has done well to utilise the Andaman Islands to foster maritime diplomatic ties with Singapore, Indonesia and Australia.

8. The Constabulary Role, exemplified by the Indian Coast Guard, too, is significant for India's maritime diplomacy. Given India's federal structure and its vast coastline, it is essential to involve the governments of India's coastal states and Union Territories. Different political parties in power at centre and state often cause lack of coordination and this is something that needs to be addressed.

9. Exercise SEA VIGIL, which was held for the first time in January of 2019, is a landmark step in enhancing India's coastal security. This should be made the flagship maritime exercise.

10. Technical Cooperation has been another important component of India's maritime defence diplomacy. In operational terms, India has been both a provider and beneficiary of naval infrastructure. This fulfils an important objective of India's defence diplomacy, namely, to enhance the capacity and technical knowhow of its defence services.

11. India has done well to discretely hold discussions with Australia and USA. It is also able to acquire hardware from Russia. This is a process that is worth continuing in years ahead.

12. Japan is emerging as an important extra-regional partner. The two countries should leverage their respective capacities and capabilities to advance technical cooperation and joint assistance throughout the maritime reaches of South Asia. The AAGC is a common point of convergence and needs to be integrated into the IORA.

13. The INSTC is an important mechanism for India's outreach to both, Central Asia and Eastern/Central Europe. Chabahar port offers an ideal maritime gateway and its development needs to be pursued in right earnest.

14. International Organisations are generally weak in the maritime domain. There is a pressing need to enhance the role of IORA, IOC and BIMSTEC. The ADMM Plus needs to be strongly leveraged to further regional cooperation.

15. Soft-Power diplomacy, too, has played a significant role in India's maritime defence diplomacy. MILAN, IONS and the GMC, all provide platforms for discussions, bringing together Track 1 and Track 2 diplomacy

16. The Chennai Centre for China Studies, the National Maritime Foundation, and the Department of Defence and Strategic Studies, University of Madras, have done well to organise an International Conference on *"Securing India's Maritime Neighbourhood - Challenges and Opportunities"*. More such conferences would be relevant across other cities in peninsular India.

Conclusion

Two main parameters of India's maritime defence diplomacy are increasing cooperation with partners and signalling intent to rivals. The underlying objective is shaping the maritime environment in a manner that is favourable to India. This article has been written toward dispelling concerns by some scholars of India's lack of effective military diplomacy. The primary geographic focus is the Indian Ocean Rim and adjacent territories and, as the foregoing paragraphs have shown, India has been reasonably successful in its efforts. There have also been a number of Indian initiatives that area relevant to New Delhi's attempt to shape the not just the regional maritime space but the global one as well. In both cases, several of these initiatives need to be continued. In the years ahead, India might encounter the same challenges or different ones, but in all foreseeable cases, robust international partnerships will need to be forged and/or strengthened, as it will not be possible for India to deal with them singlehandedly.

Endnotes

1   Vasan, R.S, (2018), Indian Navy's 'CAMPING' Expeditions in the Indian Ocean Region, National Maritime Foundation

2   Indian Navy, (2016), Ensuring Secure Seas, India's Maritime Security Strategy, Pg. 31-33

3   Parmar, S.S., (2014), Maritime Security in the Indian Ocean an Indian Perspective, *Journal of Defence Studies*, Vol. 8, No. 1, January–March 2014, pp. 49–63

4   Singh, Z.D., Foreign Policy and Sea Power: India's Maritime Role Flux, *Journal of Defence Studies*, Vol. 11, No. 4, October-December 2017, Pp. 29

5   Chatterji, S.K., (2015), Narendra Modi's Active Indian Ocean Diplomacy https://thediplomat.com/2015/03/narendra-modis-active-indian-ocean-diplomacy/

6   Singh, Z.D., Ibid.

7   Vasan, R.S., (2017), Time for India to activate its Maritime Fulcrum in the Indo-Pacific Area to serve its strategic interests, C3S Article no: 0066/2017, Chennai Centre for China Studies https://www.c3sindia.org/defence-security/time-for-india-to-activate-its-maritime-fulcrum-in-the-indo-pacific-area-to-serve-its-strategic-interests-by-commodore-r-s-vasan-in-retd/

8   Khurana. G.S., (2018), BIMSTEC and Maritime Security: Issues, Imperatives and the Way Ahead

9   Indian Navy, (2016), Ensuring Secure Seas, India's Maritime Security Strategy, Pg. 17-21

10 Indian Navy, (2016), Ibid., Pg. 5

11 Indian Navy, (2016), Ibid., Pg. 5

12 Indian Navy, (2016), Ibid., Pg. 6, Pg. 33-35

13 Baruah, D., Delhi's new Indian Ocean diplomacy, https://www.lowyinstitute.org/the-interpreter/delhi-s-new-indian-ocean-diplomacy

Singh, A., (2018), China's strategic ambitions seen in the Hambantota port in Sri Lanka https://www.orfonline.org/research/chinas-strategic-ambitions-seen-in-the-hambantota-port-in-sri-lanka/

Shrikhande, S., (2018), Making India's Sea Power Formidable and Future-Ready, ORF Occasional Paper 152

14 Sathiya Moorthy, N., (2018), Recalibrating India's ties with China and Pakistan, ORF Raisina Debates https://www.orfonline.org/expert-speak/re-calibrating-indias-ties-with-china-and-pakistan-46066/

15 Singh, A,K., (2018): Emerging Contours of Maritime Security Architecture under the Belt and Road Initiative, *Journal of Defence Studies*, Vol. 12, No. 4, October-December 2018, pp. 35-55

Singh, A.K., (2017), Unpacking China's White Paper on Maritime Cooperation under BRI, Issue Brief, IDSA

16 Singh, A., (2018a), Decoding Chinese submarine 'sightings' in South Asia, ORF Commentaries, https://www.orfonline.org/research/decoding-chinese-submarine-sightings-in-south-asia/

17 Parmar, S.S., (2014), Ibid. Pg. 57

18 Parmar, S.S., Naval Balance of Power and Freedom of Navigation: Maritime Power Praxis in Vice Admiral Pradeep Chauhan and Captain (Dr) Gurpreet S Khurana eds., **National Maritime Power: Concepts Constituents and Catalysts** (New Delhi: NMF/ Pentagon Press 2018), Pg. 6

19 Singh Z.D., Ibid, Pg. 35

20 Pakistan Navy Website, Exercise Aman 2019, https://aman.paknavy.gov.pk/Home.aspx

21 The News International, Pakistan Navy's Multinational Maritime Exercise 'AMAN-19' concludes, 12 February 2019 https://www.thenews.com.pk/latest/431208-pakistan-navys-multinational-maritime-exercise-aman-19-concludes

22 WION News, Indian Navy says INS Vikramaditya, nuclear submarines were deployed in northern Arabian Sea after Pulwama terror attack https://www.wionews.com/india-news/indian-navy-says-ins-vikramaditya-nuclear-submarines-deployed-in-northern-arabian-sea-amid-indo-pak-tensions-203846?fbclid=IwAR1qdWcZFj2sLMCcvhSQJBD-K54-8CbB1Yuyp5G7NdgqWzt3sL8JZgpmOms

24 Indian Navy, (2015), **Indian Maritime Doctrine** 2009, updated online version 2015, Naval Strategic Publication NSP. 1.1, Pg. 50

25 Indian Navy, (2015), **Indian Maritime Doctrine** 2009, updated online version 2015, Naval Strategic Publication NSP. 1.1, Pg. 91

26 Indian Navy Website, https://www.indiannavy.nic.in/content/role-navy

27 Khurana, G.S. (2019), Multilateral Structures in the Indian Ocean: Review and Way Ahead, *Maritime Affairs*, Vol. 14, No. 1, Pp. 11-23

28 Indian Navy, (2016), **Ensuring Secure Seas**, India's Maritime Security Strategy, Pg. 78

29 Muthanna, K.A., (2011), Military Diplomacy, *Journal of Defence Studies*, Vol 5, No 1., Pp. 1-15

30 Malik, V.P., (2013), India's Military Conflicts and Diplomacy, Harper Collins, Pg. 180.

31 Malik, Ibid., Pg. 181

32 Headquarters Integrated Defence Staff, (2017), **Joint Doctrine Indian Armed Forces**, JP-01/2017, Pg. 21-22

33 Jaishankar, D., (2016), India's Military Diplomacy, in Singh S., and Das P., (Eds.), **Defence Primer: India at 75**, Pp 18-25, Observer Research Foundation

34 Malik, Ibid., Pg. 181-183

36 Indian Navy, (2016), Ibid., Pg. 82

37 Padmaja, G., (2018), Revisiting 'SAGAR' – India's Template for Cooperation in the Indian Ocean Region, National Maritime Foundation

38 Padmaja, G., (2017), India and Mauritius: Cooperating to Ensure Collective Maritime Security, National Maritime Foundation, Pg. 3

39 Padmaja, G., (2017), Pg. 4

40 Padmaja, G., (2018), Pg. 4

41 Chhibber A (2017). "China's belt and road initiative and India's options: Competitive cooperation". *Journal of Infrastructure, Policy and Development*, 1(2): x–x.

42 Padmaja, G., (2018), Pg. 4

43 Indian Navy, (2015), Ibid., Pg. 105

44 Indian Navy, (2016), Ibid., Pg. 84

45 Indian Navy, Initiatives to Strengthen Coastal Security, https://www.indiannavy.nic.in/content/initiatives-strengthen-coastal-security

46 Indian Coast Guard, Coastal Security, https://www.indiancoastguard.gov.in/content/1727_3_CosstalSecurity.aspx

47 Singh, A, (2018b), India's coastal security: An assessment, https://www.orfonline.org/expert-speak/indias-coastal-security-an-assessment-45692/

48 Indian Navy Website Maharashtra Coastal Security Exercise, https://www.indiannavy.nic.in/content/maharashtra-coastal-security-exercise

Coastal Security Exercise 'Sagar Kavach' https://www.indiannavy.nic.in/content/coastal-security-exercise-%E2%80%98sagar-kavach%E2%80%99

49 Exercise "Sagar Kavach" Conducted off the Coast of Kerala, Mahe and Lakshadweep Islands https://www.indiannavy.nic.in/content/exercise-%E2%80%9Csagar-kavach%E2%80%9D-conducted-coast-kerala-mahe-and-lakshadweep-islands

Singh, A. (2017), India's Coastal Security Paradox, ORF Special Report 52

50 Singh, A. (2017), Ibid., Pg. 10

51 Govt. of India, Press Information Bureau, (2019), Indian Navy Coordinates Largest Ever Coastal Defence Exercise Ten Years After "26/11", http://pib.nic.in/PressReleaseIframePage.aspx?PRID=1560995

52 Govt. of India, Press Information Bureau, (2017), Indian Navy Concludes Theatre Level Exercise TROPEX 2017, http://pib.nic.in/newsite/PrintRelease.aspx?relid=158689

53 Indian Navy Website, TROPEX 17, https://www.indiannavy.nic.in/content/tropex-17

Saberwal, A., (2016), Time to Revitalise and Expand the Trilateral Maritime Security Cooperation between India, Sri Lanka and Maldives, IDSA Comment https://idsa.in/idsacomments/trilateral-maritime-security-cooperation-india-sri-lanka-maldives_asaberwal_220316

54 Kapoor, R.V., Making fishing in Palk Bay 'safe', ORF Website https://www.orfonline.org/expert-speak/making-fishing-in-palk-bay-safe/

55 Singh, A., (2018), China's strategic ambitions seen in the Hambantota port in Sri Lanka https://www.orfonline.org/research/chinas-strategic-ambitions-seen-in-the-hambantota-port-in-sri-lanka/

56 Padmaja, G., (2016), Maldives President Visits India: Bilateral Partnership for Regional Security, National Maritime Foundation

57 Singh, Z.D., Ibid. Pg. 25

58 WION Gravitas: Maldives decides to return naval helicopter gifted by India, http://www.wionews.com/videos/wion-gravitas-maldives-decides-to-return-naval-helicopter-gifted-by-india-128389

59 First Post, Maldives returns helicopter gifted by India: A look at how ties between the two nations have deteriorated in 2018, https://www.firstpost.com/india/maldives-returns-helicopter-gifted-by-india-a-look-at-how-ties-between-the-two-nations-have-deteriorated-in-2018-4417923.html

60 Soami, R., (2018), Should India Bail Out Debt-ridden Maldives? National Maritime Foundation

61 Vasan, R.S, (2018), Ibid., Pg. 2

62 Indian Navy, BNS Somudra Joy on a Goodwill Visit to Visakhapatnam, https://www.indiannavy.nic.in/content/bns-somudra-joy-goodwill-visit-visakhapatnam

63 Vasan, R.S, (2018), Ibid., Pg. 3

64 Khurana, G.S., (2018), Ibid.

65 Vasan, R.S, (2018), Ibid.

66 Indian Navy, (2007), Freedom to Use the Seas: India's Maritime Military Strategy, Pg. 32

67   Singh, A., (2017), India's middle eastern naval diplomacy, http://www.orfonline.org/research/india-middle-eastern-naval-diplomacy/

68   Vasan, R.S, (2018), Pg. 3-4

69   Quamar, Md. M., (2018), India and the UAE: Progress towards 'Comprehensive Strategic Partnership', Issue Brief, IDSA, Pg. 8

70   Singh, A., (2017), Ibid.

71   Singh, A., (2017), Ibid.

72   Singh, A, (2017), Ibid.

73   Iyer, R., (2018), Filling in the North-South Trade Corridor's Missing Links, *The Diplomat*, https://thediplomat.com/2018/02/filling-in-the-north-south-trade-corridors-missing-links/

74   Singh, A., (2015), The Indian Navy's Arabian Gulf Diplomacy, IDSA https://idsa.in/idsacomments/TheIndianNavysArabianGulfDiplomacy_asingh_240915

75   Agarwal, R., Security in the Gulf Region: India's Concerns, Vulnerabilities, Interests and Engagement Options, in Dahiya R., (eds.), ***Developments in the Gulf Region,*** Prospects and Challenges for India in the Next Two Decades, Chapter 2, Pg. 34-64

Singh, A., (2017), Ibid.

76   Singh, Z.D., Ibid, Pg. 25

77   Maritime Security: India to Give Dornier to Seychelles, Sign 4 Pacts, http://www.indiawrites.org/maritime-security-india-to-give-dornier-to-seychelles-sign-4-pacts/

78   Vasan, R.S, (2018), Ibid., Pg. 3

79   Indian Navy Website, Indian Navy to Host Bilateral Exercise 'Varuna' with French Navy, https://www.indiannavy.nic.in/content/indian-navy-host-bilateral-exercise-varuna-french-navy-0

80   Indian Navy Website, IN Ships enters Saint Denis Port, Reunion Island France, https://www.indiannavy.nic.in/content/ships-enters-saint-denis-port

81   Vasan, R.S., (2018a), The French Connection in the Indian Ocean, Chennai Centre for China Studies, Article No. 016/2018, https://www.c3sindia.org/defence-security/the-french-connection-in-the-indian-ocean-by-commodore-r-seshadri-vasan-in-retd/

82   Behal, A., India and France: Towards a new maritime partnership, ORF Website, https://www.orfonline.org/expert-speak/43376-india-and-france-towards-a-new-maritime-partnership/

83 Indian Ocean Commission, http://commissionoceanindien.org/accueil/

84 Behal, A., Ibid.

85 Indian Navy, (2016), Ibid., Pg. 87

86 U.S. Embassy Website, (2018), U.S., JMSDF and Indian Naval Forces Conclude Malabar 2018, Release #032-18, https://in.usembassy.gov/u-s-jmsdf-and-indian-naval-forces-conclude-malabar-2018/

87 Panda, A., (2018), Russia, India Conclude Indra Navy 2018 Naval Exercise, *The Diplomat,* https://thediplomat.com/2018/12/russia-india-conclude-indra-navy-2018-naval-exercise/

88 Indian Navy (2018), INDRA Navy-18 Concludes in Bay of Bengal, https://www.indiannavy.nic.in/content/indra-navy-18-concludes-bay-bengal

89 Indian Navy (2018), Konkan Exercise https://www.indiannavy.nic.in/content/konkan-2018

90 United Kingdom Royal Navy Website, (2019), British and Indian Navies Join Forces in Channel, https://www.royalnavy.mod.uk/news-and-latest-activity/news/2019/august/15/190815-british-and-indian-navies-join-forces-in-channel

91 European Union External Action website, https://eunavfor.eu/mission/

92 ASEAN Website, ASEAN Defence Ministers Meeting, https://admm.asean.org/

93 ASEAN Website, About the ASEAN Defence Ministers' Meeting (ADMM-Plus) https://admm.asean.org/index.php/about-admm/about-admm-plus/2013-01-22-11-01-22.html

94 Indian Navy Website, Indian Naval Ships Kolkata and Shakti at South Korea to Participate in ADMM-PLUS, https://www.indiannavy.nic.in/content/indian-naval-ships-kolkata-and-shakti-south-korea-participate-admm-plus

95 Australian Navy Website, Success takes part in ADMM+ exercise, http://news.navy.gov.au/en/May2019/IPE19/5235/Success-takes-part-in-ADMM-exercise.htm#.XXpUBCgzbIU

96 United States Navy, (2019), Commander Pacific Fleet website, ADMM-Plus exercise strengthens maritime security, https://www.cpf.navy.mil/news.aspx/110741

97 Seawright, A., (2018), ADMM-Plus: The Promise and Pitfalls of an ASEAN-led Security Forum, CSIS Website , https://www.csis.org/analysis/admm-plus-promise-and-pitfalls-asean-led-security-forum

98 Indian Navy, (2016), Ibid., Pg. 86

99   Singh, Z.D., Pg. 34

100 Indian Navy Website, MILAN 2018 https://www.indiannavy.nic.in/content/milan-18

101 WION News, Maldives says no to Indian Naval exercise, http://www.wionews.com/videos/maldives-says-no-to-indian-naval-exercise-8718

102 Indian Navy Website, IONS 10th Anniversary Celebrations to Commence Today, https://www.indiannavy.nic.in/node/21302

103 Padmaja, G., (2017), Pg. 4

104 https://www.indiannavy.nic.in/node/20856

105 https://www.iora.int/en

106 Khurana, G.S. (2019), Ibid.

107 Khurana, G.S. (2019), Ibid.

108 Khurana, G.S. (2019), Ibid.

109 Khurana, G.S. (2019), Ibid.

110 Indian Navy Website, IONS Working Group Meeting on HADR Held at Visakhapatnam, https://www.indiannavy.nic.in/node/21097

111 Indian Navy Website, INS Tarangini Returns After Voyage Across the World, https://www.indiannavy.nic.in/content/ins-tarangini-returns-after-voyage-across-world

112 Pradhan, P.K., India and the Gulf: Strengthening Political and Strategic Ties, in Daihya R., (eds.), (2015), Developments in the Gulf Region, Prospects and Challenges for India in the Next Two Decades, Pg. 11

113 Pradhan, P.K., India and the Gulf: Strengthening Political and Strategic Ties, in Daihya R., (eds.), (2015), Developments in the Gulf Region, Prospects and Challenges for India in the Next Two Decades, Pg. 11

114 Indian Navy Website, Royal Navy of Oman Delegation Visits SNC https://www.indiannavy.nic.in/node/20797

115 Quamar, Md. M., (2018), Ibid.

116 Indian Navy Website, Royal Navy of Oman Delegation Visits SNC https://www.indiannavy.nic.in/node/20797

117 Quamar, Md. M., (2018), Ibid.

118 Quamar, Md. M., Ibid. Pg. 6

119 Ishida, Y., (2015) China's OBOR Initiative and Japan's Response: The Abe Doctrine, Free and Open Indo-Pacific Strategy and Japan- India Strategic Partnership, in Panda, J., and Basu, T., (Eds.), China-India-Japan in the Indo-Pacific, Institute of Defence Studies and Analysis, Pp., 159-189

120 Iyer, S.L.D., (2018) Japanese Naval Diplomacy in the Indian Ocean: Prospects and Possibilities, NMF

121 Kashyap, K., (2018) INSTC–India Breaches: The Great Wall of Pakistan, Issue Brief No. 137, CLAWS Iyer, S.L.D., (2018) Japanese Naval Diplomacy in the Indian Ocean: Prospects and Possibilities, NMF

122 Iyer, S.L.D., (2018) Japanese Naval Diplomacy in the Indian Ocean: Prospects and Possibilities, NMF

123 Jain, P.K., (2018): Japan's development assistance to India: a strategic edge, Japan Forum, DOI: 10.1080/09555803.2018.1530283

124 Gady, F.S., India, Japan Begin Negotiations Over Military Base Sharing Agreement, https://thediplomat.com/2018/10/india-japan-begin-negotiations-over-military-base-sharing-agreement/

125 Asia Africa Growth Corridor, http://aagc.ris.org.in/

126 Panda, J.P., (2015), Soft Balancing: Asia-Africa Growth Corridor (AAGC), India-Japan Arch in contrast to the Belt and Road Initiative (BRI) and China's Rising Influence in Panda, J., and Basu, T., (Eds.), China-India-Japan in the Indo-Pacific, Institute of Defence Studies and Analysis, Pp. 261-292, Pg. 274

127 Khurana, G.S. (2019), Ibid. Pg. 13

128 Lasius, J., (2017), Is Asia-Africa growth corridor the answer to China's BRI? https://www.orfonline.org/expert-speak/is-asia-africa-growth-corridor-answer-to-chinas-bri/

129 Khurana, G.S. (2019), Ibid., Pg. 13

130 Indian Navy Website, Chief of Royal Australian Navy Visits Indian Naval Academy, https://www.indiannavy.nic.in/content/chief-royal-australian-navy-visits-indian-naval-academy

131 Indian Navy Website, Admiral Sunil Lanba, Chairman Chiefs of Staff Committee and Chief of the Naval Staff to Visit United States of America, https://www.indiannavy.nic.in/content/admiral-sunil-lanba-chairman-chiefs-staff-committee-and-chief-naval-staff-visit-united

132 Indian Navy, US Ambassador Visits Western Naval Command, https://www.indiannavy.nic.in/node/20791

133 Dave, A., India and Russia: Ties that Bind, *Commentary*, 12 November 2018, RUSI, https://rusi.org/commentary/india-and-russia-ties-bind

134 Kaura, A., India's Strategic Links with the US: Differing Visions, Different Impact, *Commentary*, 4 June 2018, RUSI, https://rusi.org/commentary/indias-strategic-links-us-differing-visions-different-impact

China's Rise and Expanding Footprint in India's Neighbourhood

Commodore Sushant Dam

The global perception of China from the outside is much diffused and misplaced, which is either biased by the Western commentary or by Chinese party-controlled media propaganda. The objective and holistic assessment of China as a country lies somewhere in between these extremes. Even people who have spent considerable time in China honestly acknowledge that their understanding of China has numerous voids, due to data opacity and lack of reliable information.

In China, the political leadership considers survival of the party as the single-most important factor. Internal security, in terms of political stability, social unrest, separatist movements, demographic imbalance and economic headwinds are considered by Beijing to be far more critical than external challenges.

Amongst the external challenges, those which impinge upon China's core interests are oriented towards the Western Pacific. China's policy on unification of Taiwan is non-negotiable and they will go to any extent — including risking a direct conflict with United States — on this issue. The current situation in the Korean peninsula is an active issue that the Chinese are, at present, most concerned with. North Korea provides Chinese a critical buffer from South Korea, where US forces are deployed. Chinese would continue to demand denuclearisation and demilitarisation of the Korean peninsula. Any conflict in the peninsula, would also lead to a large influx of North Korean refugees. China is also trying to be assertive in the East China Sea and South China Sea enhancing its island claims, constructing huge militarised artificial features, and trying to erode the US-Japanese influence in the western Pacific Ocean. The Chinese realise the vulnerability of their Sea Line of Communication in the Indian Ocean

Region (IOR) and have been expanding their footprint in this area by way of naval deployments, maritime infrastructure, dual-use ports, and establishing naval bases.

Politically, President Xi Jinping (XJP) has established himself as one of the most powerful Chinese leaders, almost at par with Chairman Mao Tse Tung and Deng Xiaoping. He further consolidated his political position during the 19th Party Congress in 2017 by incorporating his thoughts on *"Socialism with Chinese Characteristics for a New Era"* into the Party Constitution and abolishing the ten-year limit on presidential terms.[1] Since 2012, he has also removed many political and Peoples Liberation Army (PLA) leaders from their positions, under the anti-graft campaign. These days, many in China say that either one is 'loyal' to President Xi Jinping or 'corrupt'. He has been able to effectively rein-in the power of the PLA and consolidate his hold on the Central Military Commission (CMC). He resolutely purged two Vice Chairmen of the CMC after 2012 and General Fang Fenghui and Zhang Yang in 2017. China's twin Centenary Goals (of 2021 and 2050) have been further refined by XJP's strategic goals for the PLA for the modernisation of the national defence and armed forces by 2035, and the People's Armed Forces transformation into a world-class military by 2050.[2]

China is also expanding its diplomatic footprint globally and Chinese diplomats have been on overdrive globally ever since President Xi Jinping has taken over the helm. President XJP's visits to specific countries across the globe offer a good indicator of where China's priorities lie. He visited more than 40 countries in the first 1000 day of assuming power.[3]

Source: Mercator Institute for China Studies

The macro-contours of Chinese relationship with India and her South Asian neighbours may be summarised as follows:

(a) As vibrant and stable democratic and economic power, India figures on top of China's engagement calculus. In particular, the Chinese consider India as a progressive country and a land of economic opportunities.

(b) Pakistan continues to be an "all-weather friend" of China's and a strategic tool to keep India engaged in a South Asian imbroglio.

(c) Afghanistan is important to China due to the internal security situation in Xinjiang province, especially after the drawdown of US forces.

(d) Other South Asian countries are being engaged by China to enhance her geopolitical and geostrategic position in the IOR. In recent times, Chinese political interference in Sri Lanka and Maldives has received a pushback.

A few important drivers underpinning China's expanding footprint in India's neighbourhood are as follows:

(a) Support in international organisations for China's core interests.

(b) Enabler for sustained economic growth.

(c) Ensuring a secure periphery and SLOC-protection in the IOR.

(d) Protecting overseas interests such as investments and the Chinese Diaspora.

(e) Expanding China's military footprint.

(f) Achieving great power status.

In the 40th year following the economic reforms initiated by Chairman Deng Xiaoping, the Chinese economy has made a formidable leap and would be at number one place by 2030 overtaking the United States.[4] As compared to the size of Chinese economy, no South Asian country, other than India, appears even as a fraction. We do keep hearing about the slowing down of the Chinese economic growth in recent years, but even a conservative assessment indicates that for a 12 trillion economy, even a 6.5% GDP growth rate is good enough.[5] If we compare South Asian GDP-growth rates, India at an impressive 7.3% GDP growth is only a 2.5 trillion economy.[6] Nepal, Pakistan, Sri Lanka and Afghanistan's growth continues to be low due to prevailing internal political, financial, security and social challenges. In terms of per capita GDP, other than Maldives, all other South Asia courtiers score less than 50% of the Chinese per capita GDP of $8700.[7]

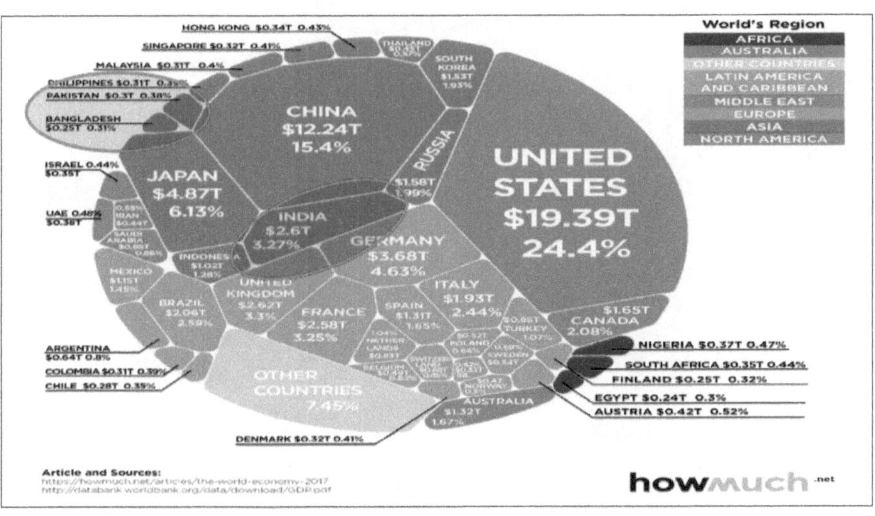

Regarding overseas direct investment, the Chinese are investing more elsewhere — in South-east Asia, Europe, Oceania and the Americas — than in South Asia. Chinese exports to South Asian countries, other than India, are also miniscule as compared to exports from China to the rest of the world. On the other hand, China is a major trading partner for Pakistan, Bangladesh, Myanmar and Sri Lanka. India is the only big emerging economy in South Asia and this explains the Chinese keenness to economically engage with India. Although India is a major trading partner of China, our bilateral trade of over $ 84 billion, suffers a trade deficit of over $ 50 Bn.[8]

No discussion on China is complete without referring to the Belt and Road Initiative (BRI), which is seen by some as a major geopolitical initiative that admirably serves that country's economic interests. A large number of MoUs and projects have been initiated by China in India's neighbourhood under the BRI 'brand'. Indeed, the BRI has several characteristics of neo-colonialism — for instance, exporting overcapacity, access to markets, exploiting key resources, and, establishing a foothold overseas. China's domination of the local economy of a BRI participant country makes the host country heavily indebted, thus exerting pressure on political, labour, social and security ecosystems of the country concerned. Chinese overseas direct investments in other parts of the world far exceed those in South Asia.[9] Pakistan, for example, is the biggest recipient of Chinese investment in our neighbourhood under the China-Pakistan Economic Corridor

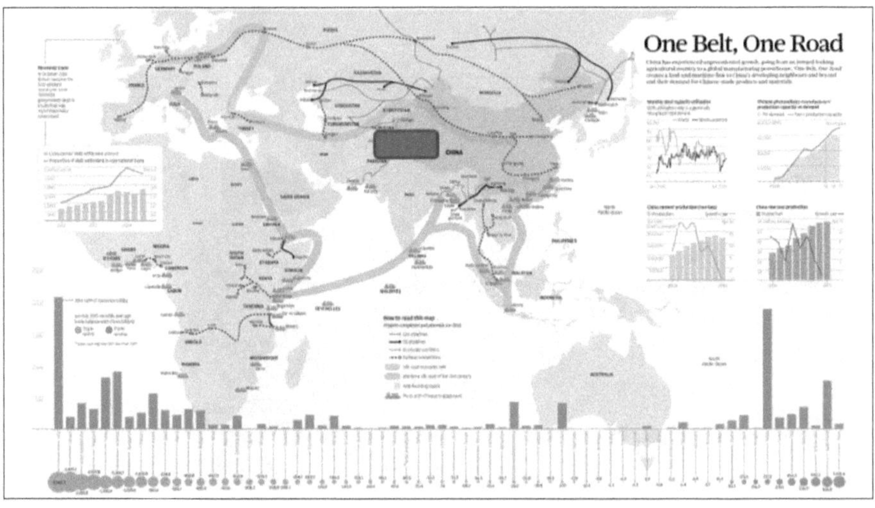

Source: South China Monitor

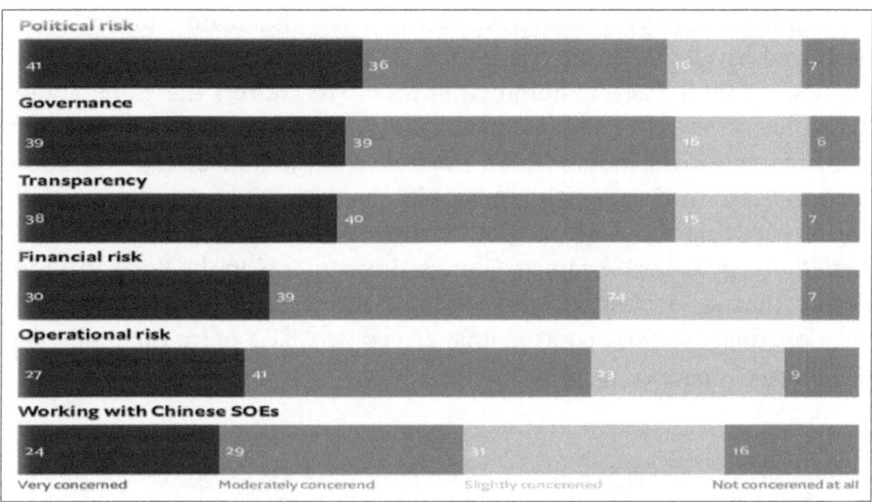

(CPEC), in respect of which the government of India has clearly expressed grave concerns due to territorial and sovereignty issues, as it passes through the Pakistan occupied Kashmir. *In order that Indians do not begin to accept the PoK as legitimate territory of Pakistan, this project needs to be referred-to throughout the Indian media and in official or unofficial writings by Indians as the 'China-Pakistan-Occupied-Kashmir Economic Corridor (CPOKEC) and not as the CPEC.* An analysis of the BRI projects indicates a wide spectrum of risks to these projects in the host countries. Many BRI participating countries have ended up in a debt trap. In fact, recent analysis shows that about 23 BRI participant countries are under high debt risk and 8 are caught in a severe debt trap.[10]

Many of the Chinese soft-power initiatives come with hard edges and are seen as subversive mechanisms for Chinese ideology, propaganda and indoctrination. The Chinese Diaspora mainly dominates Southeast Asia, as with the exception of Myanmar, none of India's immediate neighbours have a significant Chinese presence. Globally, about 135 Confucius Institutes are active in 51 countries along the Belt and Road.[11] A large number of Chinese students go to foreign universities, but their main destinations are the US, the UK, Europe and Australia. On the other hand, a large number of students from South Asia study in Chinese Universities under various scholarship schemes. This is a method adopted by China to gain favourable policy decisions in the countries-of-origin of these students. Chinese tourists made 145 million overseas trips in 2017, spending an estimated $115 billion ($ 5565 per head).[12] In India's own immediate neighbourhood, the Maldives and Sri Lanka are the main destinations for Chinese tourists.

Chinese energy and SLOC security are the main vulnerabilities perceived by China within the Indian Ocean. India sits astride all these SLOCs, comprehensively dominating them. To address the vulnerability, China has invested-in and, in many cases, even taken over, strategic port infrastructure in the Indian Ocean. Port takeovers in India's neighbourhood, such as those in Gwadar, Colombo, Hambantota, Chittagong and Sittwe, are of particular concern to New Delhi. An analysis, titled *"Harbored Ambitions"* by C4ADS, depicts Chinese investments in the ports in Indo-Pacific that serve Beijing's geo-strategic interests in terms of strategic location, dual use, State control, financial control, lack of transparency, and benefit to Chinese companies.[13]

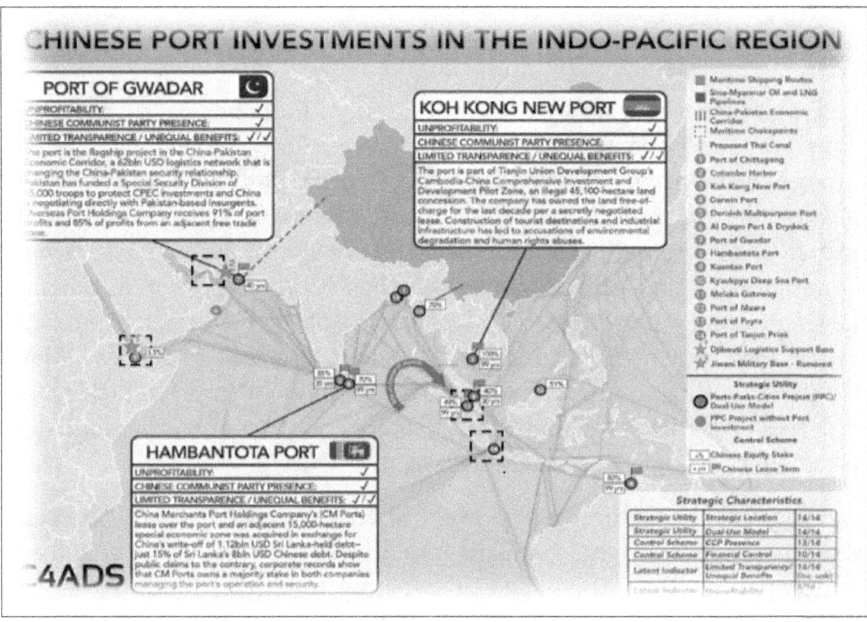

Source C4ADS

Analytic Dimension	Strategic Location	Development Model	CCP Presence	Financial Control	Transparency	Benefit Distribution	Profitability
Strategic Characteristic	Strategic Location	Dual-Use Model	CCP Presence	Financial Control	Limited Transparency	Unequal Benefits	Unprofitable
Classification	Strategic Utility	Strategic Utility	Control Scheme	Control Scheme	Latent Indicator	Latent Indicator	Latent Indicator
Port							
Port of Chittagong, Bangladesh	✓	✓	✓	unk	✓	unk	X
Colombo Harbour, Sri Lanka	✓	✓	✓	✓	✓	✓	X
Koh Kong New Port, Cambodia	✓	✓	✓	✓	✓	✓	unk
Darwin Port, Australia	✓	✓	✓	✓	✓	✓	X
Doraleh Multipurpose Port, Djibout	✓	✓	✓	✓	✓	unk	X
Al Duqm Port & Drydock, Oman	✓	✓	✓	unk	✓	unk	X
Port of Gwadar, Pakistan	✓	✓	✓	✓	✓	✓	✓
Hambantota Port, Sri Lanka	✓	✓	✓	✓	✓	✓	✓
Kuantan Port, Malaysia	✓	✓	✓	✓	✓	unk	unk
Kyaukpyu Deep Sea Port, Myanmar	✓	✓	✓	✓	✓	✓	unk
Melaka Gateway, Malaysia	✓	✓	✓	✓	✓	unk	✓
Port of Muara, Brunei	✓	✓	✓	✓	✓	unk	unk
Port of Payra, Bangladesh	✓	✓	✓	X	✓	unk	unk
Port of Tanjun Priok, Indonesia	✓	✓	unk	unk	✓	unk	X
Port Klang, Malaysia	✓						
Sittwe Port, Myanmar	✓			FAILED PORT DEALS			
Sondia Port, Bangladesh	✓						
Total Counts	15	14	13	10	15	14 (incl. unknown)	8 (incl. unknown)

Source C4ADS

In 2017, China established its first overseas naval base in Djibouti, and additional ones could be established in the near future including the Jiwani-Gwadar-Turbat triangle, as also some locations along the east coast of Africa. China has also increased her military diplomatic interaction and exercises in India's neighbourhood. As per a SIPRI analysis, about 75% of Chinese arms are exported to three India's neighbours, viz., Pakistan,

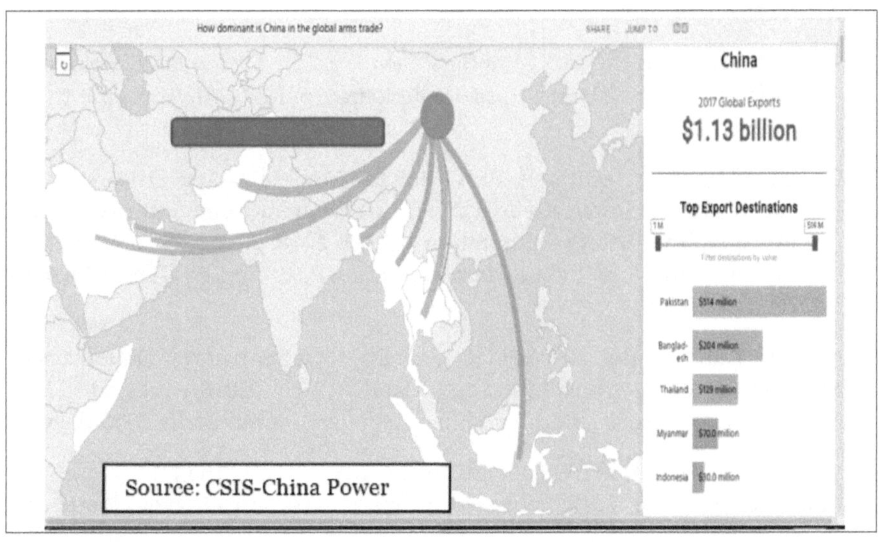

Bangladesh and Myanmar.[14] These include modern warships, submarines, fighter aircraft, tanks and artillery guns. In the last ten years, Chinese naval presence in the Indian Ocean has increased significantly. The Chinese navy has undertaken as many as 31 anti-piracy escort missions and six or seven submarine deployments. At any time three to six Chinese warships and research vessels are present in the India Ocean. During these deployments, Chinese warships and submarines regularly make port calls in India's neighbourhood. It is amply clear that the Chinese are trying hard to constrict India's strategic freedom of manoeuvre space in the Indian Ocean. The Indian Navy closely monitors maritime activities in the Indian Ocean through its 'mission-based deployments'.

China consider itself a rising power and tries to establish a favourable equation with other Great Powers such as the USA and Russia, whereas, India has positioned itself as a regional power even though it is emerging as a global player. In the foreseeable future, India-China relations could well be underpinned by cooperation on global issues, competition on economic issues and confrontation on security issues. The international community widely respects the strength, trust, stability and poise of the strong Indian elephant as compared to assertive, aggressive, hegemonic and untrustworthy Chinese Dragon.

Endnotes

1   Ankit Panda, Welcome to Xi Jinping's New Era, The Diplomat. 27 Feb 2018. Accessed 10 Mar 2019. https://thediplomat.com/2018/02/welcome-to-xi-jinpings-new-era/

2   Cortez A. Cooper, Testimony-PLA Military Modernization: Drivers, Force Restructuring, and Implications, U.S. -China Economic and Security Review Commission, The RAND Corporation. 15 Feb 2018. Accessed 10 Mar 2019. https://www.rand.org/content/dam/rand/pubs/testimonies/CT400/CT488/RAND_CT488.pdf

3   Nibil Alsabah, Around the World in 1,000 Days Xi's Superpower Diplomacy in Practice, The Mercator Institute of china Studies. 29 Jun 2016. Accessed 15 Mar 2019. https://www.merics.org/en/china-mapping/around-world-1000-days

4   SimonKennedy, China Will Overtake the U.S. in Less Than 15 Years, The Bloomberg. 25 sep 2018. Accessed 15 Mar 2019. https://www.bloomberg.

com/news/articles/2018-09-25/hsbc-sees-china-economy-set-to-pass-u-s-as-number-one-by-2030

5   The World Bank In China, The World bank. 08 Apr 2019. Accessed 10 Mar 2019. https://www.worldbank.org/en/country/china/overview

6   India to grow at 7.3% in 2019, 2020: Moody's, The Economics Time, 01 mar 2019. Accessed 10 Mar 2019. https://economictimes.indiatimes.com/news/economy/indicators/india-to-grow-at-7-3-in-2019-2020-moodys/articleshow/68213958.cms

7   List of countries by GDP (nominal) per capita, Wikipedia. Accessed 15 Mar 2019.   https://en.wikipedia.org/wiki/List_of_countries_by_GDP_(nominal)_per_capita

8   India expresses concern over widening trade deficit with China, The economic Times. 20 Mar 2019. Accessed 21 Mar 2019. https://economictimes.indiatimes.com/news/economy/foreign-trade/india-expresses-concern-over-widening-trade-deficit-with-china/articleshow/68496361.cms?from=mdr

9   China: Five facts about outward direct investment and their implication for future trend, BBVA Bancomer Team. 21 Mar 2019. Accessed 22 Mar 2019. https://www.fxstreet.com/analysis/china-five-facts-about-outward-direct-investment-and-their-implication-for-future-trend-201903210827

10 John Hurley, Scott Morris, and Gailyn Portelance, Examining the Debt Implications of the Belt and Road Initiative from a Policy Perspective, Center for Global Development. Mar 2018. Accessed 10 Mar 2019. https://www.cgdev.org/sites/default/files/examining-debt-implications-belt-and-road-initiative-policy-perspective.pdf

11   Five Years of Sheer Endeavour: What Data Says about Confucius Institute (2012-2017), Confucius Institute Headquarters (Hanban). 26 Oct 2017. Accessed 10 Mar 2019. http://english.hanban.org/article/2017-10/26/content_703508.htm

12   A profile of Chinese Outbound Travellers, Dragontrail Interactive. Accessed 10 Mar 2019.   https://dragontrail.com/resources/videos-presentations/infographic-a-profile-of-chinese-outbound-travelers

13   Devin Thorne and Ben Spevack, Harboured Ambitions: How China's Port Investments are Strategically Shaping the Indo-Pacific, C4ADS. Apr 2108. Accessed 10 Mar 2019. https://static1.squarespace.com/static/566ef8b4d8af107232d5358a/t/5ad5e20ef950b777a94b55c3/1523966489456/Harbored+Ambitions.pdf

14   How dominant is China in the global arms trade?, China Power, Center for Strategic and International Studies. Accessed 10 Mar 2019. https://chinapower.csis.org/china-global-arms-trade/

Commercial & Military Applications of Maritime Silk Road

Lt Gen S.L. Narasimhan PVSM, AVSM, VSM (Retd.)

Introduction

On o7 September 2013, President Xi Jinping made a speech titled, "**To Promote people to people friendship and create a better future**", at Kazakhstan's Nazarbayev University, wherein he outlined the One Belt One Road initiative.[1] He proposed that *"In order to make the economic ties closer, mutual cooperation with each other and space of development between the Eurasian countries, we can innovate the mode of cooperation and jointly build the silk road economic belt step by step to mutually form overall regional cooperation"*. He further highlighted five tenets of the initiative as follows: -

(a) **To Strengthen Policy Connection**. The countries in the region can connect with each other on economic development strategies and make plans and measures for regional cooperation through consultations.

(b) **To Improve Road Connectivity**. To open transportations channel from the Pacific Sea to the Baltic Sea and gradually form a transportation network that connects East Asia, West Asia and South Asia.

(c) **To Promote Trade Facilitation**. All parties should discuss issues concerning trade and investment and make appropriate arrangements.

(d) **To Enhance Monitoring**. All parties should promote the realisation of exchange and settlement of local currency and increase the ability to fend off financial risks and make the region more economically competitive in the world.

(e) **To Strengthen the People to People Exchanges**. All parties should strengthen the friendly exchanges between their people to promote understanding and friendship with each other.

2.   Out of the five tenets enumerated by him, the first one did not take place at all. However, China nevertheless felt that other countries should join this initiative. This has been one of the bones of contention between India and China. India maintains that this approach was announced unilaterally and therefore it is a singularly Chinese approach and not a joint one. The third tenet, which stipulates that all parties should discuss issues concerning trade and investment, is again an issue that has been given a go by. The fourth one, which involves promotion and realisation and settlement in local currency is something that China is aspiring for and for which she works bilaterally with other countries. This is to obviate the present dependence upon the US dollar and gradually displace it as the currency for international trade. When the financial crisis struck the world in 2008, China openly stated that there should be an alternative currency to the US Dollar.[2]

3.   The logic for the 'One Belt One Road' (OBOR) initiative, which comprises the 'Maritime Silk Route' and the 'Silk Route Economic Belt' is twofold. One is economic and the second is strategic. The economic rationale of the OBOR is four-fold. In 2008, a financial crisis struck the world. China, which was depending upon on export-related growth, saw a substantial reduction in the growth of her export-oriented economy.[3] This resulted in China trying to improve domestic consumption. However, China failed in this endeavour.[4] Consequently, the global financial crisis and lack of improvement in domestic consumption created excess capacity in China. This, combined with the global need for investment in infrastructure, gave rise to the 'One Belt One Road' initiative. Secondly, in order to sustain its economic growth, China wanted to enter new markets and sources for raw materials.[5] Fourthly, in keeping with the second Centenary Goal of being an important power (if not the most important one) by 2049, China set out to achieve dominance both strategically and commercially. Another strategic logic for the OBOR initiative is China's location and her restricted access to the Indian Ocean. This was amply articulated by Mr. Hu Jintao, former president of China, in November 2003, as "the Malacca Dilemma".[6]

4.   Initially, the 'Silk Road Economic Belt' comprised a single axis, leading from China to Europe. Over a period of time, however, it has grown into six different axes.[7] However, the 'Maritime Silk Route' has remained

a link between China and the Indian Ocean and thence, through the Red Sea, into the Mediterranean Sea and on to Atlantic Ocean. It appears that China intends to gain control of the entry and exit points of the various seas in the world by acquiring a number of ports and / or terminals. China's aim appears to be to control commerce with others through these ports and terminals.

Map Showing China's Influence

The stars marked in the map above are indicative of the influence of China in those countries or the ports that China has acquired or is in the process of acquiring. In the past few years, China has acquired 29 ports in fifteen countries and the COSCO company of China has bought 47 terminals in 13 countries. In the recent past, Italy was first amongst European Countries to sign a Memorandum of Understanding on the 'One Belt One Road' with China, and Rome has offered the ports of Genoa and Trieste to the latter. Combined with Haifa in Israel, Piraeus in Greece, and the effort to buy the port of Sines in Portugal, China will have a significant presence across the entire Mediterranean Sea.

5.   The Maritime Silk Route also corresponds to China's import through transit routes. The Malacca Strait caters for 82% of China's oil imports and 30% of its natural gas imports. Similarly, the imports of crude and natural gas from Africa and Atlantic ports of America, Gulf of Aden and Red Sea, Straits of Hormuz correspond to 26%, 3%; 3%, 4%; 43% and 18% respectively.

6.   **Importance of the Indian Ocean Region.** All except one of the One Belt One Road routes run towards west of China, either to Eurasia or through Indian Ocean region. Secondly, the Indian Ocean acts as conduit between Atlantic and Pacific Oceans. Thirdly, in the Indian Ocean region, countries are low in GDP, lacking in political stability and infrastructure development. Therefore, they need financial support for improving their development status. Fourthly, the Indian Ocean region is host to energy-rich West Asian and resource-rich Africa. Fifthly, all the countries in the Indian Ocean region enjoy a demographic dividend. Therefore, the area has prospects for investment and it is also an attractive and a large market for the future. And lastly, there is an absence of a strong regional security architecture like NATO. All these factors make the Indian Ocean region an attractive area for China to venture into.

7.   China resorted to investments in ports like Djibouti. She has also won a contract to build the Melaka Port in Malaysia.[8] In addition to its investment in ports, China has been carrying out deep sea mining in the Indian Ocean with the aim of mining rare earths. It has also been exporting military equipment to countries like Thailand, Bangladesh, Pakistan and Sri Lanka. China has been trying hard for the construction of a waterway across Kra Isthmus.[9] Since 2008, China started participating in anti-piracy patrols in the Gulf of Aden. The piracy off the coast of Somalia gave an incentive and impetus for China to enter the Indian Ocean region. With its investment in the ports of Hambantota and Gwadar, China seems to be increasing its permanent presence in the Indian Ocean region.

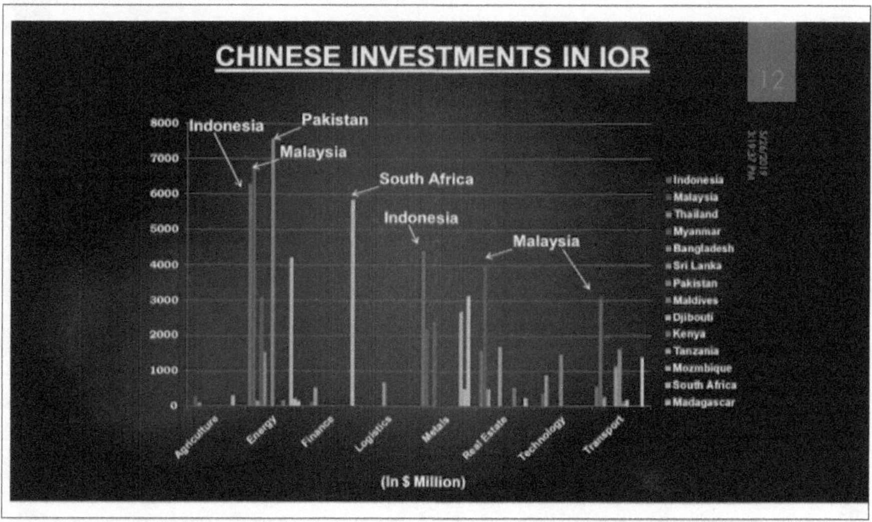

8.	**China-Pakistan Economic Corridor**. The geographic location of China impinges adversely on her desire to become a maritime power. Therefore, it has been making efforts to create corridors to have access to Indian Ocean Region. The China-Pakistan Economic Corridor (CPEC) is important from that perspective. Beijing's efforts to create a China-Myanmar Economic Corridor, linking Sittwe to China, is also an effort in this direction. From the initial commitment of USD 46 billion, the China Pakistan Economic Corridor has become a USD 62 billion project. Of this, Gwadar Port alone is expected to get USD 792 million in investment and is expected to be converted into a maritime hub. China is also planning a Chinese township in Gwadar at a cost of $ 150 million.[10] The draft long-term plan of the China Pakistan Economic Corridor was leaked, in the summer of 2017, by the Pakistan newspaper "The Dawn". The plan revealed China's effort to increase its influence in Pakistan and also its plans to acquire agricultural land.[11] However, after Imran Khan became the Prime Minister of Pakistan, there has been a review and some pushback against at least some of the projects that China was to execute as part of CPEC.

9.	A number of countries have been pushing back against One Belt One Road projects. A map, prepared by "Gateway House", the Mumbai-based think-tank, shows this pushback against Chinese projects.

10.   **Commercial Implications of One Belt One Road Initiative**. Seven commercial implications of the OBOR can be drawn from the foregoing arguments. First, with the acquisitions of ports and terminals, China will have increased control of commerce.[12] Secondly, it will help in ensuring a supply of natural resources and rare earths to China. Thirdly, the financial assistance and implementation of projects by China will increase the dependence of recipient countries on China.[13] Fourthly, it helps China in gaining a foothold in all these countries. With the spread of projects all over South Asia, Africa and Europe, it will automatically increase the Chinese influence in these regions. Fifthly, China is also looking for food security for its citizens. It has acquired agricultural land in a number of countries, probably with a view to grow food there.[14] It is a well-known fact that only 11% of China's land is arable. In order to ensure availability of food for her citizens, China has to outsource production of food by utilising the agricultural land that has been acquired by her in other countries. Sixthly, it is an easier route to gain political advantage in the countries in which China is investing in various projects, and lastly, the projects that are being undertaken as part of the OBOR initiative gives China legitimacy to her military presence in the garb of protecting her national interests.[15]

11.   **Military Implications**. The Maritime Silk Road, which is part of the OBOR initiative also has a number of military implications. Six aspects of this need particular mention. First of all, it enables China to create assets that can also be used militarily when the time comes.[16] Secondly, in its 2015 Defence White Paper, China clearly articulated that the role of PLA will be enhanced to protect Chinese interests, thereby indicating that the PLA may have a global role to protect Chinese interests. Thirdly, the spread of OBOR projects and the acquisitions related to it gives PLA a chance to expand its presence globally[17]. Fourthly, as part of the military reforms that were announced in November 2015 by President Xi Jinping, China has plans to increase the marine corps strength to 100,000 from the present 10,000[18] (Chan, 2017). This initiative combined with the operationalisation of aircraft carrier battle groups of China will enable it to have expeditionary capabilities. For an effective expeditionary capability, China needs a support system across the globe. The Maritime Silk Route will enable China to have that support system. Fifthly, China has been carrying out military exercises with a number of countries that are part of the Maritime Silk Route. This will help to improve the operational capability of the Chinese armed forces. Lastly, China has been exporting military platforms to countries along the Maritime Silk Route. The

importance of supplying military equipment is that it makes the recipient country dependent on the supplier of such equipment for a long time in terms of maintenance, supply of spares, training, etc. Thus, the recipient countries will have an increasing dependence on China.

Conclusion.

12.　　China's One Belt One Road initiative, which is a combination of the Silk Route Economic Belt and the Maritime Silk Route was initially conceived as a geoeconomic initiative. As it progressed, however, this initiative began assuming wider geopolitical and geostrategic overtones. This is mainly because China did not follow a consultative process for the One Belt One Road initiative. Moreover, the award of contracts for the projects in this initiative was not done in a transparent manner and international standards were not adhered-to. Most contracts were awarded to Chinese companies. These aspects have moved this ambitious project from the geoeconomic to the geopolitical arena. The OBOR initiative is here to stay. It is also likely that it may increase the influence of China across the continents. The commercial viability of many of the projects have been under question. This OBOR initiative will pan-out to other parts of the world over a period of time and needs to be watched closely.

Endnotes

1　Jinping, X. (2013, September 07). *President Xi Jinping Delivers Important Speech and Proposes to Build a Silk Road Economic Belt with Central Asian Countries.* Retrieved from Ministry of Foreign Affairs of Peoples Republic of China: https://www.fmprc.gov.cn/mfa_eng/topics_665678/xjpfwzysiesgjtfhshzzfh_665686/t1076334.shtml

2　Anderlini, J. (2009, March 24). China calls for new reserve currency. *Financial Times.* Retrieved from https://www.ft.com/content/7851925a-17a2-11de-8c9d-0000779fd2ac

3　Morrison, W. M. (2009). *China and the Global Financial Crisis: Implications for the United States.* Washington DC: Congressional Research Service. Retrieved from https://fas.org/sgp/crs/row/RS22984.pdf

4　Prasad, E. (2015). *The path to sustainable growth in China.* Washington DC: Brookings Institution. Retrieved from https://www.brookings.edu/testimonies/the-path-to-sustainable-growth-in-china/

5　Djankov, S. (2016, March). China's Belt and Road Initiative - Motives, Scope And Challenges. (S. M. SIMEON DJANKOV, Ed.) *Peterson Institute for Internationsl Economics.* Retrieved from https://piie.com/system/files/documents/piieb16-2_1.pdf

6   Storey, I. (2006, April 12). China's Malacca Dilemma. *China Brief,* 6(8). Retrieved from https://jamestown.org/program/chinas-malacca-dilemma/

7   Wade, G. (2016). *China's 'One Belt, One Road' initiative.* Parliament of Australia. Retrieved from https://www.aph.gov.au/About_Parliament/Parliamentary_Departments/Parliamentary_Library/pubs/BriefingBook45p/ChinasRoad

8   Maresca, T. (2017, July 05). China's growing ambitions in Malaysia raise questions about Beijing's true motive. *USA Today.* Retrieved from https://www.usatoday.com/story/news/world/2017/07/05/melaka-malaysia-china-project/423027001/

9   Yee, C. K. (2018, April 08). China to build Kra Canal across Thailand to bypass Malacca Strait. *China Daily Mail.* Retrieved from https://chinadailymail.com/2018/04/08/china-to-build-kra-canal-across-thailand-to-bypass-malacca-strait/

10 Chinese-only colony' in Pakistan to house 5 lakh workers. Retrieved from https://www.businesstoday.in/current/world/chinese-colony-in-pakistan-international-port-city-cpec-gwadar/story/281497.html

11 Husain, K. (2017, June 21). Exclusive: CPEC Master Plan Revealed. *The Dawn.* Retrieved from https://www.dawn.com/news/1333101

12 Zail, C. P. (2018, June 05). With Acquisition of California Port, China Broadens Influence on US Commerce. *AMAC.* Retrieved from https://amac.us/with-acquisition-of-california-port-china-broadens-influence-on-us-commerce/

13 Taj, H. (2019, May). China's new Silk Road or debt-trap diplomacy? *Global Risks Insights.* Retrieved from https://globalriskinsights.com/2019/05/china-debt-diplomacy/

14 China, voracious buyer of foreign agricultural land. (2018, February 25). *The Express Tribune.* Retrieved from https://tribune.com.pk/story/1644418/3-china-voracious-buyer-foreign-agricultural-land/

15 Lily Kuo, N. K. (2018, July 30). What is China's Belt and Road Initiative? *The Guardian.* Retrieved from https://www.theguardian.com/cities/ng-interactive/2018/jul/30/what-china-belt-road-initiative-silk-road-explainer

16 Green, M. J. (2018). *China's Maritime Silk Road: Strategic and Economic Implications for the Indo-Pacific Region.* Centre for Strategic and International Studies. Retrieved from https://www.csis.org/analysis/chinas-maritime-silk-road

17 *How will the Belt and Road Initiative advance China's interests?* (2017, May). Retrieved from China Power: https://chinapower.csis.org/china-belt-and-road-initiative/

18 Chan, M. (2017, March 13). As overseas ambitions expand, China plans 400 per cent increase to marine corps numbers, sources say. *South China Morning Post.* Retrieved from https://www.scmp.com/news/china/diplomacy-defence/article/2078245/overseas-ambitions-expand-china-plans-400pc-increase

Integrated Coastal Security Management — After the Mumbai Terror Attack

Gp Capt AV Chandrasekaran, IAF (Retd.)

On 27 Nov 08, India was rudely awakened by the worst *fedayeen* attack on Indian soil. The series of attacks in South Mumbai unfolded into a huge hostage crisis, as militants, holed-up in the iconic hotels, Taj and Trident, went about their job with clinical efficiency. This attack was a fallout of the negligent maritime surveillance along India's vast and porous coastal stretch. The assassins of India's late Prime Minister, Shri Rajiv Gandhi, also came through the sea from Sri Lanka and so did the explosives that ignited Mumbai in 1993. The vastness of India's maritime zones has seen an increased proliferation of criminal and terrorist networks that has vitiated the security scene and is cause of concern for Indian security agencies.

With coastal security proving to be the nation's *Achilles' Heel,* which has been repeatedly exposed and exploited, it is imperative that the collective might of the nation be amalgamated into a mission to safeguard the country's shoreline. Admiral Sureesh Mehta, the former Chief of the Naval Staff, explicitly stated, *"history has taught India two bitter lessons: firstly, that neglect of maritime power led to loss of sovereignty, and secondly, that it takes many decades to restore maritime power after a period of neglect and decline"*.[1] Regrettably, for many decades after Independence, the country did not quite grow out of its continental mind-set and focus remained primarily upon developments in India's land-neighbourhood.

A slew of measures was hurriedly taken to plug the gaping holes in the coastal security. The measures adopted were primarily due to a harsh review by the Pradhan Committee, consisting of Shri RD Pradhan (former Home Secretary, Government of India) and Shri V Balachandran, (former Special Secretary in the Cabinet Secretariat, Government of India), both of whom probed the causes of the Mumbai attack and, in their recommendations, brought out that coastal security was woefully inadequate, and there was a definite lack of operational coordination between the state-level coastal police and the Indian Coast Guard, and also gross inadequacy in the training and equipment of the police force. It is over a decade since the infamous Mumbai attack and a dispassionate dissection of the current state of readiness still leaves much to be desired. Despite an overhaul of India's coastal defence architecture, prompting a three-tier security arrangement, with the navy, the coast guard, and the marine police jointly safeguarding India's "near seas", the coastal security project remains work in progress. There are gaps that beg urgent attention to prevent yet another seaborne attack.

Big-Ticket Initiatives

The Indian Government had embarked upon an ambitious plan to overhaul the country's security apparatus to make it more robust and capable of responding to any security situation at short notice. Some of the important decisions taken and implemented are summarised in the succeeding paragraphs.

1. Role of Indian Navy: In April of 2009, after a great deal of deliberation, the Indian Navy was placed in charge of overall maritime security. This responsibility included both coastal and offshore security, and the navy was to be assisted by the Indian Coast Guard (ICG), state marine police forces, and other central and state agencies designated for the purpose. The Indian Coast Guard, in addition, was designated as the authority responsible for coastal security in the country's Territorial Sea, including areas to be patrolled by the coastal police. Further, to ensure that assets were optimally deployed with minimum time lapse for emergent requirements and to ensure synergy between the two organisations, the Indian Navy was authorised to control all navy and coast guard joint operations.[2]

2. Coastal Radars: The Ministry of Home Affairs (MHA), Government of India, planned to integrate the entire coastline into a single radar network which could seamlessly monitor movements in the sea. The government entrusted Bharat Electronics Limited (BEL), an India Public Sector Undertaking (PSU), with the responsibility of establishing a chain of 46 static radar sensors along the entire coastline. The project, known as the Coastal Surveillance Network (CSN), comprises a 'chain of static sensors' (CSS) including radar, Automatic Identification System (AIS), Long-Range Identification and Tracking (LRIT), day-and-night cameras, and, communication systems. Vessel Traffic Management System (VTMS) radars in ports along the coastline also facilitate surveillance of port areas. The installation of these radars help in maintaining a network of coastal surveillance radars across the region, leading to heightened Intelligence, Surveillance, and Reconnaissance (ISR) capabilities and Maritime Domain Awareness (MDA) for the Indian Navy and the Indian Coast Guard.[3] The radar stations were also fitted with high-resolution cameras with a range of 10 nautical miles.

3. Automatic Identification Systems (AIS): The Directorate General of Lighthouses and Lightships (DGLL), Government of India, established a national AIS network by setting up 74 shore stations on existing lighthouses along the Indian coast, primarily for facilitating aids to marine navigation and tracking of Safety of Life at Sea (SOLAS) vessels. This facility would provide an overall image of AIS-compliant vessels along the Indian coastline. Thus, apart from effective security-management, the AIS network would aid navigation and facilitate the creation of maritime domain awareness along the coastline. A total of six Regional Control Centres (RCCs), located at regional headquarters at Jamnagar, Mumbai, Kochi, Chennai, Kolkata, and Vishakhapatnam, were also established for the smooth flow of data. In addition, two Coastal Control Centres (CCCs) located at Deep Bhavan, Mumbai, and Dolphin's Nose Lighthouse, Vishakhapatnam, were created. The National Data Centre (NDC), located at Deep Bhavan, Mumbai, the simulator located at Dolphin's Nose Lighthouse, Vishakhapatnam, and the viewing terminals for the Indian Navy at the Directorate of Net Centric Operations (DNCO), New Delhi, along with Joint Operations Centres (JOCs) at Mumbai and Vishakhapatnam, enhanced the overall operational efficiency. The viewing terminals for the ICG, located at Coast Guard Headquarters (CGHQ), New Delhi, and, for the Directorate General of Shipping located at the Long Range Identification and Tracking (LRIT) Data Centre, in Jahaz Bhavan, Mumbai, were also operationalised.[4] There are now a total of 74 AIS receivers along the Indian coast and these are capable of tracking 30,000 to 40,000 merchant ships transiting through the Indian Ocean. AIS is mandatory for all merchant ships above 300 tonnes Dead Weight Tonnage (DWT) and helps monitoring agencies to keep track of shipping and detect suspicious ships.

4. Command, Control, and Coordination Centre: The Indian Navy, through the CCC Centre, will be able to track the real-time movement of ships and fishing boats plying in the waters all along India's 7,500-km-long coastline. It has set up a Command Centre in Gurgaon, which will receive real-time radar feeds and pictures taken by high-definition cameras, satellites and maritime surveillance aircraft. The footage will be exactly the same as captured by 46 coastal radar stations now operating in the remotest corners of the country. This is broadly termed the 'Information Management Analysis Centre' (IMAC). This command centre will enable the Indian Navy and other stakeholders in coastal security to take effective action in case a rogue ship or boat is detected. This Rupees 450-Crore project, also known as the 'National Command, Control, Communication and Intelligence Centre' (NC3I), was launched soon after the 26/11 attacks in Mumbai. The Command Centre, which is the nodal centre of the NC3I network, will go a long way in plugging these gaps through around-the-clock surveillance by radars, high-definition electro-optic cameras, and satellites. An operator, sitting at his console in the Gurgaon centre, can access real-time information on his computer screen about traffic of ships and boats in his designated zone, be it in the waters of Chennai or off remote spots in the Andaman and Nicobar Islands. In the aftermath of the Mumbai terror attacks, at least 46 coastal radar stations at strategic locations in all the nine littoral states continuously monitor the coastal seas. With the main centre at Gurgaon, which is 80% indigenised, becoming functional, the officer on watch will get the same information and/or visual data as seen by his counterparts manning the coastal radar stations. All stations, core centres and main command posts are connected with a high-tech computer network, through a specially-developed Coastal Surveillance and Decision Support software system, designed and managed by the Navy. The 'Decision-making' or Decision-Support Software' (DSS), as it is termed, has been procured from the US-based company Raytheon, but has been customised by Indian Naval IT software-experts, who have developed their own algorithms. After being duly certified by the Scientific Analyst Group (SAG) under the DRDO, it is considered hack-proof.[5]

5. Information Management and Analysis Centre: The Information Management and Analysis Centre (IMAC) was inaugurated by the then Defence Minister, Shri Manohar Parikkar, on 23 November 2014. The facility is located in Gurgaon within the National Capital Region (NCR), and is a joint venture of the Indian Navy, the Indian Coast Guard, and BEL. This is primarily to ensure improved coastal surveillance and near fool-proof coastal security. It will be operationally under the Indian Navy but functionally under the National Security Advisor (NSA).[6] This has been primarily established to be the single-point assessment centre interlinking the chain of radars installed. It will function as the nodal centre for the National Command, Control, Communications, and Intelligence Network (NC3I Network), which will link all the 20 Naval and 31 Coast Guard monitoring stations with the IMAC thereby generating a real-time picture of India's coastal waters. The system currently comprises 46 radars, with the remote hubs of the system being linked with the centre by high-speed optical fibre networks and satellite link-ups as a backup. In addition to the coastal radars and optical sensors, it also seeks and draws information from the Automatic Identification System (AIS) installed in merchant ships and has a comprehensive database for the analysis of traffic.

6. NATGRID (National Intelligence Grid): The NATGRID is primarily a national, computerised, information-sharing network. This agency is expected to be the binding factor for all intelligence agencies by linking all databases of all departments of the Government of India, in order to collect real-time intelligence so as to thwart any terror attempts. The intelligence gathered would be disseminated to involved agencies for identifying, capturing and prosecuting terrorists. Ten Central Government 'user' agencies, including the Intelligence Bureau (IB) will be able to electronically access 21 sensitive databases, in several areas such as banks, credit card trails and accounts, the internet, cell phones, immigration data, motor vehicle departments, the railways, the National Crime Records Bureau, SEBI, the income tax department, etc. This, coupled with the Crime and Criminal Tracking Network System (CCTNS), would integrate central and state crime-data. If NATGRID succeeds in becoming fully functional, it is expected to yield a '360-degree profile' of any given suspect.[7]

7. Sagar Prahari Bal: The Sagar Prahari Bal (SPB) meaning 'Ocean Sentinels', is an elite unit of the Indian Navy, and was formed in March 2009. The force is entrusted with the primary responsibility of providing seaward protection to Indian Naval harbours, jetties, and coastal installations. It consists of approximately 2,000 personnel and is equipped with around 80 high-speed patrol boats. The fast interceptor boats have a maximum speed of 50 nautical miles per hour and would be used by the Navy to intercept suspicious boats along the, subjecting them to inspection and verification. They will also be used for preventing crimes such as poaching and smuggling, apart from counter-terror operations. The sailors are trained at the INS *Shivaji*, a naval training and engineering base, near Lonavla, Pune. The SPB maintains security at all major and minor ports in India and carries out around-the-clock patrolling including shallow-water operations by day, while during the night it carries out seaward anti-terrorist patrols for the security of naval assets, besides high-speed interception of all suspicious vessels.

Promising Protocols

In addition to these major inductions and creations, certain small yet very vital actions were undertaken by the Government of India. These measures included both, the human resource as well as the induction of various types of specialised equipment, so as to enhance the efficacy of maritime security. Some of these are:

1. Radiation Portal Monitor: It would be operationally unwise to assume that only conventional weapons would be used as a means of carrying out terror attacks on Indian soil. With an ever-increasing number of non-State actors seeking access to nuclear and radiological materials, a radiological and/or nuclear attack has become a serious threat. The Government of India has sought to induct devices not only to deter attacks but to detect the basic materials needed for a radiological and/or nuclear attack.[8] These devices will monitor major ports of entry in an effort to minimise the threat of an individual or group smuggling radiological and/or nuclear material into the country. Terror outfits such as the *Lashkar*, JeM and *Al Qaeda* have deep links with the Pakistani intelligence setup which is known for its nuclear proliferation to various rogue nations. Hence, India remains greatly concerned about the possibility of a dirty bomb smuggled through containers and a subsequent detonation at its critical infrastructure and has installed Radiation Portal Monitors (RPMs) at various ports. These are passive, non-intrusive devices used to screen objects and persons passing through them for nuclear and radiological materials. These devices can detect various types of radiation emanating from nuclear devices, dirty bombs, and special nuclear materials. They are built to sense ionizing radiation emitted through cargo containers, including gamma radiation and some neutron emissions. The detectors can be made part of a 'discreet fixed-mount detection system' that can be set to scan smaller containers and even people. In addition, video monitoring equipment can also be made integral to such devices. These monitors have been installed in the Jawaharlal Nehru Port Trust (JNPT), and the ports of Mumbai, Kandla, New Mangalore, Cochin, Tuticorin, Ennore, Chennai, Vizag, Paradip and Kolkata.[9]

2. Increase in the intake of Police Forces: A shortage of police personnel has often been blamed for rising crime in in India. From insurgency to rising crimes against women, the blame is usually placed on a skewed police-to-people ratio, and high vacancies in police forces. In the aftermath of the Mumbai attack (26/11) the probe committee found a huge difference in the sanctioned strength and the actual strength in the Maharashtra

Police with the shortage being 11, 503 personnel! The situation is not any better in other major states either. In addition to being short in numbers, policemen are ill-trained, ill-equipped and desperately short of modern technologies for effective policing. State police forces had 24% vacancies (about 5.5 lakh vacancies) in January 2016. Hence, while the sanctioned police strength was 181 police per lakh persons in 2016, the actual strength was 138 policemen. The figure is an average across the country. It is pertinent to note that the United Nations recommended standard is 250 police per lakh persons.[10] This invariably leads to an overburdened police force. It was also disheartening to note that states with better economic resources were spending much less than those with poorer ones. While prosperous states like Maharashtra and Tamil Nadu spent only 3% and 3.1% of their state budget, smaller states like Manipur and Nagaland spend 8.1% and 7.2% of their budget, respectively.[11] This is testimony to the low importance that states accord to their police force, despite the latter being a crucial element in the security wellbeing of the country.

In order to mitigate this problem, there has been a substantial increase in the intake of the police force in the aftermath of 26/11 Mumbai attacks. Although the shortfalls remain, the gaps between the sanctioned and the actual strength has narrowed. In addition to the Maharashtra Police, several states in India have formed their own commando forces, specially trained and equipped for anti-terrorist operations. In addition, police forces of most vulnerable coastal states have been provided with advanced weapons, bullet-proof vests, and amphibious vehicles for seaward coastal patrolling. CCTV cameras have been placed at all vantage points, and additional coastal police stations have been sanctioned. Five National Security Guard (NSG) hubs — in Chennai, Ahmedabad, Mumbai, Hyderabad and Kolkata — have been set-up for a rapid response from this elite force. Creating NSG hubs in all four corners of the country is meant to facilitate the rapid deployment of the NSG commandos for counter-terror and counter-hijack operations. The response time taken by the commando force for countering the Mumbai terror attacks in 2008 had come under criticism and therefore the government had decided to station the commandos at various locations so that crucial time was not lost in transit.

3. Multi Agency Centre (MAC): The Multi Agency Centre (MAC) was established in 2002 but only had a limited role to play. It was revamped in 2009, after the 26/11 attack, to streamline intelligence gathering and sharing. However, it is interesting to note that the MAC is not entrusted with responsibility for intelligence-gathering. MAC, which functions under the Intelligence Bureau, is the nodal body at the Centre for sharing intelligence inputs on a daily basis. All agencies are expected to share information with MAC. The intelligence thus gathered by MAC is then shared with all other concerned agencies in states. Each designated agency, and all Central Police Organisations, have an officer deputed who is responsible for coordinating with MAC and sharing intelligence on a daily basis. Similarly, at the state level, there is a Subsidiary Multi Agency Centre (SMAC) functioning under a similar mandate.[12]

The National Committee for Strengthening Maritime and Coastal Security (NCSMCS) is a national-level forum and an apex review mechanism for maritime and coastal security, in which all concerned ministries and government agencies are represented. The Indian Navy, the Indian Coast Guard, and the State Marine Police, along with other agencies such as the Customs, and the Port Trusts, patrol the Maritime Zones of India (MZI), islands, and the adjacent seas, using ships and aircraft to detect and check infiltration through the sea routes. Since '26/11' the Government has taken a number of measures to strengthen coastal, offshore and maritime security. Broadly, these measures include capacity augmentation of maritime security agencies for surveillance and patrol of the nation's maritime zones; enhanced technical surveillance of coastal and offshore areas; the establishment of mechanisms for inter-agency coordination; increased regulation of activities in the maritime zones; as also integration of the fishing and coastal communities. Besides, state-wise Standard Operating Procedures (SOPs) for coordination among various agencies on coastal security issues have been formulated. Coastal security exercises are being conducted regularly, by the Indian Navy and the Indian Coast Guard, to assess the effectiveness of existing mechanisms and to address gaps.[13]

The Centre has taken considerable steps and had invested a huge amount in evolving a secure coastal security infrastructure. In the decade since 26/11, there is definitely better synergy amongst the country's intelligence agencies, and a faster exchange of information. The system to have the country's most potent anti-terror force, the NSG, pre-positioned in different places to tackle any potential terror attack, in order to ensure rapidity of response, is truly welcome. Some states like Maharashtra, Andhra Pradesh and Delhi, to name just three, have raised well-trained counter-terror-forces of their own.

In many cases, however, the initiatives have been well planned but, unfortunately, implementation on the ground has been far from resounding. The overall situation cannot be said to be satisfactory and the reforms have not gone far. Major initiatives like the National Counter Terrorism Centre (NCTC) and the National Intelligence Grid are struggling to get off the ground primarily due to lack of political consensus. This brings to the fore, perhaps the most significant challenge to India: the politicisation of the terrorism debate in the country. The fractious nature of Indian politics has made it difficult for the country to evolve a coherent response to terrorism. There is no political consensus across the political spectrum on how best to fight terrorism and extremism. India, which has a complex, and often difficult Centre-state relationship, has not been able to effectively coordinate the joint actions required from both the bodies and hence, the implementation of counter-terrorism plans have not yielded quite the requisite efficacy.

4. **Flaws in Security Architecture:** While the idea behind MAC is to integrate intelligence, the flip side is that if poor or inaccurate intelligence has been gathered, it, too, gets 'integrated' across all agencies, as it is difficult to establish the veracity in quick time. Ground-level intelligence is often poor and needs to be improved through a dynamic approach. Another drawback is that while MAC collects all the intelligence and passes it on, there is no follow-up on whether there has been any action. There is no mechanism to monitor inputs sent to the states or other agencies. This leaves a gap in the intelligence network. This was precisely what happened during the Mumbai attacks, and despite advance intelligence warnings there was no action from the Maharashtra Police nor was there a follow up by the intelligence agencies which provided the intelligence inputs. Despite these limitations the lateral flow of intelligence has increased considerably. However, in the event of a crisis, individual states still need to formally request central help, which could slow down response times. The security of ports remains patchy: coastal police still lack adequate equipment and, in 2016, an Indian Intelligence Bureau audit concluded that 187 out of 227 minor ports still lacked any meaningful security overlay. The port of Tuticorin in Tamil Nadu, which is sensitive due to the proximity of Sri Lanka, continues to be an especially weak link in the security chain of southern India, and yet, this is only one of many ports that remain poorly guarded.

The Government of India has stipulated that the hulls and/or superstructure boats of all states be colour-coded. At the state level, there are plans to mandate specific colour-combinations for mechanised fishing boats to paint on their cabins, hulls, wheelhouses and superstructure, to facilitate identification from the surface as well as from the air. Likewise, each boat's registration number and name will have to be painted black at two places — on the roof of the cabin and near the stem.[14] The implementation challenges are not small. Maharashtra alone, the state that bore the brunt of the seaborne attack, has some 12,000 mechanised boats and 11,000 non mechanised ones. Consequently, except in the states of Gujarat and Tamil Nadu (the latter also uses a diesel subsidy to ensure compliance), compliance remains low, including in Maharashtra. In very great measure, it is vote-bank politics and populism that prevent meaningful implementation.

Fishing boats that are over 20 metres in length are required to be fitted with a DRDO-developed, smaller version of the Automatic Identification System (AIS) that has been mandated for ships (of tonnage exceeding 300 Deadweight Tonnes). In the latter case, vessel- and positional information, unique to each ship, is picked-up by shore-based radars and AIS receivers. However, smaller boats with lengths less than 20 metres, have no such requirements. Many fishermen are reluctant to get the DRDO-developed AIS fitted in their vessels for fear that if their location is monitored, it might compromise jealously-guarded information on fishing grounds, and, at a somewhat more sinister level, preclude their present freedom to engage in illegal, unreported and unregulated (IUU) fishing. Fisherman are also required to have biometric identification but there are no checks on compliance. In any case, out of some 4.5 lakh fishing boats in use along the coastline by fishermen, only two lakh have been registered. All of this is especially galling because the Mumbai attackers came ashore at a small fishing village near the city, and on a small boat.

As many as 194 coastal police stations have been set up, but only 204 of the 429 boats/vessels sanctioned have actually been inducted and only 23 of the 60 jetties sanctioned have been actually been constructed in the coastal states. Likewise, the coastal police stations put together have been provided only 284 jeeps and 554 motorcycles. There is an acute shortage of policeman posted in the coastal police stations thereby leading to a cumulative shortfall of over 80 per cent in patrolling effort, especially at night.[15]

The coastal police stations do not have adequate maritime capabilities, and a lack of coordination with other stakeholders is a persistent problem. These issues continue to dog the security architecture for the coastline, leading to diminished physical checks of fishing vessels. Despite setting up of Marine Police Stations in all the nine coastal states, the coastal police in most of these states are dependent on jetties and piers of other related departments like the Fisheries Department. The cost of operating the jetties is high — often prohibitively so. This is why in several states, even such jetties as have been provided are poorly utilised. There is a lack of adequate training to the coastal police. It is ironical that most policemen assigned to coastal police stations do not even know how to swim.[16]

Maintenance of patrol boats is also a costly affair, even where the boats are small (6 to 12 tonnes). According to a report from the Home Ministry, many coastal states have asked the Centre to devise a mechanism for the periodic maintenance of their patrol boats. There have been inordinate delays in the acquisition of land and in the setting-up of support-infrastructure such as barracks and staff quarters, and in all too many cases, these are simply absent.

State governments also have a 'free rider' mentality — a feeling that coastal security is the responsibility of the Centre — and hence remain largely uninterested in finding mechanisms through which to fund the costs. A posting to the marine police is considered a punishment, as it does not yield the perks that go with normal crime duties.[17]

A review of coastal security projects, which was carried out as recently as in 2017 by the Comptroller and Auditor General (CAG), has raised serious concerns. It has pointed out that the majority of projects are way astern of their timelines and schedules and less than half the allocated funds have been utilised. The vulnerable Andaman & Nicobar Islands were sanctioned Rs 32 Crores for enhancing and strengthening the coastal security, but only Rs. 14 Crore had been spent, which was disheartening to say the least. Another example of apathy in implementation concerns the utilisation of funds sanctioned by the Home Ministry, in November 2010, for purchase of 10 large vessels and 23 Rigid Inflatable Boats (RIBs), that were to be procured at a cost of Rs 302 Crore. These vessels were considered essential for surveillance along the coastline and were required to be stationed at ten predesignated strategic locations where Maritime Operational Centres (MOCs) were to be set up. The CAG report of 2017 stated that tenders were floated only in 2016 and finalised only in 2017 — that is, after a gap of six to seven years.

Under the coastal security scheme, a total of ten Maritime Operations Centres (MOCs) were to be set up as 'nerve centres' for the conduct of surveillance, patrols, and raids (where warranted), in the far flung and scattered islands of the A&N chain, and all preparatory works were to be completed by March 2011. Six years later, only one of out of the planned ten could be operationalised — at Kadamat, 75 km north of Port Blair.[18]

Vulnerability Assessment

The shortfalls in coastal security need urgent attention. There are about 3,600 fishing villages spread across the country. It is estimated that about 2.5 crore people live in and around 50 km off these coasts. There is also approximately 4,120 square kilometres of dense mangroves in these regions. These facts exponentially increase the risk of terrorists using this vast area for their nefarious activities.

The use of Waterborne Improvised Explosives (WBIED) cannot be ruled out. The most notable and widely known use of a WBIED was the attack by *Al Qaeda* affiliates on the USS *Cole*, in Aden, on 12 October 2000. An innocuous-looking small vessel, carrying a shaped charge with between 200 and 300 kg of explosives, simply drifted alongside the USS Cole and detonated. The explosion and resultant damage led to 17 fatalities, with a further 39 being wounded. The attack stunned the world as US warships had hitherto been considered to be impregnable. The USS Cole incident was not the first, nor most recent use of these tactics against shipping. Assorted anti-Israeli militant groups were known to have made use of small speedboats for suicide attacks way back 1973; and the Liberation Tigers of Tamil Eelam, widely known as the Tamil Tigers or LTTE, conducted at least ten small-boat suicide attacks against Sri Lanka warships in the period from 1990 to 2008. In several of these instances, including, of course, the attack on the USS Cole, WBIED were used as an asymmetric force-multiplier, generally by non-State elements against conventional, State-forces. India has several vital assets located all along its coast, including a number naval offshore and on shore establishments, nuclear plants, oil wells, ports, and merchant ships. All these present valuable and viable targets for terrorists, who have no qualms in carrying out suicide attacks.

One of the gravest maritime risks facing the nation is the potential of a terrorist group to obtain a WMD and detonate it within the confines of an Indian port city, military installation, or industrial facility. Closely aligned with this is the potential for the maritime domain to be used as a transportation medium for such a weapon, weapon materials, or components, with an eventual target farther inland. The sheer volume of sea traffic makes this job relatively easy for a determined terrorist. A study by the United Nations has revealed that organised crime, trafficking and smuggling are increasingly linked to global patterns of violence. Drugs and arms-smuggling is rife in much of the Indian Ocean.

The sea provides an easy way for international crime syndicates, unscrupulous traders and non-state actors to distribute their wares, or to provide belligerents with highly sophisticated weapons. While the entire coast of the India is vulnerable to clandestine landings of contraband, the Gujarat-Maharashtra coastline, the Tamil Nadu coast, the Sundarbans in West Bengal, and, the Andaman and Nicobar Islands, have been particularly prone to such activities.[19]

Standoff waterborne attacks, which include the use of Man Portable Air Defence Systems (MANPADS), through the use of a small vessels are considered to be credible threats. In November 2005, a cruise ship 100 nautical miles off the coast of Somalia was attacked by two 25-foot rigid hull inflatable boats. Although the attack was repulsed, it generated a lot of publicity. The effective exploitation of a small vessel as a stand-off attack platform provides numerous benefits for terrorists. These include greater operational security, improved access to targets (bypassing shore-side security measures), and, a fast means of escape. Cargo emanating from or bound for Indian ports is transported by numerous ships, vessels, and barges, via the inland and coastal waterway systems and the seas and oceans. Key energy-resources, such as coal for electrical power plants, crude-oil and petroleum-products, and, food grain, move on these waterway systems daily. Even a minor but successful attack would generate a significant impact on the insurance rates for cargo and general transportation.

Recommendations

1. Intelligence-gathering, using human intelligence (HUMINT), communication-intelligence (COMINT), and satellite-intelligence (SATINT), all need to be strengthened so that precise information can lead to timely action.

2. The role of the Joint Terrorism Task Force in port-security needs greater clarification. There is, currently, much disagreement over jurisdiction for the guarding of assets, between the ICG and the CISF. These issues need to be ironed out and SOPs formulated that clearly spell out the roles, responsibilities, limits, and, coordination-functions of individual security agencies.

3. There needs to be a system of regular background checks carried out on employees working in ports and coastal installations of consequence, in order to ensure that no 'insider-help' is available to inimical forces.

4. The status of landward- and seaward-perimeter patrols around ports and coastal installations of consequence, needs regular monitoring to ensure that there is no complacency.

5. The strict enforcement of access-control, using retina-, facial- and hand-geometry scans for entry into ports and coastal installations of consequence, must be instituted and maintained. Personnel should be debarred from using individual private vehicles inside such locations. Instead, port/establishment authorities should organise inhouse vehicular transport for conveying the workforce to and from their specific places of work. Worker identification numbers, using colour codes should also be given to ensure that no unauthorised person gains access to areas for which he or she is not security-cleared.

6. Regular training needs to be imparted by simulating various contingencies and ensuring their positive response during real-time situations.

Way Ahead

1. Threat-assessment and Contingency-planning. A realistic threat-assessment needs to be carried out on all out vital areas and vital points along the Indian coast. After a thorough study, a comprehensive implementation-plan needs to be formulated to counter all possible contingencies.

2. Silent 'Ship-to-Shore' Alert. In case a suspicious movement towards a vital coastal asset is observed by a ship, there should a quick and silent ship-to-shore alert mechanism in place so as to ambush the incoming attacker.

3. Avoidance of Duplication of Resource-acquisition. In far too many cases there is a duplication of purchase on assets for various organisations. An internal exchange of plans on probable procurements by the agencies needs to be carried out to avoid this and, in so doing, providing significant benefit to the exchequer.

4. Ensure Commonality of Communication Equipment. Communication equipment available with various agencies needs to be standardised, thereby ensuring easier compatibility and easing servicing and maintenance problems.

5. Strengthen Technological Capacity and Capability. There is no substitute for human intelligence, but at the same time, there is no gainsaying the fact that coastal security services and systems need to be technologically upgraded to meet the contemporary and future challenges. The equipment sought should be sourced in India itself, thereby reducing dependence on imports.

6. Enhance Readiness. It is essential to conduct joint exercises such as the SAGAR KAVACH series, and the recent SEA-VIGIL that was held on 22 and 23 January 2019, in order to check the efficacy of the coastal security architecture and its preparedness to tackle emergent situations.

7. Avoid Turf Wars. All concerned agencies should be clear about their jurisdiction and need to be actively discouraged from intruding-into or unduly-influencing functional requirements proposed by the other agencies.

8. Rehearse SOPs. SOPs for various responses needs frequent but clear amplification and need to be validated through the regular conduct of joint exercises.

Conclusion

Terrorism today stalks the maritime environment in a deeply disturbing fashion. Terrorists, increasing numbers, have begun to realise and recognise that maritime infrastructure is the soft underbelly of States and can be attacked with relative impunity and minimal effort. More significantly, these attacks have the capacity and capability to disrupt and destroy maritime enterprise and threaten the peaceful use of the seas. This is a wakeup call for naval forces and coast guard organisations to enhance their respective capacity and capability to counter the menace of terrorism from the sea. There is also an absolute necessity for India develop closer relations with friendly navies on intelligence sharing and vital actions.

Endnotes

1   Changing Roles of Navies in the Contemporary World Order with Specific Reference to the Indian Navy Sureesh Mehta*, April 2009, Volume 3, Issue 2, IDSA, Journal of Defence Studies.

2   10 years after 26/11 attack: Is India's maritime, coastal security any better? Anil Bhatt, The Asian Age, 30 January 2019 accessed on 13 March 2019.

3   India Unveils New Coastal Surveillance Radar Network, Ankit Panda, 26 March 2015, The Diplomat,https://thediplomat.com/2015/03/india-unveils-new-coastal-surveillance-radar-network/ accessed on 23 March 2019.

4   Smart border management: Indian coastal and maritime security, September 2017, Price Waterhouse Coopers, Study Paper, https://www.pwc.in/assets/pdfs/publications/2017/smart-border-management-indian-coastal-and-maritime-security.pdf, accessed on 01 April 2019.

5   Maritime Surveillance goes hi-tech, Huma Siddiqui, Financial Express, 08 December 2014, https://www.financialexpress.com/economy/maritime-surveillance-goes-hi-tech/16692/ accessed on 12 June 19.

6   Raksha Mantri Shri Manohar Parrikar Inaugurates IMAC, a Navy-CG Joint Operations Centre,https://www.indiannavy.nic.in/content/raksha-mantri-shri-manohar-parrikar-inaugurates-imac-navy-cg-joint-operations-centre

7   NAT GRID will prove to be a security nightmare, V Balachandran, The Sunday Guardian, 13 July 2019. http://www.sunday-guardian.com/analysis/natgrid-will-prove-to-be-a-security-nightmare accessed on 13 July 2019.

8   The Changing Face of Maritime Terrorism, Abhijit Singh, https://www.orfonline.org/research/the-changing-face-of-maritime-terrorism/ accessed on 31 May 2019.

9   India to Deploy Radiation Sensors at Ports, Borders, 26 April 2010. https://www.nti.org/gsn/article/india-to-deploy-radiation-sensors-at-ports-borders/ accessed on 24 April 2019.

10 India's Ratio of 138 Policeman Personnel per lakh of population fifth lowest among 71 countries. https://economictimes.indiatimes.com/news/defence/indias-ratio-of-138-police-personnel-per-lakh-of-population-fifth-lowest-among-71-countries/articleshow/48264737.cms?from=mdr, accessed on 19 May 19.

11 Modernization of Police Forces in Indian States, https://www.prsindia.org/theprsblog/modernization-police-forces-indian-states, accessed on 19 May 2019.

12 Government of India Ministry of Home Affairs Rajya Sabha Unstarred Question No.2988 To Be Answered on the 6th August, 2014/Sravana 15, 1936 (Saka) Strengthening Internal Security and Intelligence Sharing Mechanism 2988. Shrimati Sasikala Pushpa: Answer A to C by Kiren Rijiju Union state Minister for Home Affairs.

13 Press Information Bureau, Ministry of Defence Government of India, 05 March 2018. http://pib.nic.in/newsite/PrintRelease.aspx?relid=176953 accessed on 04 April 2019.

14 Government Of India Ministry of Home Affairs Rajya Sabha Unstarred Question No.2301 To Be Answered on The 18th March, 2015/Phalguna 27, 1936 (Saka) Infiltration Through Sea Route https://mha.gov.in/MHA1/Par2017/pdfs/par2015-pdfs/rs-040315/2301.pdf Answer for Question 2301 is in serial Number XVII.

15 Indian Coastal Security Paradox, Abhijit Singh. Observer Research Foundation New Delhi, Special Report. https://www.orfonline.org/research/india-coastal-security-paradox/ accessed on 19 May 2019.

16 Why Marine Police remain the Weakest Link in India's Coastal Security System, Pushpita Das, 26 November 2014. https://idsa.in/idsacomments/WhyMarinePoliceremainstheweakestlink_pdas_261114 accessed on 23 May 2019.

17 Still at Sea against Terror, Asutosha Acharya, 11 June 2009, Outlook. https://www.outlookindia.com/website/story/still-at-sea-against-terror/261005 accessed on 19 May 2019.

18 Patrolling and Security Issues, CAG report. https://cag.gov.in/sites/default/files/audit_report_files/Union_Performance_Defence_Services_Role_and_Functioning_Indian_Coast_guard_7_2011_chapter_5.pdf accessed on 19 May 2019.

19 High Seas Crime Becoming More Sophisticated, Endangering Lives, International Security, Speakers Tell Security Council, High Seas Crime Becoming More Sophisticated, Endangering Lives, International Security, Speakers Tell Security Council, 05 February 2019.https://www.un.org/press/en/2019/sc13691.doc.htm, accessed on 13 May 2019.

Kautilya's Prescription and Relevance for India's Neighbourhood Management

Maj Gen G. Murali, Indian Army (Retd.)

Introduction

There is considerable evidence in the country's ancient scriptures, dating back to the Vedic age, of India's maritime prowess. For more than 3000 years, despite the copious exchanges of commerce between civilizations, which were diverse in terms of culture, language and philosophies, the Indian Ocean region has remained orderly and peaceful. The Rig Veda Samhita frequently mentions boats and ships, while Kautilya's *Arthashastra* shows the Admiralty to have been a separate department of the War Office of the Mauryan Empire. The establishment of trade with the Roman empire by South India finds mention in *Sangam* literature. Kautilya distinguishes between ocean routes (*Samudra samyanapatha*), coastal traffic (*kulapatha*), and river routes.[1] Inadequate research of ancient Indian scriptures and ancient Indian history leads us to the wrong conclusion that we were poor at recorded history (historiography).

India's neighbourhood comprises both a sea of opportunities and lands of locked potential. In the words of that great Indian statesman, diplomat and visionary, Sardar KM Panikkar, "*Millenniums before Columbus sailed the Atlantic and Magellan crossed the Pacific, the Indian Ocean had become a thoroughfare of commercial and cultural traffic.[2]*"

The twin phenomena of power transition from the west to the east on the one hand, and power diffusion from State to non-State actors on the other, has resulted in a geopolitical shift especially in the maritime security domain of the Indian Ocean Region (IOR). The result is what we currently refer-to as the 'Indo-Pacific'. The Indo-Pacific has been described as a biogeographic region, comprising the Indian Ocean and the western and central Pacific Ocean, including the South China Sea.[3] The vastness of the land and sea expanses of the IOR, including its littoral and islandic States, creates several security challenges for sustained economic activities and growth. The Indo-Pacific region has become the centre of 21ˢᵗ Century geopolitics, wherein regional as well as external powers are actively competing and/or collaborating to expand their own influence and counter the influence of other players. Against this competitive background lies the necessity for India to secure its national interests and manage the neighbourhood in a manner that will enable it to project itself as a participative, cooperative, but powerful entity.

The clue to addressing this challenge lies in ancient Indian scriptures such as Kautilya's *Arthashastra*, which articulates foreign policy as being one amongst seven primary constituents of governance, and, distinguishes between bilateral relations and multilateral ones, as a function of State behaviour that itself is contingent upon differentials in the power levels. The ancients knew the potential of the seas in promoting trade, as well as in the spatial expansion of the kingdom. The emergence of India's policies regarding its neighbourhood and the IOR have their roots in these ancient scriptures.

The Indian Ocean Region (IOR)

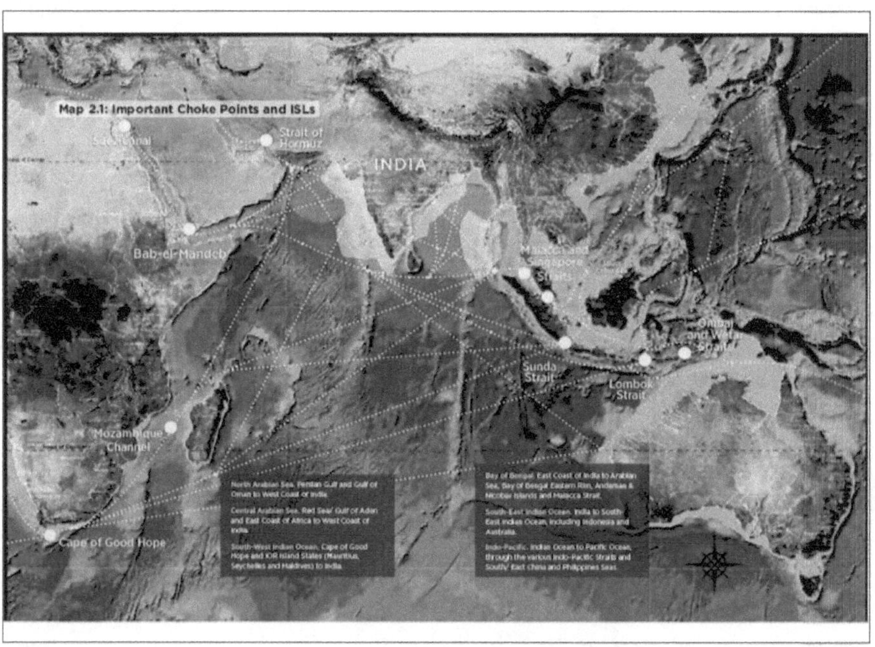

Image: courtesy India Foundation
http://52.66.16.81/wp-content/uploads/2016/09/Image1-1.jpg

Historicity. Dr Vincent, in his book, *"The Commerce and Navigation of the Ancients"*, mentions how the commercial intercourse of India with Mediterranean countries and Africa led to the requirement of protecting the sea-lines of communication (SLOCs) from piracy.[4] The Admiralty, as a department of administration in the Mauryan Empire, consisted of a *Navadyaksha* – a superintendent of ships. He was tasked with examining accounts related to navigation and maintaining security over different kinds of water bodies. India's tryst with the seas continued well into the middle ages, with coastal kingdoms flourishing in the peninsula. The *Yuktikalpataru, written by King* Bhoja (c. 1010 CE - 1055 CE) of Malwa, is the only ancient Indian work dealing in detail with the subject of shipping.[5] Inadequate scholarship and research of ancient scriptures has many contemporary Indians to incorrectly conclude that we had a sketchy historiography. A far more detailed study and analysis of the subject in Indian vernacular languages is required, in order to bring out the true richness of Indian historiography.

Threat Perception. The IOR connects the West with the East and is a passage for half the world's trade, yet remains ungoverned in that it lacks the institutional mechanisms required in today's world order. While India may desire to assert its supremacy in IOR, it cannot do so without developing a sophisticated analysis of threats vs necessity (interests). Threats in IOR are both traditional as well as non-traditional. Globalisation exacerbates crime such as drug- and human-trafficking, gunrunning, piracy, and so on. The region includes littoral and small island States such as the Seychelles, Maldives, as also failing or failed States that are extremely vulnerable to environmental degradation, natural calamities, and exploitation leading to erosion of sovereignty. Against this backdrop must be viewed the growing militarisation of the region. All these, taken in aggregate, make up the spectrum of threats. Countering these threats essential for ensuring that we are able to transition, both as a country, as also as a region, to a 'blue economy' — an concept that seeks to preserve the ocean, along with its littoral and islandic States, from environmental and cultural degradation, while simultaneously legislating a controlled use of marine wealth. It underpins the thinking behind the Commonwealth Blue Charter, highlighting, in particular, the close linkages between the ocean, climate change, and the wellbeing of the people of the Commonwealth.[6] Para 30 of the Commonwealth Charter enjoins us to *"look forward to a 'blue' Commonwealth future in which every member of the Commonwealth sees fair ocean governance, more prosperous maritime and marine industries, sustainable ocean use, and secure marine space across the Commonwealth".[7]*

Given the wide canvas of the IOR and the complex spectrum of threats that must be faced in an intensely competitive environment, India has to choose between claiming a right of dominance in the region by historical ties with the littoral nations and its geostrategic location on the one hand, and, proving prove its credibility by demonstrating its '**Capacity and Capability**' as a responsible power, on the other. It is evident that if one is to possess the power of persuasion, one has to have credibility and demonstrated abilities for succeeding. Whatever be the policy choice, the path to securing the IOR lies in participation, entente, and cooperation among the littorals, and in strengthening regional alliances/strategic partnerships.

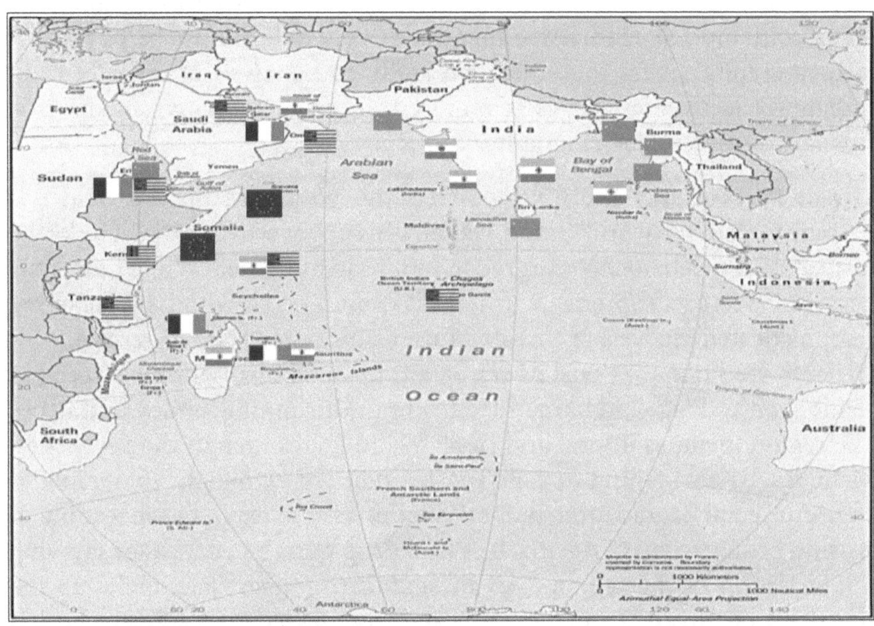

The repeated mention of the 'Indo-Pacific' in India's Maritime Security Strategy (published in October 2015) reflects a geostrategic shift in which New Delhi not only 'looks' but also 'acts' East.[8] It is against such a backdrop that the tenets of Kautilya's *Arthashastra* can show the course for the future.

Kautilya's Prescription. Kautilya conceived six internal constituents of state (*Saptanga* Theory) — king, ministers, fortified city, countryside, treasury, army — and one external constituent — *Mitra* or 'friend', which he considered to be the most critical, to interpreted in the context of foreign relation with another kingdom. International relations have a symbiotic relationship with national security and foreign policy. Foreign policy is a fundamental tool to ensure national security and hence is an essential component of the national security strategy. Kautilya conceptualised international relations as state behaviour that was contingent on relative strength. Kautilya, in the *Arthashastra*, is subtle in his dilation upon the different facets of power. According to him, "Strength is Power; happiness is the objective".[9] The treatise defines power in terms of three kinds — *mantrashakti* with its adjunct of the power of counsel and diplomacy (as also intellectual propensity), *prabhava shakti* (a rich treasury and a strong army) and *utsahashakti* (energy and drive of the king) (*Arthashastra Sutra* 6.2.30-34). The kingdom's power is a sum of the internal elements of the state and the three forms of power. Kautilya states that the strength that a state can bring to bear in promoting its own interests vis-à-vis the interests of other kingdoms, depends on how close to ideal the internal constituents are. This may be interpreted as the need for internal consolidation of the empire before adopting a means to acquire wealth and prosperity for the kingdom. It is not enough to possess power or capacity but one must be able to select a process to utilise one's potential to secure the people and the kingdom. If power is capacity, then the ideational ability becomes 'Capability', which involves a process (foreign policy) with ideational (diplomatic) expertise. The ideational ability of a country is its ability to persuade others, based on the foundation of its inherent strategic culture. Thus 'capability' is the sum of 'capacity' (*prakriti* = power) and 'process' (doctrine, policy, and conduct) with which a kingdom or nation addresses issues and handles situations. Together, these give a nation-state the power of persuasion. Application of resources, along with diplomacy, provides a security strategy with which to achieve the desired end-state.

The *Arthashastra* gives the guiding principles of foreign policy and the 'Six Methods'. The *Sadhgunyas* (six methods), is a classification of six different policies, based on a permutation of situations, outlined by Kautilya as the framework of foreign policy, which is pivotal on the differential power of other states. All six operate through four primary mechanisms (*Chatur-upayas*). The four mechanisms (*upayas*), viz., *saman*, *dana*, *bheda*, and *danda*, are means of overcoming opposition.[10] They also sum-up the means that are helpful as tools of hard- and soft-power. In arriving at the right policy for a given situation, the *Arthashastra* describes the Theory of *Rajamandala*, which is, essentially, an appreciation of the current environment and the identification of friend and foe. Kangle describes policy options contingent upon a supreme criterion of state interest, and expediency to decide the choice of policy that is most advantageous under a given set of circumstances. According to Kautilya, diplomacy is *entente* whose nature depends upon the strength and resources of the parties concerned.[11] The relationship of non-intervention and overt action is to be understood as a deliberate policy-choice of intervention when needed, so as not to get entangled with situations that are detrimental to national growth. Within the two stages of non-intervention *versus* covert action and active policy, lies the imperative of making progress in terms of economic prosperity or building allies and bridging relations with other kingdoms through the exercise of adroit diplomacy. The universality of these two tenets is the fact that all nations aspire to be powerful and influential and yet require an economic stimulus to achieve power. A state's position is determined by its relative progress or relative decline vis-à-vis other states in the neighbourhood.[12] Relative progress or decline is the determinant of relative power.

In her confirmation hearings, the-then US Secretary of State, Hillary Clinton, said, *"America cannot solve the most pressing problems on our own, and the world cannot solve them without America..."* We must use what has been called 'smart power', the full range of tools at our disposal.[13] 'Smart power' is a term developed in 2003 to counter the misperception that soft power alone can produce effective foreign policy.[14] The ultimate goal of creating capacities and capabilities was, however, conquest, and prevailing over others so as to have peace and prosperity (*yogakshema*). It was a theory, set against a background of anarchy, to achieve the goal of success in creating wealth and, consequently, lasting peace. While, contemporary 'measurable' aspects of power such as the economy, territory, etc., are similar to what Kautilya said, the 'intangibles' — of will, competence, and behaviour — have a relationship to intellectual power, which is '*Mantrashakti*', or strength of persuasion through counsel and the strategic culture of the kingdom.

Modern theorists such as Ray Cline define power in terms of a sum of the population, territory, economy, and military, multiplied by its strategy and will. In 1979, Waltz had outlined the *"size of population and territory, resource endowment, economic capability, military strength, political stability and competence"* as crucial ingredients of national strength. Nearly all the international studies conducted on measuring the power of nations have confined themselves to these significant variables.[15]

Policy Framework

Any security framework of the IOR has to account for a geographic expanse starting from the eastern coast of Africa, and encompassing West Asia, the island nations of the Indian Ocean, and the countries of Southeast Asia. The concept of securing the region is not limited to physical security, but encompasses the protection of the biodiversity of the ocean, the sustenance of trade, and, having a standardised mechanism for the sharing of natural resources of the deep seabed. Each of these components of securing the IOR is to be seen as a single comprehensive entity and as a collective responsibility of the littorals and the nations that depend on IOR for economic development. The words of Ms Sushma Swaraj bear recalling: *"As we envisage the Indian Ocean as an engine for growth and prosperity in our region and beyond, it is of utmost importance that these waters remain safe and secure. We consider it imperative that those who live in this region bear the primary responsibility for the peace, stability, and prosperity of the Indian Ocean."*[16] The purpose of all policy is to secure an increase in one's power, principally at the cost of one's natural enemies. The interest of one's State is the supreme criterion, and 'suitability' is to decide which policy would be most advantageous under the prevailing circumstances.

Since its Independence, India has remained a staunch supporter of the Non-Aligned Movement (NAM), and never entered into military alliances with any other power but yet, has signed strategic partnerships with several world powers. A strategic partnership (modern-day *entente*) is a long-term interaction between two countries, based on political, economic, social and historical factors. Such a partnership manifests itself in a variety of relationships. The Indian Ocean Region (IOR) is of great value to India as also to the rest of the world. Considering its economic necessity to India, Ms Sushma Swaraj had mentioned in the Indian Ocean Conference, 2017 that, *"India sees the region as not just a water body, but also a global stage for continued economic, social, and cultural dialogue."*[17] She went on to state, *"...our response to security challenges in the Indian Ocean will be based on our national capabilities, complemented by participation in relevant regional platforms."* India's Foreign Secretary, Dr S Jaishankar, in his address — once again at the Indian Ocean Conference, 2017, categorised India's approach to its contribution and participation into four broad themes, viz., (a) hinterland linkages and strengthening regionalism; (b) maritime contributions and support; (c) linking South Asia to South East Asia through an Act East policy and to the Gulf through a Think West approach, and (d) assume larger responsibilities as a net provider of security, with an integrated approach reflected in the SAGAR (Security and Growth for All in the Region) vision.[18] *What* one sees from the official Indian stance in public conferences, seminars and symposia, is that India values a participatory and enabling role. Its policies conform to the world's perception that countries of this region must facilitate the IOR being an engine of economic growth, to develop a security architecture that strengthens the culture of cooperation and collective action, and, to counter threats and promote a regional rules-based organisational architecture. India has demonstrated that it is responsible and not hegemonistic. Going by Kautilya's elucidation on power, *balamsaktihsukhamsiddhih* (Strength is power; happiness is the objective of using power), India has demonstrated legitimacy and authority in the use of force where it was needed. It attaches great importance to cooperative endeavours in the fields of 'maritime domain awareness' (MDA), coastal surveillance, and 'white shipping', and regional initiatives that significantly contribute to critical oceanic security and safety. If, however, it has to be a net provider of security, then the mismatch of India's perception of its capacities and power has to be addressed.

The current Indian naval strategy is driven by the idea "that the vast Indian Ocean is its *mare nostrum*…that the entire triangle of the Indian Ocean is their nation's rightful and exclusive sphere of interest".[19] India's naval aspirations are growing in conformity with its growing maritime commitments, but lack adequate emphasis on the development of sea power. Our focus must shift to the dominance of seas while being adequately balanced on land and air. What, then, should be pragmatic aspirations of India? It should seek to establish an enhanced naval operational presence in the IOR, which is inherently hard-power, but one that functions within a cooperative framework. A collaborative structure is a projection of the nation being a provider and does not have any hegemonic aspirations like China. India can, indeed, be a 'net provider of security' in the IOR and this is an achievable goal. India's involvement in rescue missions, the capability to carry out Out-of-Area Contingency (OOAC) operations, the success of maritime cooperative action against piracy in and around the Gulf of Aden, are all examples of the benefits of a collaborative approach, and many such instances are manifestations of our capabilities. At the regional level, the consolidation of cooperative arrangements and strengthening existing partnerships such as BIMSTEC, SAARC, ASEAN, etc., holds the key to India providing leadership and infrastructural support to its maritime neighbourhood. Considering the enormity of the aspiration, a deadline to achieve this by 2047 should, perhaps, be the way ahead.

Conclusion

There is a well-known argument connecting economics and security in international relations: military allies are likely to trade more with one another than non-allies.[20] A review of alliance treaties and diplomatic history suggests that, under certain conditions, States may tie together alliance agreements and economic agreements.[21] When nations explicitly link alliance agreements with economic cooperation, one would expect to see increased economic exchange coinciding with coordinated security policies. India views the security of the IOR as a collective responsibility of the users as well as the littoral States. Given the economic importance of the region, not just to India, but to the rest of the world as well, Kautilya's prescription of cooperative alliances as the fulcrum, on which the promotion of trade as a means of wealth for the people rests, finds relevance today. India needs to be an effective leader and provider in the IOR, a perception shared by the West. It has, however, to build its capacities to match its capabilities of intellectual power. The future lies in getting nations whose interests are aligned (or even overlap) to work together on global and regional challenges in a non-formal but effective way. That would mean somewhat different agendas and conversations, with a more open mind and an appreciation for what each player can bring to the table. This trend is visible already in naval exercises, strategic consultations or infrastructure projects. Stability and order cannot be built solely upon the strength of capabilities. The discipline of law must temper it.

Endnotes

1   V. R. Dikshitar, "Aerial and Naval Warfare," in War in Ancient India (Madras: Macmillan and Co Limited, 1944), 284. https://archive.org/details/in.ernet.dli.2015.512231/page/n313

2   Panikkar KM. *India and the Indian Ocean: An Essay on the Influence of Sea Power on Indian History*. (London, George Allen and Unwin Ltd, 1945)

3   PTI, "Trump signs legislation enhancing U.S. leadership in Indo-Pacific region into law", *Economic Times* (Chennai), January 01 2019, https://economictimes.indiatimes.com/news/defence/trump-signs-legislation-enhancing-us-leadership-in-indo-pacific-region-into-law/articleshow/67332642.cms

4   Dikshitar, *War in Ancient India*, 285.

5   Lal, Dr A. "Naval Warfare in Ancient India." *Ancient History Encyclopedia*. Last modified August 15, 2018. Accessed March 08, 2019. https://www.ancient.eu/article/1259/

6   The Commonwealth Secretariat, *Commonwealth Blue Charter*, at The Commonwealth Heads of Government Meeting, U.K. April 20 2018, accessed March 12 2019, chrome-extension://oemmndcbldboiebfnladdacbdfmadadm/file:///Users/mm/Desktop/Blue_Charter_07062018.pdf

7   Commonwealth Blue Charter, 8

8   Pejsova Eva, "Scrambling for the Indian Ocean", *European Union Institute for Security Studies (EUISS)*, February 2016, 2, Accessed March 12 2019. doi:10.2815/910250 https://www.academia.edu/37753232/Brief_4_Indian_Ocean

9   (Rangarajan, p 525).

10 Kangle R.P, *The Kautilya Arthasastra, Part III, First Ed* (Delhi: Motilal Banarsidass, 1965), 255.

11 Dikshitar, "War in Ancient India", p 330.

12 Rangarajan L.N., *The Arthasastra*, (New Delhi: Penguin Books, 1992), 511.

13 Joseph S. Nye, "Get Smart Combining Hard and Soft Power," *Foreign Policy* 88, no. July 04 2009: Accessed March 12 2019. https://www.foreignaffairs.com/articles/2009-07-01/get-smart

14 Nye, 1.

15 Zorawar Daulat Singh: "The Complexity of Measuring National Power", *Journal of Defence Studies*, Vol-6, Issue-2. 94-99 (2012), Accessed 10 Mar2019. http://

www.idsa.in/jds/6_2_2012_TheComplexityofMeasuringNationalPower_
ZorawarDSingh

16 Sushma Swaraj, "SAGAR – India's Vision for the Indian Ocean Region," *India Foundation* 5, no. 6 (November 2017): 8, Accessed March 10, 2019. http://
indiafoundation.in/wp-content/uploads/2017/12/India-Foundation-Journal-
Nov-Dec-2017final.pdf

17 Sushma Swaraj, 9.

18 Jaishankar.S, "Nurturing Growth and Resurgence in IOR", *India Foundation* 5, no. 6 (November 2017): 18, Accessed March 10, 2019,http://indiafoundation.
in/wp-content/uploads/2017/12/India-Foundation-Journal-Nov-Dec-
2017final.pdf

19 Pant, Harsh V. "India in the Indian Ocean: Growing Mismatch between Ambitions and Capabilities." *Pacific Affairs* 82, no. 2 (2009): 279-97. http://
www.jstor.org/stable/25608866. Accessed March 13 2019. https://www.jstor.
org/stable/25608866?read-now=1&refreqid=excelsior%3A3fc20d0c983e2a47f
24407f3801780e6&seq=13#page_scan_tab_contents

20 Andrew G. Long and Brett A. Leeds, "Trading for Security: Military Alliances and Economic Agreements*," Journal of Peace Research 43, no. 4 (July 2006):
433-451, doi:10.1177/0022343306065884.

21 Long and Leeds, " Trading for Security,"

Sustainable Fisheries and Best Management Practices in the Bay of Bengal

Dr Yugraj Singh Yadava

Introduction

Global marine 'capture fisheries' have increased manifold since the 1950s. Fish production has increased from about 16.8 million tonnes in 1950 to about 90.9 million tonnes in 2016. This has contributed immensely to global food and nutritional security. The *per capita* supply of fish from marine sources[1] has increased from about 9.0 kg in 1961 to about 20 kg in 2015, and is expected to reach 21.5 kg by 2024. Since 1961, the average annual increase in global fish consumption (3.2%) has outpaced population growth (1.6 %). More than 3.1 billion people depend on fish for at least 20 per cent for their total animal protein intake, and a further 1.3 billion people for 15 per cent of animal protein uptake.

The world population in 2018 was estimated at 7.0 billion and is estimated to increase to 9.7 billion by 2050. Similarly, the demand for fish and seafood products is likely to increase from 171.0 million metric tonnes in 2016 to 261.2 million metric tonnes in 2030 (estimated). The fisheries sector employs over 110 million people worldwide. Direct and indirect employment opportunities are created along the value chain for about 200 million people. A heightened demand for fish and fishery products could translate into increased decent employment opportunities in this sector.

Fish and fisheries products are also amongst the most widely traded commodities. The global fisheries trade now stands at about USD 145 billion per year, which has increased from about USD 8 billion in 1976 (FAO 2012). In 2016, about 35 per cent of global fish-production entered international trade in various forms either for human consumption or for non-edible purposes. Developing countries play a key role in the trade of fish and fisheries products, and the growth rate of exports from developing countries has increased faster than from developed ones.

In 2016, 85 per cent of the global population engaged in fisheries and aquaculture sectors were in Asia. During the same period, overall, women accounted for nearly 14 per cent of all people directly engaged in the fisheries and aquaculture primary sector. Over 90 per cent of people employed globally in capture fisheries and related activities can be classified as small-scale fishers and over 90 per cent of these fishers live in developing countries. It is also seen that the small-scale fisheries support the livelihoods and wellbeing of over five hundred million people worldwide.[2] This is both an indicator of importance of the sector as well as of the pressure on fisheries.

The Bay of Bengal Large Marine Ecosystem (BOBLME)

Large Marine Ecosystems (LMEs) are regions of the world's oceans, encompassing coastal areas from river basins and estuaries to the seaward boundaries of continental shelves and the outer margins of the major ocean current systems. They are relatively large regions, covering 200,000 km^2 or more, and are characterised by distinct bathymetry, hydrography, productivity, and trophically-dependent populations.[3] There are 66 of them, worldwide and it is estimated that they produce about 80 per cent of global annual marine fishery biomass. In addition, LMEs contribute USD 12.6 trillion in goods and services each year to the global economy.

The BOBLME includes the Bay of Bengal itself, the Andaman Sea, the Strait of Malacca, and the Indian Ocean down to Two-degrees South of the equator. Apart from the high seas area, the BOBLME comprises the coastal areas, islands, reefs, continental shelves and coastal and marine waters of the northern part of the island of Sumatra in Indonesia (the provinces of Aceh, Riau, North Sumatra and West Sumatra), the west coast of peninsular Malaysia, the west coast of Thailand, Myanmar, and Bangladesh, the east coast of India, the Andaman and Nicobar Islands of India, Sri Lanka, and the Maldives (Fig 1).

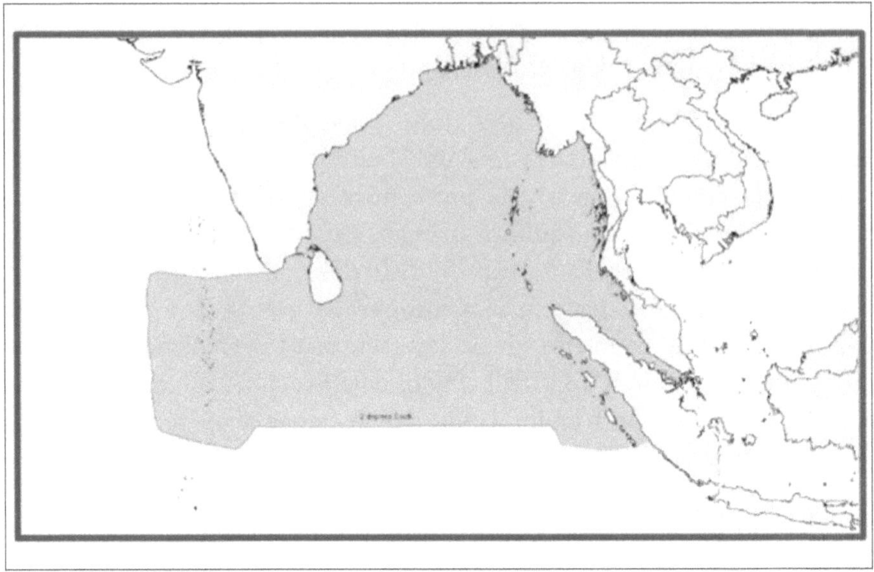

Figure 1: The Bay of Bengal Large Marine Ecosystem

The total maritime area of the BOBLME is 6.2 million km², with depths ranging between 2000 metres and over 4000 metres in most of its central area. The total area of the Exclusive Economic Zones (EEZs) of the countries within this LME is 4.3 million km², with a combined coastline of 14,000 km.

About 66 per cent of the BOBLME lies within the EEZs of BOBLME countries. Consequently, a significant portion of the BOBLME is subject to national jurisdiction. The BOBLME countries with the greatest extent of estimated EEZ area in the BOBLME as defined are, from largest to smallest: India, Maldives, Myanmar, Sri Lanka, Indonesia, Thailand, Bangladesh and Malaysia.

The BOBLME receives drainage form many large rivers including the Ganga, the Brahmaputra, and the Meghna which drain across Bangladesh and India, the Ayeyarwady and Thanlwin rivers in the east from Myanmar, and, the Mahanadi, Godavari, Krishna and Cauvery in the west, from India. These rivers discharge huge quantities of fresh water and large quantities of silt into the coastal and offshore regions. The Ganges-Brahmaputra-Meghna basin, which covers nearly 1.75 million square kilometres, and spreads over five countries, is the second largest hydrologic region in the world. Monsoonal rains and floods have a strong influence on BOBLME dynamics, resulting in seasonal gyres, and a warm, low salinity, nutrient- and oxygen-rich surface layer, down to a depth of 100 m.

Fisheries in the BOBLME

The BOBLME is characterised by high biodiversity and its fisheries resources are of considerable social and economic importance to its bordering countries. The BOBLME is also the home of three important critical habitats, viz., mangroves (11.9% of the world's holdings), coral reefs (8.0% of the world's holdings), and vast seagrass beds. Besides this, a large number of endangered and vulnerable species such as the dugong, whale shark and many species of sharks and rays are also found in the BOBLME.

It is estimated that the BOBLME countries have some 2.2 million fishers and the sector provides employment to about 4.5 million people. The number of fishing boats are estimated to exceed 415,000. In all BOBLME countries, with the exception of India, fish and seafood products make a significant contribution to the animal proteins that are consumed (Maldives (76%), Indonesia (62%), Bangladesh (57%) and Sri Lanka (52%).

Despite having a long and rich tradition of fishing and, especially in recent decades, relatively good fisheries legislation and policies, fisheries management is weak in most BOBLME countries. 'Open access' to fisheries seems to be main constraint, although there are many controls practiced through local customs and social controls. Resulting from open access, the resources are heavily exploited — beyond their sustainable limits in several cases. To cite an example, about 50 per cent of the major commercial fish stocks are over-exploited, resulting in smaller sizes of individuals entering the fishery year after year. Further, the following indicators also point towards a situation of over-exploitation of the fisheries resources, especially in coastal inshore waters:

- Stagnating or declining fish-production from marine waters in many BOBLME countries.

- Harvesting of large quantities of top predators (sharks, rays, etc.), resulting in changes in species-composition and "fishing down the food web";

- Landings equal to or greater than the estimated potential yields;

- Catching of juvenile fish in several species; and

- Declining production and productivity.

Table 1 provides an overview of fisheries issues relevant to BOBLME countries, and their impact on transboundary attributes of the LME's fishery resources.

Table 1: Overexploitation, overfishing/over-capacity, open access regime in the BOBLME

Issues	Trans-boundary nature of issues
1. Decline in overall availability of fish[4] resources; [4] 2. Changes in species composition of catches 3. High proportion of juvenile fish in the catch; 4. Changes in marine biodiversity, especially though loss of vulnerable and endangered species.	• Many fish stocks shared among BOBLME countries either through transboundary migration of fish or larvae; • Fishing overlaps national jurisdictions, both legally and illegally - overcapacity and overfishing in one location forces a migration of fishers and vessels to other locations; • All countries (to a lesser or greater degree) are experiencing difficulties in implementing fisheries management, especially the ecosystem approach; • BOBLME countries contribute significantly to the global problem of loss of vulnerable and endangered species.

Socio-economics and Trade

Despite the large size and populations of many BOBLME countries, most have, with the exception of India, relatively small economies. All these economies are decreasing their reliance on the agriculture sector (including fisheries), with growth in the industry- and service-sectors driving the long-term growth of their respective GDPs. Other than in the Maldives, the contribution of fisheries to GDP is relatively low in BOBLME countries. However, despite this low GDP, marine living resources are extremely important for the livelihood of millions of people and their communities, in particular as a source of food. All BOBLME countries consider fisheries sector as an engine of growth, providing livelihood, food and nutritional security, and promoting economic growth and development, including through the increased exploitation of these living resources. As a result, all governments of the region have set ambitious marine-production targets, which in many cases, do not acknowledge the biological limits to production inherent in these renewable resources and also competing uses by the other economic sectors such as tourism, shipping, mining, and, oil and gas exploration.

The principal social factors affecting BOBLME countries include population growth, increasing migration to the coast, and, lack of alternatives for securing food, livelihood and shelter (space and materials) in the poor rural coastal communities. The sheer number of people is probably the most important driver of all key issues arising in the region. The human population is still growing in the region from an already large base (now about 1.78 billion) and it is expected that the region's human population will exceed 2.0 billion by 2020. The coastal population of 450 million is also expected to increase, both as a result of the overall population increase, and as a consequence of migration and urbanisation to the coast. With densities averaging about 410 people per square kilometre regionally, of which at least 30 per cent overall will be concentrated along the coasts, the pressure on the coastal and marine environment of the BOBLME is likely to be one of the highest in the world (Kaly, 2004).

The increasing levels of industrialisation in some coastal zones of the BOBLME have attracted new waves of human migrants and have resulted in new residential and industrial zones being set-up outside of the existing towns and cities. Such developments can displace existing coastal communities, especially where they are made up of groups such as fishers who often have little political influence. People are moving from inland areas to the coast and also from rural areas to urban areas in search of employment and a better life.

The already significant production, collection and disposal of domestic sewage and solid-waste are exacerbated by the increasing number of tourists to the coastal regions, over and above the indigenous population-growth. For example, in Maldives, the number of tourists arriving per year is greater than the resident population. Similarly, it is estimated that 20 million tourists per year visit Thailand's Andaman Sea area.

Besides all the above-mentioned aspects, issues arising from climate-change are likely to further exacerbate the situation in BOBLME countries. These changes may be broadly summarised as: (i) ocean acidification; (ii) sea-level change (rises in most areas); (iii) rising sea-surface temperatures; (iv) changes in rainfall (decrease in some areas and increase in others); and (v) increased frequency or intensity of storms and cyclones.

Conclusion

Marine waters in BOBLME countries are largely viewed as common resources and fisheries is carried out by practitioners who are likely to follow the tenets of 'revenue maximising'. To ensure the sustainability of the stocks so that they do not collapse, major stakeholders need to be actively involved in introducing responsible fisheries. Partnerships — between governments (at all levels) and major stakeholders — hold the key to improving the management of these resources and securing the potential social and economic benefits that are on offer. This will require human capacity-building at all levels, the development of institutions that engender trust, and true participation of all stakeholders in the development and implementation of new policies and reforms.

Second, there is need to improve fisheries Monitoring, Control and Surveillance (MCS). While MCS, in the beginning, might appear to be daunting, especially in the backdrop of a predominant small-scale fisheries sector, in the long run it can be highly rewarding. A disciplined fisheries sector will be a win-win situation for all. The sector needs to work in a cooperative environment, involving all stakeholders, understanding each other's requirements, and finding solutions that meet the needs.

Third, BOBLME countries need both, LME-wide and bilateral cooperation mechanisms. The BOBLME has many sub-ecosystems that need cooperation between two or three countries to manage the resources. For example, the Gulf of Mannar is shared between India and Sri Lanka, the Sundarbans Mangrove Forests between Bangladesh and India, and the Myeik Archipelago between India, Myanmar and Thailand. Such sub-regional cooperation could be extremely useful for building strong regional cooperation amongst all BOBLME countries.

Fourth, there are several political arrangements between BOBLME countries, such as the Bay of Bengal Initiative for Multi-Sectoral Technical and Economic Cooperation (BIMSTEC) — whose membership includes Bangladesh, India, Myanmar, Sri Lanka, Thailand, Nepal and Bhutan — and the South Asian Association for Regional Cooperation (SAARC), which is a regional intergovernmental organisation and a geopolitical 'union' of states in South Asia. Its member states include Afghanistan, Bangladesh, Bhutan, India, the Maldives, Nepal, Pakistan and Sri Lanka. Similarly, the ASEAN (Association of Southeast Asian Nations) is a regional intergovernmental organisation comprising ten countries in Southeast Asia, which promotes intergovernmental cooperation and facilitates economic, political, security, military, educational and sociocultural integration among its members and other countries in Asia. It is essential that the subject of fisheries becomes an important agenda in the work programmes of these sub-regional entities.

Fifth (and finally), the BOBLME region also has several Regional Fisheries and Environment Bodies such as the Asia-Pacific Fisheries commission (APFIC), the Bay of Bengal Programme for Inter-Governmental Organisation (BOBP-IGO), the Indian Ocean Tuna Commission (IOTC), the South Asia Cooperative Environment Programme (SACEP) and the Southeast Asian Fisheries Development Centre (SEAFDEC). It is essential that these bodies work in tandem to provide the necessary science and policy support to the BOBLME countries so that the fisheries resources and the environment health of the LME can be sustained.

Endnotes

1   Estimated from FAO State of Fisheries and Aquaculture (SOFIA), 2018.

2   World Bank/FAO/WorldFish Centre, 2010. The hidden harvests: the global contribution of capture fisheries. In: Conference Edition, Washington, DC, USA.

3   Global Environment System Website, Large Marine Ecosystems , https://www.thegef.org/topics/large-marine-ecosystems

4   Fish includes finfish, crustaceans, molluscs and any aquatic animal which is harvested.

Mercantile Marine as a Force Multiplier for Prosperity and Security

SS Bangara, Master Mariner

The merchant marine plays only a modest role in directly securing India's maritime neighbourhood. On the other hand, its indirect contribution to security — largely through the economic dimension) is significant. This paper seeks to explore the economic dimension of merchant ships and, in doing so, endeavours to bring out the resultant contribution to maritime security.

Global Maritime Shipping.[1] Shipping is the life blood of the global economy. Without shipping, intercontinental trade, the bulk transport of raw materials, and, the import and export of affordable food and manufactured goods, would simply not be possible. The international shipping industry is responsible for the carriage of around 90% of world trade.[2] Seaborne trade continues to expand, bringing benefits to consumers across the world through competitive freight costs. Thanks to the growing efficiency of shipping as a mode of transport, and, increased economic liberalisation, the prospects for the industry's further growth continue to be strong.

There are over 50,000 merchant ships trading internationally, transporting every kind of cargo. The world merchant fleet is registered in over 150 nations, and manned by over a million seafarers of virtually every nationality.[3] Merchant ships are technically sophisticated, high value assets (some of the larger hi-tech vessels can cost over US $200 million to build), and their operation generates an estimated annual income of over half a trillion US dollars in freight rates.[4]

Global Regulation. Globalisation has had the effect of propelling shipping to even greater prominence — making it a catalyst for world peace and prosperity. A less-acknowledged reality, however, is that ships operate in a very fragile marine environment, fraught with inherent perils, which requires that social costs be borne, and calls for investments to ensure safety of the ships and their crew, as also to ensure environmental protection. On the positive side, shipping is the least environmentally damaging form of commercial transport and, compared with land-based industry, is a comparatively minor contributor to environmental pollution.

The International Maritime Organization[5] (IMO), which is tasked with the responsibility of minimising the social cost of shipping, has established a clear mandate to strive for cleaner oceans and safer ships. Ships that operate outside these standards are deemed to be substandard and, therefore, pose the greatest risks. Flag States, Port States, and Coastal States have the most to lose in the event of a maritime catastrophe. They, therefore, along with shipowners, have explicit legal responsibilities to enforce the provisions of the various IMO conventions.

The IMO has produced a profusion of regulations, that have been tailored to promote safe and efficient shipping. However, several impediments remain. In the wake of a maritime disaster, there is often a knee-jerk reaction on the part of governments, caused by real or perceived public pressure. Added to this is the fact that a few States confer nationality on vessels for the sole purpose of garnering economic benefit. Vessels registered in such States are commonly said to be flying "Flags of Convenience".

Indian Merchant Marine. The Indian shipping industry plays a crucial role in the Indian economy. Around 95 % of India's external merchandise trade (by volume) and 70% (by value) is done through maritime transport.[6] India has a coastline of 7,516 kilometres, forming one of the largest peninsulas in the world. It is studded with 12 major ports and 200 notified non-major ones (also referred-to as 'minor' and 'intermediate' ports).

In 2018, Indian ports handled about 16 million TEU (Twenty Foot Equivalent Units) of containers, of which nearly 70% was 'gateway' container cargo (meaning that it was destined for that port itself) while 25% was transhipped. Transhipment is the act of off-loading a container from a large container ship (generally at a 'hub' port) and loading it onto a second, smaller feeder ship to be carried to the final port of discharge. Obviously, the reverse can also be done. Global vessel-sizes have significantly increased in the last decade and most main 'liner' vessels have capacities of 10,000 TEU or more, with the largest reaching a capacity of 20,000 TEU.[7] Indeed, it has recently been reported that COSCO, the third largest container operator in the world, is considering ordering a 25,000 TEU ship from a State-owned shipyard in China.

Large container ships need deep-draught ports that offer depths in excess of 18-metres to berth. India's terminals offer, at the most, about 15 metres depth at the berth —that too, only in very few terminals. Consequently, a quarter of all containers are transhipped through ports in other countries. Colombo (Sri Lanka), Singapore and Port Klang (Malaysia) handle more than 80% of India's transhipment cargo. Of this, Colombo alone handles about 43%.[8] It is interesting to note that Colombo achieved a record throughput of around 7 million TEU in 2018. Sri Lanka itself has very few exports and Colombo's container terminals rely heavily on transhipment, which is a huge source of revenue.

However, transhipment adds to the cost of handling cargo because of the extra port-handling charges. It has been estimated that the Indian port industry loses up to Rs 1,500 crore per year in revenue on transhipment cargo that is either originating-from or destined-for India. The additional cost is about US$ 80-100, or Rs 5,600-7,000, per TEU, which would not be incurred, if the container could be imported/exported directly from an Indian port.

SAGARMALA Project. Through its ambitious SAGARMALA Project, the Government of India wants to transform the country's ports and reduce logistic costs for domestic as well as import/export cargo by optimising infrastructure investments. The government has planned six mega-ports under the SAGARMALA project, viz., the Vizhinjam International Seaport (Kerala), Colachel Seaport (Tamil Nadu), Vadhavan Port (Maharashtra), Tadadi Port (Karnataka), Machilipatnam Port (Andhra Pradesh), and Sagar Island Port (West Bengal). A study done in September 2016 estimates that the resultant cost-saving could range from US$ 5.2 billion (Rs 35,000 crore) to US$ 5.9 billion (40,000) crore per year, by 2025

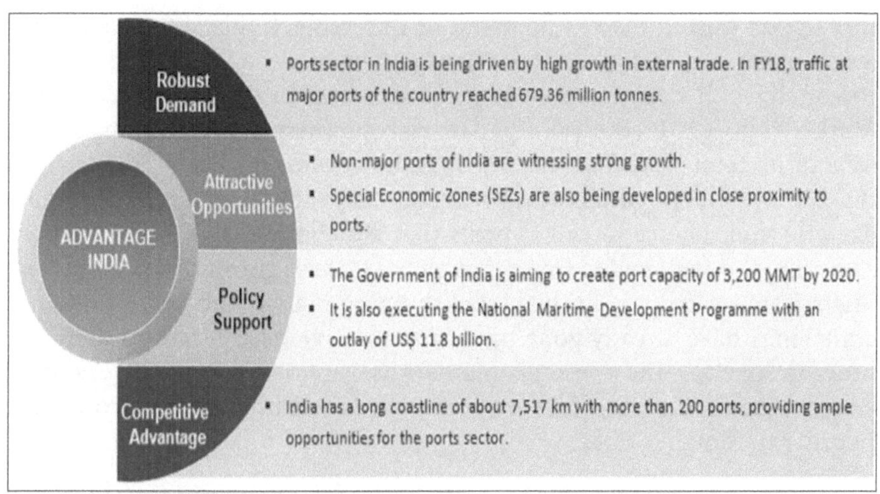

While the Indian Government is focussing in the right direction with SAGARMALA and inland waterways, the author takes the liberty to offer a perspective that although the government has proposed and set-up numerous terminals, connectivity to these terminals has been consistently ignored. Those in the shipping industry are painfully aware of the congestion, bottlenecks and lack of connectivity in the past — and, above all, the bureaucratic hurdles and the lack of understanding and support rendered by both bureaucrats and regulators. **Why cannot professionals be given a free hand to make policy-decisions and improve efficiency and performance?**

Transhipment Ports. In discussing India's plans for the development of transhipment ports it is quite apparent that there has been very little understanding of this issue, even at the highest levels, which has inevitably led to high levels of frustration amongst investors and operators alike. For instance, Enayam Port, having received governmental go-ahead, is likely to be an unviable venture since it is barely 36 km away from the Vizhinjam transhipment port, which is being built with private funds from the Adani Ports and Special Economic Zone Ltd. (APSEZ).[9] Likewise, Vizhinjam Port is only 225 km from the government-owned Vallarpadam Port, where the Dubai-based company, DP World, has been operating India's first container transhipment terminal for the last six years.[10] Three transhipment ports, so close to one another are certainly not needed. The requirement can be managed with just two – Vallarpadam and Vizhinjam — on the west coast. It is also pertinent to note that even these ports will take a minimum of five years to make any difference in the country's transhipment business. From his personal experience as a Trustee on the Board of Cochin Port for three years during the development of this project, this author is acutely aware of the efforts that the Port Management and the Board, had to make to convince all concerned. Further, according to the Indian Container Market Report 2017, the Vallarpadam transhipment port is running at only 49% of its total installed capacity. It is, however, growing.[11] That said, it must never be forgotten that international shipowners will invariably exercise their choice to call at ports that are commercially viable – more so during the challenging times that global trade is currently experiencing. There is an oversupply in the global shipping market and some container companies have already gone bankrupt, or have been forces to merge in order to survive. The present container rates are not remunerative, and, as a consequence, shipping lines are becoming more and more cost-conscious in order to remain viable.

Tariffs play an important role in the global competitiveness of India's terminals. Efficient service with quick turnarounds, and, above all, deep depths that will allow mega carriers to call at Indian ports directly, should be a priority. Although India's transhipment tariff is lower than that at Colombo, the vessel-related charges or marine charges at Indian ports are four times higher than those in Colombo. For instance, the marine charges for a 24-hour stay for a 5,000-TEU capacity ship is about US$ 40,000 in India *versus* US$ 10,000 in Colombo. The marine charges are low in Colombo because, unlike the case in India, the Sri Lankan government funds basic infrastructure, including dredging. In contrast, the Indian government expects ports to pay for dredging, which is, in fact, a huge component of the tariff, and hence, is inevitably passed on to the end-users. India needs to make its tariffs practical for the country's shippers and importers to complete in the world arena.

If coastal shipping is used to complement road and rail transport in India, it could lead to significant savings in logistic-costs. The SAGARMALA project also aims to shift the movement of coal to the coastal route, which could cut electricity costs by up to 35 per cent. This is particularly true for coastal power plants in Andhra Pradesh and Karnataka, which presently receive coal by rail. The shipping of coal via ports can lead to estimated savings of about US$ 1.4 billion (Rs 10,000 crore) in the power sector.

India Inland Maritime Transport. The Shipping Minister's focus on inland waterways is indeed a welcome move. Recently, the worlds' largest container company, Maersk, moved 16 shipping containers, from Varanasi to Kolkata and back, on National Waterway 1, which was set-up with the technical and financial assistance of the World Bank, at an estimated cost of

5,369 crore Rupees. Rivers such as the Ganga, the Bhagirathi, the Hooghly, the Brahmaputra, all offer exciting and significant potential. It is pertinent to note that Pepsico, Emami Agrotech, IFFCO Fertilizers, and Dabur India, had moved their containers on the river Ganga. The same is the case with rivers in Goa, the backwaters of Kerala, inland waters in Mumbai, and the deltaic regions of the Godavari-Krishna rivers. A question that merits serious consideration is whether the powerful road transporters lobby will permit this to succeed. It can be expected that they will resort to periodical strikes and hold the various governments to ransom. Besides, implementation of road infrastructure is more 'visible' to the voters than inland waterways or terminals, so whether the Government will have the political will to expedite these inland waterways projects is a question that only time will tell.

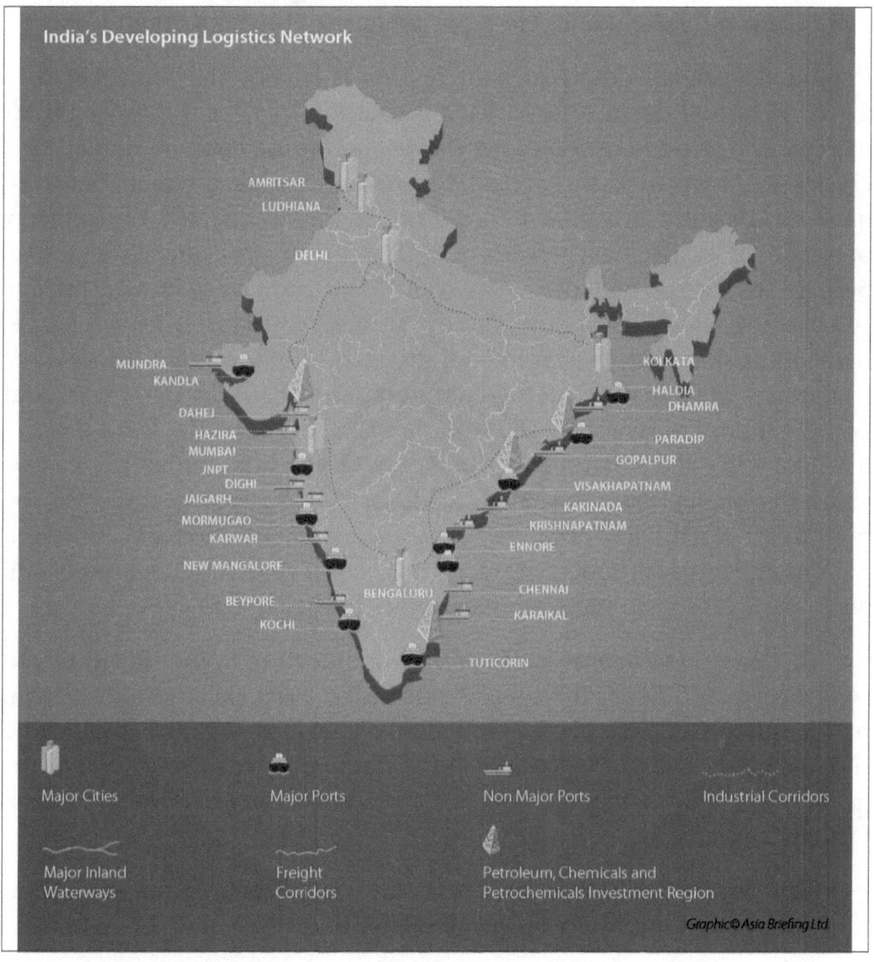

India's Cabotage Law, under the Merchant Shipping Act, 1958, permitted only Indian-flagged ships or ships chartered by Indian companies to service the Indian coast. The relaxation of the cabotage law, announced by the Ministry of Shipping of India on May 22 2018, relates in particular to the shipping of agricultural-, fisheries-, animal husbandry, and horticultural-commodities.[12] In practice, this means that international shipping companies would be able to move EXIM containers along India's coast.

A separate cause for concern is that from 01 January 2020, the IMO MARPOL Annex VI regulation on limiting the sulphur content of bunker fuel to a maximum of 0.5% will enter into force.[13] At present, the global sulphur-content cap on bunker fuel is 3.5% — a level considered easy to comply-with by vessel operators. This will bring significant increases in fuel prices, and freight rates are expected to rise correspondingly.

Regional Security. The merchant marine is traditionally considered as a second line of defence for a maritime nation — after the Navy. India's merchant marine contributes in the economic defence of India. The challenges facing maritime security in the Indian Ocean region, however, have significantly broadened. Traditional threats include the military presence of belligerent powers and consequent strategic rivalry, and, perhaps terrorism and piracy as well. Non-traditional threats include IUU fishing, illegal smuggling, and the adverse impacts of climate change, involving a sharp increase in natural disasters with the consequent loss of traditional livelihood of coastal communities. These disruptions impact island nations in this part of the world particularly severely. For a country like India, the island nations of the Indian Ocean hold immense strategic value in shaping the geopolitical contours of the region and ensuring maritime security and order. A close partnership between these island nations and larger littoral countries thus becomes a practical necessity and plays a critical role in maintaining stability in the region.

A strong governance- and security-architecture in the Indian Ocean is necessary, and ought to be a global priority. New Delhi's Indian Ocean policy, articulates India's vision for building a security regional architecture that includes *"safeguarding mainland and islands, strengthening capacities of maritime neighbours and advancing peace and security"* in the Indian Ocean Region.

The Indian islands of the Andaman and Nicobar chain, as well as those of the Lakshadweep chain, have significantly helped in enhancing the country's maritime prowess. The Andaman and Nicobar Islands are positioned right across the northern funnel of the Strait of Malacca and are less than 90 nautical miles from Aceh Province in Indonesia. This enables India to closely observe military and economic activities in and around the Strait of Malacca, which is the main maritime entry point of western Pacific countries into the Indian Ocean. To its west, India enjoys exclusive rights over nearly 400,000 square kilometres of Exclusive Economic Zone (EEZ) due to the Lakshadweep islands. Farther west from India lie the islands of Socotra (Yemen), Madagascar, Mauritius, and the Seychelles. All of them have gained strategic importance, standing as they do at the crossroads of Europe, Africa, and South Asia. While Socotra is strategically located at the mouth of the Gulf of Aden, which connects the Suez Canal with Indian Ocean, the maritime zones of Madagascar, Mauritius, the Maldives, and Seychelles encompass over a million square kilometres of ocean, which gives them exclusive rights over the living and non-living resources within this vast expanse. India seeks to bolster its economic and strategic relations with these island-States in order to favourably influence the dynamics of the Indian Ocean. Other chapters in the book cover this issue more comprehensively.

Sri Lanka. Another critically important island State, Sri Lanka presently has three container terminals in Colombo, while an additional 'East Container Terminal' is under negotiation. Sri Lanka is also working on setting-up additional infrastructure in Hambantota, to supplement the Car Carrier Terminals that are already in place. However, the economic rationale for Hambantota is fundamentally weak, given existing capacity and expansion plans at Colombo port, fuelling concerns that it could become a Chinese naval facility. It can hardly be forgotten that faced with an inability to repay its debt, Sri Lanka gave China a controlling equity stake and a 99-year lease for Hambantota port, which it handed over in December 2017. The challenge for Sri Lanka's partners is to avoid throwing good money after bad. India, for example, has expressed interest in taking over the international airport near Hambantota port. Officials have suggested it could be used as a flight school. The prospect of turning a failing project around is difficult to resist. However, if that attempt is unsuccessful, India risks assuming the reputational damage that China would otherwise suffer. Likewise, Indian and Japanese interest in port facilities in Trincomalee, on Sri Lanka's east coast, should be tempered by Sri Lanka's debt levels and the existence of competing ports in the region.

Seafarers. There are around 53,000 merchant ships trading internationally. Of these, some 11,000 ships were bulk carriers.[14] The worldwide population of seafarers serving on internationally trading merchant ships is estimated at 1.65 million seafarers, of which 774,000 are officers and 873,500 are ratings, which proves that the merchant marine generates quite significant employment opportunities worldwide. Additionally, a career at sea pays far better than a career ashore and, therefore, the merchant marine further contributes to the global economy by increasing the purchasing power of those employed by it. Indian seafarers on Indian and Foreign flag vessels number 209,000 as of February 2019. China, the Philippines, Indonesia, the Russian Federation and Ukraine are estimated to be the five largest supply countries for all seafarers (officers and ratings). The Philippines is the biggest supplier of ratings, followed by China, Indonesia, the Russian Federation and Ukraine. China is the biggest supplier of officers, followed by the Philippines, India, Indonesia and the Russian Federation. Noteworthy is that the 200,000 Indian seafarers engaged in International Shipping remit all their earnings into India to sustain their families and save for their future, which may not be the case with other industries.[15] The shipping industry and its relevant stakeholders cannot expect there

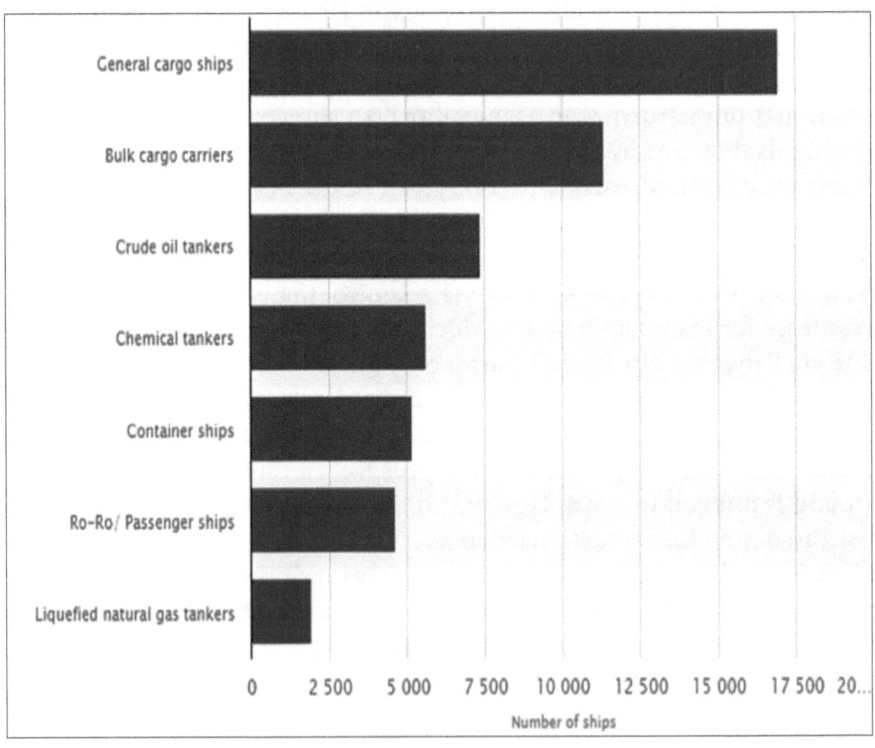

to be an abundant supply of qualified and competent seafarers without concerted efforts and measures to address key manpower issues, through the promotion of careers at sea, enhancement of maritime education and training worldwide, and, addressing the retention of seafarers.

Conclusion

In conclusion, it is highlighted that the shipping industry in India does meet all international standards and, besides attracting huge amounts of money from international investors, contributes heavily toward the Indian economy by way of shipping and shipping-related activities, which include logistics, supply chain management, ports, terminals, etc.

Endnotes

1   International Chamber of Shipping, Shipping Facts, http://www.ics-shipping.org/shipping-facts/shipping-facts

2   International Chamber of Shipping, Shipping and World Trade, http://www.ics-shipping.org/shipping-facts/shipping-and-world-trade

3   International Chamber of Shipping, Shipping and World Trade, http://www.ics-shipping.org/shipping-facts/shipping-and-world-trade

4   International Chamber of Shipping, Shipping Facts, http://www.ics-shipping.org/shipping-facts/shipping-facts

5   International Maritime Organisation, www.imo.org

6   Indian Navy, (2016), Ensuring Secure Seas, India's Maritime Security Strategy, Pg. 25

7   V.O.Chidambaranar Port Trust, Preparation of Rapid Techno-Economic Feasibility Report for Development of Colachel Port in Tamilnadu, Report by Boston Consulting Group, Pg. 30

8   V.O.Chidambaranar Port Trust, Preparation of Rapid Techno-Economic Feasibility Report for Development of Colachel Port in Tamilnadu, Report by Boston Consulting Group, Pg. 81

9   Live Mint Website, What is the ideal distance between two ports?, 7 October 2016, https://www.livemint.com/Opinion/vgefHtNgoR79iTJsSnzPKN/What-is-the-ideal-distance-between-two-ports.html

10 DP World Website, Our Locations, https://www.dpworld.com/what-we-do/our-locations/Subcontinent/India/cochin

11 Behera, S.K., (2017), India Container Markets Report, Drewry, Pg. 8

12 Ministry of Shipping,Relaxation under Section 407 of the Merchant Shipping Act, 1958, forcoastal movement of agriculture, horticulture, fisheries and animal husbandry commodities. NO. SW-14020/5/2009-MG/SA (Vol 9), http://www.dgshipping.gov.in/WriteReadData/News/201805230236156996537GeneralOrderNo02of2018_sd.pdf

13 International Maritime Organisation, Revised MARPOL Annex VI, http://www.imo.org/en/OurWork/Environment/PollutionPrevention/AirPollution/Pages/Air-Pollution.aspx

14 Statista Website, Number of ships in the world merchant fleet as of January 1, 2018, by type, https://www.statista.com/statistics/264024/number-of-merchant-ships-worldwide-by-type/

15 International Chamber of Shipping, Global Supply and Demand for Seafarers, http://www.ics-shipping.org/shipping-facts/shipping-and-world-trade/global-supply-and-demand-for-seafarers

BIMSTEC and MAUSAM: India's Answers to China's Maritime Silk Route

Dr. Binoda Kumar Mishra

Genesis of Look East/Act East Policy

India's engagement with Southeast Asia restarted from 1992. This new engagement came to be known as Look East Policy. From then on, India is, slowly but surely, getting engaged with Southeast Asia. Beginning as a sectoral dialogue partner in 1992, India became a full Dialogue Partner in 1995, a member of the ASEAN Regional Forum in 1996, a Summit Level Partner in 2002, and, finally, a member of the East Asia Summit in 2005. This 'unusually proactive' move[1] from the Indian side has generated a debate as to the objective of this Look East Policy. It has been termed a manifestation of India's assertiveness in the immediate neighbourhood and, at the same time, it has also been identified as a strategic move specifically designed to contain China in China's traditional sphere of influence. Another interpretation is that it is primarily an automatic fallout of India's expansionist attitude. Such interpretations are based more on conjectures than on an objective analysis of India's foreign policy. Therefore, in order to get rid of conjectures and to arrive at reality, one must start with an understanding of India's foreign policy approach and the place that Southeast Asia holds in India's scheme of things. Given the fact that there is a host of literature dealing with the factual evolution of India's Look East policy, this author will avoid repeating this. Rather, this paper will explain the reasons for the emergence of certain conjectures regarding Look East policy and attempt to refute them in the light of facts and logic.

India's Foreign Policy Approach and Southeast Asia

India's rich civilizational heritage, followed by two centuries of colonisation and the unique nature of freedom struggle, have all contributed to the nature of India's foreign policy and foreign policy priorities. The leaders of nascent Independent India were primarily concerned with the preservation of the country's new found political sovereignty and autonomy in international affairs, which was under constant threat in the emergent international system predominantly characterised by the Cold War. Added to this, the direct security threat created by the partition of India and an assertive China coming to India's doorstep through annexation of Tibet, created a complex scenario for India. The second major characteristic of India's foreign policy comes from India's need for a fruitful association with the developed world to ensure steady economic growth, which was of prime concern to nascent independent India. That this entailed that India avoid stepping into murky international affairs, particularly where there was a tussle between the two superpowers, was evident. Coming out from under the colonial yoke, India had developed an "anti-hegemonic foreign policy ethos."[2] Thus, India had the task of engaging nations of the industrialised West without surrendering her political autonomy. This needed either a balancing of economic engagements with other countries or creating new economic blocs. India pursued both options. She diversified her economic relations by engaging the USSR and other East European countries, and committed herself to the promotion of South-South relations to increase trade, joint ventures and collaboration with other developing countries. On the political front, India championed the idea of Non-Alignment. Within this broad framework, Southeast Asia occupied a very important place. For India, being committed as she was to the idea of South-South relations, it was almost a compulsion to factor Southeast Asia in all her foreign policy calculations. The recent memory of suffering under colonialism made India sympathetic towards freedom struggles throughout Southeast Asia. India saw these movements for independence as a natural extension of India's freedom struggle. India's sincerity was evident from the fact that in January 1949, barely one and half years into her independent existence, India organised a conference on Indonesia, which was attended by fifteen countries. India also extended support to Vietnam's struggle against the French and Malaysia's struggle against the British, though with different degrees of success. The strategic importance of the region to India's security had been driven home by Japan's swift sweep of Southeast Asia during World War II. This made India realise the strategic importance of Southeast Asia for protecting her own eastern and southern frontiers.

Thus, India, from the very beginning, intended to have some presence, if not control, in the region. The importance of the Malacca Strait and the kind of control India could exercise over that waterway was a second strategic reason for India's interest in the region. Thirdly, the rise of China certainly made India apprehensive about the future of the region and the implications for India. Particularly, the conciliatory approach of China towards States such as Pakistan, which were allies of the West, and China stealing the show at the 1955 Bangdung Conference, convinced India that China was trying to increase its sphere of influence in the region at the expense of India. In addition, the rise of communist movements in various Southeast Asian countries, particularly in Malaysia and Vietnam, were perceived as potential threats, in alliance with rising China. This concern was evident from the difference in the Indian attitude towards the Indonesian freedom struggle and the communist-led freedom movements in Malaysia and Vietnam. While India was proactive in the case of Indonesia, she was lukewarm towards the other two. Last but not the least, certain economic gains were also anticipated from interactions with Southeast Asia within the framework of South-South relations. A pattern of economic interdependence was realised, as is evident from the fact that immediately after India's Independence, Southeast Asia (the whole region) ranked third, after the United Kingdom and United States amongst India's trading partners.[3]

India's genuine interest in Southeast Asia was also evident from her desire to be part of the region in any form that the members of this region wanted. While the Association of Southeast Asian Nations (ASEAN) was in the making, the-then Foreign Minister of India, MC Chagla, during his visit to Singapore and Malaysia in May 1967, expressed India's support to the formation of ASEAN and wanted to be part of this grouping in any form that the members thought fit.[4] Suffice it here to point out that China severely criticised the formation of ASEAN and called it a 'puny counter-revolutionary alliance.'[5] But it was only in the year 1992 that India started her formal engagement with Southeast Asia as a bloc. This long gestation is generally attributed to two factors: (1) the emergent ASEAN was primarily an association of the Western Alliance; (2) India was seen as hobnobbing with Soviet Union. However, the reality is that India had always wanted to be a part of the grouping in some capacity or the other but was not invited at the inception of the grouping. Secondly, economically, India focussed on West Asia due to her need for crude-oil, on which India was heavily dependent, and thirdly, at a strategic level, Pakistan attracted most of India's foreign policy attention, being seen as the most immediate threat.

The scenario started changing from 1980s onwards, driven by five Indi-centric factors. First of all, India's efforts to engage with Southeast Asia had almost materialised in 1980 when it was about to get the status of a Dialogue Partner. *"[B]ut India's support to Vietnam's invasion of Cambodia and her subsequent recognition of the Vietnam-backed regime in Cambodia upset ASEAN."*[6] Second, around the same time, the importance of West Asia started reducing for India due to a fall in oil prices, and the Gulf War, in which both the then-superpowers were heavily invested and deeply interested. It was perceived to be against India's interest to remain involved in a region where both the superpowers were involved, as any action would have angered one or the other of them. Third, India started producing two thirds of its own oil requirement which further reduced the primacy of West Asia for India. Fourth, by becoming a group, Southeast Asia experienced steady economic growth which was seen as an opportunity for Indian surplus skilled and semi-skilled labour force; and fifth, ASEAN, on its part, started looking outside its original six members in order to obtain optimality in economic terms under the guiding vision of Dr S Rajaratnam who, in 1973, had set 'outward-looking' as a strategy that would ensure ASEAN's steady development.[7] All these were reasons enough for India to seriously pursue ASEAN and engage fruitfully, at the earliest, with this emerging regional organisation within her neighbourhood. However, a major inhibiting factor was the nature of India's economy, which was largely closed and was yet to reach a point where India could effectively gain from external economic engagement. It was the coincidence of the end of the Cold War and the liberalisation of the Indian economy, both of which occurred in the early 1990s, which created a favourable atmosphere for India to pursue her natural ambition of furthering relationship with her Southeast Asian neighbourhood.

Initiation of Look East Policy/Act East Policy

The term 'Look East', although a misnomer, gives a fairly clear expression of India's priorities. The articulation of the 'Look East Policy' was preceded by India's engagement with ASEAN in 1992, when India became a Sectoral Dialogue Partner in the fields of trade, investment, and tourism. The Singapore speech of the-then Prime Minister of India, Mr PV Narasimha Rao, which became the foundation of India's 'Look East Policy' did not specify the nature of engagement India wished to have with the Asia-Pacific, other than highlighting the economic nature of the initial engagement. It deliberately outlined merely the broad contours of India's wishes. This broad-spectrum approach has, however, created scope for misinterpretation or formation of conjectures. The first of the conjectures is that India's Look East Policy is an expression of India's assertiveness within Asia on her way to emerge as a global power. This is a logical interpretation of India's current foreign policy keeping geostrategic factors in mind and based on an unqualified assumption that India wishes to assume regional, if not global, leadership. Thus, the Look East Policy seems to be the latest attempt — after a series of earlier initiatives such as the Asian Relations Conference, the Bangdung Conference and the subsequent Non-Alignment Movement — had failed to obtain a leadership-position for India among the developing countries. In addition to these failures, India, it is argued, saw the dysfunctional nature of the South Asian Association for Regional Cooperation (SAARC) as waste in terms of furthering India's interest and ambition of enhancing her global and regional image. The final qualification for such a conjecture is that India could not move westward, given the presence of Pakistan and other Islamic countries, while an eastward movement was inhibited by powerful China, thus making Southeast the only direction that India could move to expand her sphere of influence.

The validity of such an interpretation needs to be questioned on the ground that a nation does not pursue global power ambitions under economic duress. A look at the Indian economy during the late 1980s and early 1990s, prior to her engagement with Southeast Asia, would make it clear that it was in shambles (to say the least!) and India desperately needed assistance from outside to tide over the tough economic situation in which she found herself. By no stretch of imagination would or could the pursuit of global power status have crossed the minds of Indian policy makers while formulating the Look East Policy. A circumstantial coincidence can certainly be discovered in the nature of Indian early engagement with ASEAN. The three sectors that India identified for engagement with ASEAN were those that happened to experience a sudden collapse with the collapse of the Soviet Union. With the disappearance of the USSR, India lost a major trading partner and her most important investor.[8] The balance-of-payment crisis that was thus created called for a search for new partners that would be interested in investing in India and would trade with India. Thus, at its inception, the 'Look East' engagement was more a desperate economic measure than some carefully deliberated or thoughtful step in India's foreign policy. Secondly, during the formation of ASEAN, India had clearly articulated her priority and ruled out any intention of dominating the region or any grouping.[9] On the other hand, it can be said that the Look East Policy was a measure to assuage the fear of India's intentions that was building due to India developing naval and air power – an aircraft carrier from the UK, a nuclear-powered submarine on lease from Russia, TU-142 Long-Range Maritime Reconnaissance and ASW (LRMP) aircraft, modern KILO-Class conventional submarines from Russia, etc.[10] It was feared that India was trying to exercise control over the Malacca strait and other places from her strategically located naval base in the Andaman and Nicobar Islands. Suffice it to mention here that it was the Indian Navy that made serious efforts in assuaging this fear of Southeast Asian countries "... *by undertaking a variety of confidence building measures such as bilateral and multilateral naval exercises, invitation to senior naval officers to visit the Andaman base facilities and regular port calls.*"[11]

That the 'Look East Policy' is primarily an economic initiative was clearly spelt out in the Singapore speech of Mr PV Narasimha Rao when he said, "*the Asia-Pacific could be the springboard for India's leap into the global market place.*"[12] The economic primacy within India's 'Look East Policy' is both natural and prudent. ASEAN is primarily an economic organisation. Thus, if India is to ride on ASEAN as an enabler of her broader Look East Policy, New Delhi simply has to give primacy to the economic facet of the engagement. At the same time, India, needing newer avenues for economic engagement, found ASEAN to be eminently suitable. In the words of JN Dixit, "*The economic involvement of important industrialised countries of the West and Japan with ASEAN countries makes it a catalyst through which India can have access to investment and technologies. India's initial experience with ASEAN countries shows that it is an important growing area for India investment, joint ventures and trade promotion.*"[13]

Over time, India has substantially increased her economic interaction with this economic bloc. From a negligible amount in 1990, India's share in ASEAN's total trade now stands at modest 2.6 percent.[14] Currently, ASEAN is the fourth-largest trading partner of India, with a two way trade value in excess of USD 63 billion, and can be expected to emerge as the largest trading partner soon, considering the compounded annual growth rate (CAGR) of 27 per cent since the year 2000 and the operationalisation of the India-ASEAN Free Trade Agreement from 2010.[15]

The second conjecture that is nearly ubiquitous amongst scholars looking at India's 'Look East Policy' is that India is trying to chase China out of the latter's traditional sphere of influence. This is a logical construction of the circumstances under which India initiated her 'Look East Policy', but is a grossly oversimplified analysis of the dynamics of the India-China relationship and the respective interaction of each with their immediate neighbourhood. Since the early 1980s, India increasingly realised the fact that it was China that was emerging as the principal long-term concern. China's continued support to Pakistan, the expansion of her own conventional and nuclear force, the persistence of her border dispute with India, her unrelenting posture regarding Tibet and Taiwan, and the history of Chinese support to Indian insurgents, were reasons enough for India to perceive China as a source of concern. This notwithstanding, pursuing engagement with Southeast Asian countries can no way be related to India's concerns vis-à-vis China. First of all, since the establishment of the Peoples' Republic of China, China had no strategic presence in Southeast Asia except her large diaspora. Second, the inception of ASEAN was never encouraged by China, nor did Beijing consider ASEAN to be of any importance in her future scheme of things. It is only after the end of the Cold War, and only once ASEAN showed signs of ideological neutrality, that China started cultivating Southeast Asia as a group and began engaging ASEAN. This is almost the same time that India, too, started her engagement with ASEAN. In terms of economic engagement, China's bilateral trade increased rapidly and from US\$ 8.8 billion in 1993 to UD\$ 55.4 billion by 2001.[16] In comparison, India's economic engagement with ASEAN was minimal. Thus, India attempting to chase out China cannot hold good in economic terms, as it is China that is clearly the major economic partner to ASEAN and not India. The 'India chasing China out' hypothesis is a by-product of the belief that there is a zero-sum competition between India and China. The fallacy of such theorisation is that it treats India and China as the only players and the Southeast and East Asia as a passive field wherein India and China are playing their zero-sum game. A more objective understanding entails factoring-in the significant and dynamic role of Southeast and East Asian countries based on their own perceptions of the two big regional powers, namely India and China, and their expectations from both of them. It is beyond the scope of this paper to make a detailed analysis of the role of Southeast and East Asian countries in determining the Look East Policy of India or, for that matter, China's engagement with Southeast and East Asia. It must, however, be mentioned here that, at least in economic terms Southeast and East Asian counties are looking to engage both India and China for their own economic development and to achieve the optimality that was (and is) lacking in ASEAN as a regional economy. In other words, China and India may have not reached a point to demonstrate hardware and software complementarities in their bilateral relations, but it is, nevertheless, the wish of Southeast- and East-Asian countries to gain from these complementarities in their own economic development.

A strong case is made about India's strategic engagement with Southeast- and East-Asian countries through her Look East Policy. It is argued that the realisation of the full potential of India's economic engagement with ASEAN may well lie in the future, but India's strategic engagement, at least with Southeast Asia, is complete. Again, this conjecture is based on two overly generalised assumptions: (1) there is geographical contiguity between India and Southeast Asia, making their security and strategic needs similar and compatible; (2) India intends to contain China in response to the latter's attempt to contain India.

As mentioned earlier, for India, the strategic importance of Southeast Asia was driven home by the experience of World War II. Thus, it is essential that India monitors the strategic configurations of the region for ensuring India's own safety and security. Mr KM Panikkar had, way back in 1960, pointed out that *"India's security interests cover ... Burma, Thailand, Indochina coastlines, certainly including Malaysia and Singapore."*[17] During the Cold War, this region was largely dominated by the Western alliance, leaving little space for India. The end of Cold War and subsequent signs of the USA losing interest in the region created a condition that demanded India's immediate attention. This is not to argue that India senses any threat to arise from Southeast Asia as such, but it is rightly believed in New Delhi that the developments in Southeast Asia would affect its interests directly and indirectly.[18] The region may present itself as a cohesive economic bloc, but strategically, it remains largely fragmented. There are attempts to project ASEAN as a security player on the loose grounds that a security community emerges when a group of States commonly renounce the use of force in resolving conflict.[19] In reality, of course, the security interests of the Southeast Asian nations vary widely and at times overlap, causing frictions amongst themselves. Competing claims over the Spratly Islands and the Paracel Islands, within the South China Sea, are cases in point. There are other areas of contention as well.[20] This fragmented nature of the strategic environment of the region called for a complex strategic engagement with Southeast Asian nations. Two factors currently characterise India's strategic engagement with the States in the region — first, India's determination of areas in which New Delhi can play a supportive role in assuaging security anxieties of that region; and second, India's own strategic and security calculations in the region. Since there is hardly any security and strategic convergence among the Southeast Asian States, India needs to engage these States at varying levels. This is clearly visible in the nature and degree of Indian strategic engagements. In the security sphere, it is clear that ASEAN, as a group, is interested in India for the specific congruity in security interest that its members have, namely, anxiety over China's long-term intentions. Other than this, there is no security or strategic convergence in the traditional sense of security. India, therefore, is engaged more bilaterally in the region than with ASEAN as a group. Although it has been a general practice amongst the Southeast Asian countries to resolve their disputes peacefully, there are moments when force has been projected a means to resolve conflict. For example, in March 2005, Indonesia sent warships to the Sulawesi Sea to protest Malaysia's decision to award a contract to an Anglo-Dutch firm to explore and mine the Ambalat and East Ambalat oil and gas blocks. Such incidents drive home the point that each of the Southeast Asian nations need to maintain modernised military equipment and trained personnel to deal with any future eventuality. India figures prominently as source of assistance for the modernisation of armed forces and equipment. The various defence agreements between India and individual Southeast Asian States suggest that India caters to these specific needs since *"[c]ompared with ASEAN countries, India's weapon systems are not only good in quality but also inexpensive"*.[21]

These strategic engagements of India with Southeast Asian countries are interpreted by some scholars in India — and more so in China — that India is trying to chase China out of the region. It is true that India's engagements are giving jitters to China but that is not because India wants to chase China out of the region. A realistic interpretation of India's strategic moves would be to consider the vacuum that was created by the departure of the USA at the end of the Cold War. With the US withdrawal from the Philippines, there was a possibility that the region would be thrown into strategic chaos and instability. India, on the other hand, had always wanted to keep its neighbourhoods stable by not allowing any single power to control the region. One may recall India's initiative, in 1967, to create an 'Asian Council' with the singular objective of ensuring that no power would ever be powerful enough to dominate Asia, particularly South and Southeast Asia.[22] The post-Cold War conditions provided India with the opportunity to put in place a kind of diversified security order in which no single State within or outside the region could ever become preponderant. In a sense, India intends to play the role of a balancer in the region and wants to ensure stability in the security order of the region. This balancing is not necessarily directed against any particular country. If India has security and strategic relationships with countries like Vietnam and Japan on the one hand, it has a strategic understanding with China and Russia, on the other. At a different level, India ropes in Japan, the US and Australia, who, too, have major stakes in the region, into some kind of security arrangement. Southeast Asia as a group, on its part, welcomes this role of India, as there is a convergence of Indian and ASEAN's strategic perspective, i.e., preventing any single power from dominating the region.[23]

BRI and the Maritime Silk Route

In 2013, China launched the most ambitious of its plans, namely, the 'One Belt One Road' (OBOR), whose nomenclature was later changed to the 'Belt and Road Initiative' (BRI). The BRI is the largest economic connectivity project ever launched by any country. It has both land and sea components. China's desire to connect the northern and western parts of the country with Central Asia, South Asia and Europe, through numerous land-corridors, falls under the 'Silk Road Economic Belt'. The sea component of the BRI is known as the "21st Century Maritime Silk Road" (MSR). Through the MSR, China plans to create an economic zone spanning East Asia, Southeast Asia, South Asia, Eastern and Northern Africa, the Arab world and Europe. There are good economic rationales put forward by the Chinese leadership for such an economic zone. China's President, Xi Jin Ping, has been advocating a policy of regional stability through economic development and, in one of his speeches, prior to the 13th Party Congress in 2013, he articulated China's strategy of maintaining regional stability through Chinese "peripheral diplomacy". In this context, he said, *"Maintaining stability in China's neighbourhood is the key objective of peripheral diplomacy. We must encourage and participate in the process of regional economic integration, speed up the process of building up infrastructure and connectivity. We must build the Silk Road Economic Belt and 21st Century Maritime Silk Road, creating a new regional economic order."*[24]

China is proactively pushing the '21st Century Maritime Silk Road' project by creating assets in the form of ports all along the route. The economic benefits that would accrue to the countries agreeing to be part of the Maritime Silk Route need, of course, to be weighed against the political costs the countries are to incur for being part of the Chinese scheme. Sri Lanka already has started feeling the heat of being part of the project in the form of shedding control over the port of Hambantota. There are many more ports and related infrastructure that is yet to come-up along the Maritime Silk Route. The jaw-dropping scale of the Chinese initiative has generated both positive and anxious responses from around the world. Geoeconomically, the initiative is being viewed as a Chinese attempt to change the regional economic order and replace the Bretton Woods system with a Chinese one. The huge foreign currency surplus in Chinese hands has emboldened China to conceptualise a system that would establish Chinese economic order in the region.

The associated fear that causes more anxiety than the economic fear is the strategic implication of these Chinese moves. In geostrategic terms, apprehensions abound that China not only plans to change the global economic order, but also wishes to change the strategic configuration of the world, by the centenary of the Communist Revolution, i.e., by 2049. The intensity of this fear varies among countries, largely in accordance with their own equations with China. Among countries that have maximum fears about the rise of China is India. India, in her own right aspires to be an important member of the global order and if there is any country that can impede India's progress, it is China. By virtue of her economic might, China has penetrated the conventional Indian sphere of influence, i.e., South Asia. China has already established a firm economic grip over Southeast Asia and is often seen to be flexing her military muscle in the region and refusing to participate in multilateral negotiations, even discarding verdicts of the international tribunal on contentious issues such as those that persist within the South China Sea. India, having its own historical baggage vis-à-vis China in the form of a war and unresolved border issues, has every reason to remain worried about Chinese military and growth and expansion. Chinese forays into Indian Ocean in the form of port acquisitions and the establishment of naval bases are causes of concern for India. Incidentally, both India and China share the same neighbourhood and a competition for strategic space is natural. In this competition, China has made the first move and is seemingly set to outpace India in the region. India, on her part, has to come up with plans to counter the growing Chinese influence in the region both economically and strategically.

India's Options

In a relative power calculation, China is far ahead of India, both economically and militarily. A confrontational approach, in the form of alliance-building to counter Chinese growth and expansion, may not be the best of the options available to India. Rather a seemingly co-optive and benign approach may help India's cause of nullifying or minimising Chinese influence in the region to a level that India can then deal-with. The "structural impediments"[25] that prevent India from assuming a leadership role in South Asia are not present in Southeast Asia and thus India finds much more acceptability in Southeast Asia. As has already been pointed out, Southeast Asia, too, suffers from strategic anxiety vis-a-vis China, which creates an opening for India to establish bonds with the countries of this region. India does, however, need an institutional mechanism and a vision to increase her presence in the region. In the era of multilateralism and regionalism, India has to pro-actively build multilateral arrangements with her neighbours that would ensure her progressive association with the region to the extent that it can be insulated from any kind of Chinese threat of regional hegemony.

As discussed earlier, India has been providing substance to her Look East Policy/Act East Policy sight from the early 1990s. However, because the 'Look East Policy' was a response to the economic crisis India was then in, it could not sustain a strategic dimension and, consequently, there is very little to show by way of success in the subsequent 'Act East Policy' even after a quarter century. A much better thought-out initiative has been recently conceptualised by India, one that is based on the age-old Indian contacts with Southeast Asia and beyond. This is called "Project MAUSAM".[26] Developed on the basis of the process of connectivity that existed from ancient times between India and the Indian Ocean world, Project MAUSAM seeks to reconnect the region and revitalise its cultural connectivity. Unlike the Look/Act East Policy, Project MAUSAM can be steered towards sustaining India's presence in Southeast Asia and beyond, albeit in the cultural sphere. The cultural connectivity established through this project can then be built-upon to serve India's other interests. Though the idea of MAUSAM is grounded in a good amount of historical experience, the present initiative does not seem to be drawing lessons from that very same history. One needs to understand that the ancient seafarers of India who established the connectivity between India and the extended region of Southeast and East Asia, operated from the eastern coast of India and followed geographically contiguous routes. It was, thus, easy to establish relationships and nurture them for long period of time. What India needs is to analyse the historical cultural connectivity of the region and customise Indian culture in the present context to be exported through the routes that could maintain India's cultural connectivity in the past.

While the cultural connectivity is slow to take off India can make use of a much more pragmatic institutional arrangement that exists in the form of the Bay of Bengal Initiative for Multi-Sectoral Technical and Economic Cooperation (BIMSTEC). BIMSTEC is the most natural of the regional arrangements within the common area of Bay of Bengal. Even though the early years since its inception in 1997 have not been particularly spectacular, BIMSTEC nevertheless has the potential of emerging as a very successful economic and cultural community over which India can have great influence. BIMSTEC has identified 14 sectors within which to promote cooperation amongst seven Bay of Bengal littoral countries. Of these 14 sectors, three were identified for special focus by the BIMSTEC Network of Policy Think Tanks in its second meeting held in 2015 in Bangkok. These three sectors are: Connectivity, Value-Chain development, and, People-to-People Contact. It is a given that the success of the BIMSTEC depends upon increased connectivity amongst its members. The Asian Development Bank commissioned a study called "BIMSTEC Transport Infrastructure and Logistics Study" (BTILS), which identified 166 connectivity projects, of which 65 have been identified as priority ones. These connectivity projects include all three modes of connectivity, i.e., connectivity by land, sea and air. India needs to put her weight behind these BIMSTEC arrangements and push for the early implementation of the connectivity projects identified in the BTILS, in order to give a boost to the process of regional cooperation in the region.

Neither Project MAUSAM nor BIMSTEC can match China's BRI initiative, but a successful BIMSTEC can be an effective mechanism for India to deepen its engagement with the extended neighbourhood of Southeast and East Asia. If China has deep pockets with which to invest in regional infrastructure and lure countries towards the economic opportunities that she holds out, India has the advantage of greater acceptability in the region. The hidden anxiety amongst the Southeast Asian nations vis-a-vis China places the latter in a position of relative disadvantage, making it difficult for Beijing to sustain a relationship beyond economic engagements. India, on the other hand, is welcomed to the region. If India can deliver, even minimally, on the economic front to the benefit of the countries of the region, this would go a long way in gaining goodwill for India. Such goodwill will work as a shield against China's attempt to meld the region against India's strategic interests. India's willingness to be involved and to invest in infrastructure and connectivity projects in the region would reduce the excessive reliance on Chinese capital, leading to reduced chances of Chinese domination of the region. Further, Project MAUSAM, if implemented in a calibrated manner, would lead to India's sustained relationship with the countries of the region that currently have no option but to join the Chinese bandwagon. In conclusion, it can be said that although India may not have the resources to counter the massive Chinese

BRI, India can augment her admittedly smaller resource pool by using historical knowledge, and the geopolitical and geoeconomic dynamism of the region to protect India's strategic neighbourhood from falling into the Chinese sphere of influence.

Endnotes

1   Scholars in India do not consider India to be generally proactive in her foreign policy.

2   Mohammed Ayoob, *India and Southeast Asia: Indian Perceptions and Policies*, London and New York: Routledge, 1990, p.2.

3   Ton That Thien, *India and South East Asia, 1947-1960*, Geneve: Librairie, 1963, p. 74. Cited in, M. Ayoob, p.15.

4   K. P. Saksena, *Cooperation in Development: Problems and Prospects for India and ASEAN*, New Delhi: Sage Publications, 1986, p.53.

5   "Meeting in Bangkok: Puny Counter-revolutionary Alliance," *Peking Review*, 18 August 1967. Cited in, M. Ayoob, p, 11.

6   Chulacheeb Chinwanno, "The Dragon, the Bull and the Ricestalks: The Roles of China and India in Southeast Asia," in Saw Swee-Hock, Sheng Lijun and Chin Kin Wah, (eds.), *ASEAN-China Relations: Realities and Prospects*, Singapore: Institute of Southeast Asian Studies, 2005, p. 159.

7   It was S. Rajaretnam, the Foreign Minister of Singapore and one of the founding fathers of ASEAN who advocated the idea that ASEAN, in order to achieve optimality in economy has to attract outside powers to be involved in the region. For more see, New themes for Asia. South-East Asia in transition. Singapore solution / by S. Rajaratnam, Reprinted from The Australian outlook, Dec. 1973, East Melbourne : Australian Institute of International Affairs, 1973, p. 243-260.

8   Zhao Hong, "India and China: Rivals or Partners in Southeast Asia," *Contemporary Southeast Asia*, vol. 29, no. 1, 2007, p.122.

9   M. C. Chagla's Speech at Singapore during his visit to Malaysia and Singapore in may 1967. Quoted in K. P. Saksena, *Cooperation in Development: Problems and Prospects for India and ASEAN*, New Delhi: Sage Publications, 1986, p.53.

10 G.V.C. Naidu, "Looking East: India and Southeast Asia," p.195. www.sinca.edu.tw/

11 ibid.

12 P.V. Narasimha Rao's views articulated by Sudhir Devare. See Sudhir Devare, *India and Southeast Asia: Towards Security Convergence*, Singapore: Institute of Southeast Asina Studies, New Delhi: Capital Publishing Company, 2006, p.126.

13 J.N. Dixit, *Indian Foreign Policy and Its Neighbours*, New Delhi: Gyan Publishing House, 2001, p.340.

14 *Strengthening Asean-India Partnership: Trends and Future Prospects, Export-Import Bank of India, January 2018, https://www.eximbankindia.in/Assets/Dynamic/PDF/Publication-Resources/ResearchPapers/88file.pdf*

15 Preety Bhogal, "India-ASEAN economic relations: Examining future possibilities", ORF Issue Brief, Issue No. 221, January 2018, https://www.orfonline.org/wp-content/uploads/2018/01/ORF_Issue_Brief_221_India_ASEAN.pdf

16 Vincent Wei-cheng Wang, "The Logic of China-ASEAN FTA: Economic Statecraft of 'Peaceful Ascendancy,'" in Ho Khai Leong and Samuel C. Y. Ku (eds.), *China and Southeast Asia: Global Changes and Regional Challenges*, Singapore: Institute of Southeast Asian Studies, Kaohsiung: Centre for Southeast Asian Studies, 2005, p.26.

17 K. M. Panikar, *Problems of Indian Defence*, London: Asia publishing House, 1960. Cited in Hu Shisheng, "India's Approach to ASEAN and its Regional Implications," in Saw Swee-Hock, Sheng Lijun and Chin Kin Wah (eds.), *ASEAN-China Relations: realities and Prospects*, Singapore: Institute of Southeast Asian Studies, 2005, pp.136-37.

18 Frederic Grare, "In Search of a Role", In Frederic Grare and Amitabh Mattoo (eds.), *India and ASEAN: The Politics of India's Look East Policy*, New Delhi: Manohar Publishers, 2001, p. 136.

19 For details on ASEAN as a Security Community, see Amitav Acharya, *Constructing a Security Community in ASEAN: ASEAN and the Problem of Regional Order*, London and New York: Routledge, 2001.

20 Articulating K. S. Nathan's views Sudhir Devare say's "ASEAN, unlike the European Union (EU), can be described as a 'process regionalism' as against 'product regionalism', which does not have a common security policy. Sudhir Devare, *India and Southeast Asia: Towards Security Convergence*, Singapore: Institute of Southeast Asina Studies, New Delhi: Capital Publishing Company, 2006, p.45.

21 "Hu Shisheng, "India's Approach to ASEAN and its Regional Implications," in Saw Swee-Hock, Sheng Lijun and Chin Kin Wah (eds.), *ASEAN-China Relations: realities and Prospects*, Singapore: Institute of Southeast Asian Studies, 2005, p.132.

22 "Hu Shisheng, "India's Approach to ASEAN and its Regional Implications," in Saw Swee-Hock, Sheng Lijun and Chin Kin Wah (eds.), *ASEAN-China*

Relations: realities and Prospects, Singapore: Institute of Southeast Asian Studies, 2005, p.136.

23 Zhao Gancheng, 'India's Look East Policy: A Chinese Perspective," in P.V. Rao (ed.), *India and ASEAN: Partners at Summit*, New Delhi: KW Publishers Pvt. Ltd., p.223.

24 "习近平在周边外交工作座谈会上发表重要讲话 [Xi Jinping's Important Speech at the Peripheral Diplomacy Work Conference]", Xinhua News Agency, 25 October 2013, http://news.xinhuanet.com/politics/2013-10/25/c_117878897.htm. Cited in Peter Cai, "Understanding China's Belt and Road Initiative", Lowy Institute for International Policy, March 2017, P. 3, https://www.lowyinstitute.org/sites/default/files/documents/Understanding%20China's%20Belt%20and%20Road%20Initiative_WEB_1.pdf

25 The South Asian region was and to a large extent is identified with India and Indian culture. The new modern nations of South Asia are in the process of nation-building and all of them find the issues problematic to their concept of nation are negatively related to India. Thus, there is a feeling that Indian regional leadership may lead to the obliteration of the nascent national identities these countries are trying to acquire for their new nation-states. For a detailed discussion, see, Binoda Kumar Mishra, "The Nation-State Problematic in Asia: The South Asian Experience," *Perceptions: Journal of International Affairs*, Vol. XIX, No. 1, Spring 2014, ISSN 1300-8641.

26 Project 'Mausam' is a Ministry of Culture project to be implemented by Indira Gandhi National Centre for the Arts (IGNCA), New Delhi as the nodal coordinating agency with support of Archeological Survey of India and National Museum as associate bodies, https://www.indiaculture.nic.in/project-mausam

China's Forays into the Indian Ocean: A Case of Anti-Piracy Operations

Rahul Karan Reddy

In 1978, the grounds from which the Chinese government has traditionally drawn its legitimacy shifted from an ideological one to one structured around economic performance and nationalism. The current emphasis upon China's economic development prioritises the safety and security of maritime trade and commerce, which accounts for a significant portion of Chinas imports and exports. The International Sea Lanes (ISLs) upon which her maritime trade commerce flow, are also the arteries for China's imports of crude-oil and other natural resources. Indeed, the import of crude-oil accounts for over 40% of China's oil consumption. Based upon its assessment of the prevailing security environment within the maritime domain of its interest (which is, of course, a dynamic process rather than being a one-time activity), Beijing determines the preferred orientation of its maritime trade routes, transforming these ISLs into China's 'Sea Lines of Communication' (SLOCs). Guaranteeing the security of these SLOCs and ensuring unfettered access to them has prompted a modernisation of the People's Liberation Army-Navy (PLA-N) and the Chinese Coast Guard to secure Chinese interests spread across Asia and the Indian Ocean region.

The role of the PLAN underwent a transformation under 'New Historic Missions' initiated by Hu Jintao in 2004 which changed the defensive and inward-looking orientation of the PLAN. The PLAN's strategy shifted from 'near-seas active defence' (*jinhai jiji fangyu*) to 'far-seas operations' (*yuanhai zuozhan*).[1] The political leadership at the time also expressed an interest in Military Operations Other Than War (MOOTW) which include anti-piracy operations, search and rescue, disaster relief, medical support and counter-terrorism missions, which would serve the image of China being a 'responsible stakeholder'.[2] However, the PLAN's modernisation had begun in the 1980s itself, when it evolved from a coastal force into a force capable of defending Chinese interests in the 'near seas'. The PLAN has evolved further to break out of the First and Second Island Chains, and is now enhancing its blue water capabilities to conduct operations and gain experience in the Indian Ocean. This was spelt out in the 2015 White Paper on 'Open Seas Protection', which translates into a further modernisation of the PLAN to include power projection capabilities as a 'blue water navy'.[3]

Beijing's counter-piracy operations began in December 2008, motivated by the fact that a significant amount of its energy supplies and trade traversed the International Recommended Transit Corridor (IRTC) off the coast of Somalia. The PLAN unilaterally deployed a Task Force in January 2009 to escort Chinese-flagged shipping in the Gulf of Aden but refrained from participating with other members of the coalition.[4] This began to change after China's participation and coordination with other navies through the Shared Awareness and Deconfliction (SHADE) mechanism gained momentum. The PLAN has sent a task force every year since then, reaching its 31st deployment in July 2019.[5]

Drivers of Anti-Piracy Operations

Protecting Economic and Strategic Interests. Official statements from the PLA-N and Ministry of Foreign Affairs (MOFA) indicate that Beijing is a realist actor looking to protect Chinese ships and crews with military force. China's significant overseas economic interests, initiated and planned under the framework of the Belt and Road Initiative (BRI) (which construct includes the Maritime Silk Route [MSR]) require a strong navy to protect sea lanes and ships that assure Beijing of its economic growth and energy supplies. According to Chinese sources, more than 1220 ships and 40% of China's goods and raw material trade traverse the Gulf of Aden each year. Additionally, as a massive energy consumer, China receives 45% of its imports from West Asia and 32% from Africa.[6] Escort vessels are critical to ensure the sustained supply of raw materials and energy resources. However, China's anti-piracy operations are not purely mercantilist, since a significant amount of Chinese trade is carried on foreign-owned vessels. Since piracy has fallen significantly since 2015, anti-piracy operations are no longer the main focus of the task groups in the Gulf of Aden. The PLAN's Gulf of Aden deployment has begun to engage in a diverse set of operations, including the evacuation of Chinese and foreign nationals from Yemen, Non-Combatant Evacuation Operations (NCEO) in Libya, and chemical disarmament missions in Syria.[7] These operations are an indication of the larger role Beijing envisages for the PLAN in the Indian

Ocean — a necessity for Beijing's broader strategy of developing a blue water navy.

Strategic competition with the USA drive Beijing's pursuit of a blue water navy so as to secure its overseas economic interests in the event of a blockade or localised war. The re-emergence of the QUAD has possibly alerted China to a counter-strategy spearheaded by the US, Japan, Australia and India. Additionally, the Malacca dilemma has worried Chinese strategic thinkers, who argue that China faces the risk of being isolated from supplies of energy in the event of a blockade by the US Navy. Since 80% of China's oil passes through the Malacca Strait and initiatives like the MSR require free and open SLOCs, it is in China's interest to project its sea power. The projection of power at sea has recently involved the use of diesel-electric and nuclear-powered submarines, confirming fears that China's operations in the IOR are not just in the interest of anti-piracy. China's deployment of submarines began in 2013, with a three-month patrol of a *Shang* Class nuclear powered attack submarine (SSN) in the IOR.[8] There has been a general expansion of the PLAN's operational range, evidenced by the base in Djibouti that provides China a rudimentary power-projection base capable of supporting intelligence collection, non-combatant evacuations, peacekeeping operations and anti-piracy efforts.[9] The base may be part of larger network of dual-use bases in the Indian Ocean Region that Beijing intends to develop. Beijing's interest in ports located around South Asia and Africa has raised suspicions that Beijing intends to acquire of a network of bases through the Belt and Road Initiative (BRI) and Maritime Silk Route (MSR).

A substantial naval presence in the IOR, with bases to support logistical and supply requirements, are necessary to hedge against the Indian facilities in the Andaman and Nicobar Islands which are rapidly improving. China's power projection, through the deployment of submarines ostensibly for anti-piracy missions has been noted, by the Indian Navy. Navy Chief Admiral Sunil Lanba noted at the Raisina Dialogue in 2019 stated that there were six to eight Chinese Navy ships in the Northern IOR at any given time.[10] Shortly after the deployment of a submarine in the IOR during the Doklam standoff, the Indian Navy has ordered permanent surveillance of critical sea lanes and choke points by 'mission-ready' warships. The intensifying competition between India and China has drawn-in other nations such as France, Mauritius, Seychelles, Mozambique and Oman. These deployments risk catalysing a collective reaction from regional navies such the Indian Navy, who perceive the IOR as their maritime backyard. China's forays into the IOR have not merely raised the stakes for countries in the region, but have provoked the interest of extra-regional powers as well.

Demonstrating Participation as a Responsible Stakeholder. An important driver of the anti-piracy operations is Beijing's characterisation of such missions as a demonstration of China's participation as a responsible stakeholder in the international system.[11] China has committed personnel and resources to the fight against piracy, while its task force operates alongside regional and extra-regional navies. On the other hand, ambiguous declarations against joining operations with non-Chinese command raise questions about China's intention to participate fully with the international community. However, the novelty of this approach allows Beijing to display its sovereignty at sea to Chinese citizens at home. Despite the absence of any formal institutionalisation between the EU and NATO missions and the PLAN's Gulf of Aden deployment, there are several informal mechanisms of information sharing and mutual dependence between China and the EU. Through ship to ship exchanges, port visits and combined exercises, Beijing reinforces its domestic image as a global actor. Through these mechanisms, the PLAN also gains operational insights into the workings of other navies, while maintaining its freedom to act independently.

Anti-piracy operations have created a framework for engagement between important navies in the region. These joint efforts advance the perception that Beijing's goals are non-threatening and in agreement with accepted norms of the region. China's willingness to not only participate in anti-piracy operations but to also alter their practice when deemed necessary indicates a proactive approach to multilateralism. Anti-piracy operations are also a means of confidence building between countries that have an adversarial security relationship — such as India and China. The first mention of anti-piracy in the bilateral talks between India and China was in February 2012, when both sides agreed to undertake joint operations against pirates. However, such steps have been rare since the land border issue and traditional threat perception of China prevents any progress in that direction. Nevertheless, the trend of generating diplomatic goodwill by devoting a large share of naval resources to diplomacy has been a constant factor in the interactions between the Chinese Navy and other navies.[12] Incremental soft power benefits from various facets of anti-piracy operations has created an approach that scholars are currently referring to as 'creative involvement'[13] in a region with adversarial powers.

Naval diplomacy plays an important part in China's anti-piracy operations, which have evolved new dimensions since the incidence of piracy began to decrease from 2017.

Acquiring Operational Experience in the IOR

Anti-piracy operations act as a springboard for Beijing to expand its maritime security operations, thereby expanding the range and scope of the PLAN's engagements. The enhanced domain awareness of the PLAN through various non-traditional security operations will familiarise it with the operating environment of the IOR. This is further enhanced by port calls, ship visits, fleet reviews, joint exercises and bilateral engagements. Beijing's overseas interests have propelled China beyond its land borders to focus on a mix of 'offshore waters defence' and 'far seas defence' — reflecting the high command's interest in a wider operational reach. This is also supported by China's interest in aircraft carriers, valuable for their ability to project power in distant oceans. The US Department of Defence notes that China's next-generation carriers will have greater endurance and will be able to launch various types of aircraft, which will increase the potential striking power of Chinese Carrier Battle Groups. Improvements in shipbuilding and construction have allowed Beijing to build its second aircraft carrier and these capacities are likely to be bolstered by further investing in supply ships, port access and logistic-support ships. The Chinese naval base in Djibouti contains a ship-maintenance and repair shop, which was created after an incident in 2010, when the power plant of a type-052B destroyer Guangzhou broke down while the ship was carrying out anti-piracy missions in the Gulf of Aden[14] — which indicates an adaptation of the PLAN to the IOR environment.

Conclusion

Beijing's anti-piracy operations are a demonstration of the PLAN's evolving capabilities in the IOR. The expanded capabilities of the PLA-N under the mandate first of *Hu Jintao* and then of *Xi Jinping* manifest themselves through the deployment of a succession of PLAN Task Forces in the Gulf of Aden. The broader operational reach has also constituted protecting China's overseas economic interests and investments that are expanding in the form of the BRI and MSR. Beijing continues to deploy warships in the Gulf of Aden, even though the incidence of piracy has decreased significantly, which indicates a forward strategic deployment to conduct low- to medium-intensity operations. The progressive increase in regional presence indicates the political willingness of the leadership to expand China's global profile and influence. The anti-piracy efforts demonstrate to citizens in the mainland that Beijing's efforts to protect Chinese nationals, Chinese interests and foreign nationals too, are signs of China's role as a global actor.

The acquisition of bases and intensifying naval diplomacy is forcing other actors in the region to look for allies and partners so as to balance China's increased presence. This has drawn India, Japan, Australia, Vietnam and the United States closer — a situation Beijing could avert through the use of soft power manifestations such as aid programs, high-profile gestures and Humanitarian Assistance and Disaster Relief (HADR). Normalising the Chinese presence in the IOR through naval diplomacy has given some actors in the region the opportunity to become beneficiaries of Chinese investment and aid without appearing to compromise on their own sovereignty and territorial integrity. Anti-piracy operations, on the other hand, are Beijing's projection of hard power and have stirred into action, other actors in the region who see Beijing as eroding their influence. These anti-piracy operations are significant because they signal the coming of a blue-water Chinese Navy with a significant presence in the IOR.

Endnotes

1   United States of America. US Army War College. *Assessing the People's Liberation Army in the Hu Jintao Era Assessing the People's Liberation Army in the FOR THIS AND OTHER PUBLICATIONS, VISIT US AT Hu Jintao Era.* By Roy Kamphausen, David Lai, and Travis Tanner. https://ssi.armywarcollege. edu/pdffiles/pub1201.pdf.

2   Suri, Gopal. *China's Expanding Military Maritime Footprints in the Indian Ocean Region.* Vivekananda International Foundation. https://www.vifindia. org/sites/default/files/china-s-expanding-military-maritime-footprint-in-the-indian-ocean-region-india-s-response_0.pdf.

3   Blasko, Dennis. *The 2015 Chinese Defense White Paper on Strategy in Perspective: Maritime Missions Require a Change in the PLA Mindset.* Publication no. Vol 15, Issue 2. China Brief, Jamestown Foundation. June 2015. https://jamestown.org/ program/the-2015-chinese-defense-white-paper-on-strategy-in-perspective-maritime-missions-require-a-change-in-the-pla-mindset/.

4   "Chinese Navy Sends Most Sophisticated Ships on Escort Mission off Somalia." *Xinhua,* December 2008. http://en.people. cn/90001/90776/90883/6562939.html.

5   Erickson, Andrew. "The China Anti-Piracy Bookshelf: Statistics & Implications from Ten Years' Deployment." *Andrew S. Erickson*(blog), January 2019. http://www.andrewerickson.com/2019/01/the-china-anti-piracy-bookshelf-statistics-implications-from-ten-years-deployment-counting/.

6   "China's Crude Oil Imports by Country." Chart. Statista. January 2015. https://www.statista.com/statistics/221765/chenese-oil-imports-by-country/.

7   Erickson, Andrew. "The China Anti-Piracy Bookshelf: Statistics & Implications from Ten Years' Deployment." *Andrew S. Erickson*(blog), January 2019. http://www.andrewerickson.com/2019/01/the-china-anti-piracy-bookshelf-statistics-implications-from-ten-years-deployment-counting/.

8   Singh, Abhijit. "Decoding Chinese Submarine Sightings in South Asia." *Economic Times*, November 2015. Decoding Chinese submarine 'sightings' in South Asia, eroding New Delhi's strategic primacy Read more at: //economictimes.indiatimes.com/articleshow/66631063.cms?utm_source=contentofinterest&utm_medium=text&utm_campaign=cppst.

9   Headley, Tyler. "China's Djibouti Base: A One Year Update." The Diplomat. December 07, 2018. Accessed June 23, 2019. https://thediplomat.com/2018/12/chinas-djibouti-base-a-one-year-update/.

10 Prasun Sonwalkar. "Keeping a Close Eye on Chinese Presence in Indian Ocean,' Says Admiral Lanba." *Economic Times*, March 2019. https://www.hindustantimes.com/india-news/keeping-a-close-eye-on-chinese-presence-in-indian-ocean-says-admiral-lanba/story-pr7dzln0KC1wPxLrzV182M.html.

11 Kaufman, Alison A. *China's Participation in Anti-Piracy Operations off the Horn of Africa: Drivers and Implications.*Report. Department of Political Science, Massachusetts Institute of Technology. May 2009. https://ocw.mit.edu/courses/political-science/17-408-chinese-foreign-policy-fall-2013/assignments/MIT17_408F13_ExplinigChina.pdf.

12 Ercikson, Andrew, and Austin M. Strange. "China 's Blue Soft Power." *Naval War College Review*, 6th ser., 68, no. 1 (Winter 2015): 78-79. https://digital-commons.usnwc.edu/cgi/viewcontent.cgi?referer=https://www.google.com/&httpsredir=1&article=1182&context=nwc-review.

13 Erickson, Andrew, and Austin M. Strange. "Why China's Gulf Piracy Fight Matters." *Global Public Square*(blog), January 2014. http://globalpublicsquare.blogs.cnn.com/2014/01/07/why-chinas-gulf-piracy-fight-matters/.

14 Chan, Minnie. "China's Navy Is Being Forced to Rethink Its Spending Plans as Cost of Trade War Rises." *South China Morning Post*, May 2019. https://www.scmp.com/news/china/military/article/3011872/chinas-navy-being-forced-rethink-its-spending-plans-cost-trade.

Valedictory Address

S Paramesh, PTM, TM,
Inspector General, Indian Coast Guard

Admiral Pradeep Chauhan, IN (Retd), Director-General NMF; Cmde RS Vasan, IN (Retd), Regional Director, NMF; Dr M Venkataramanan, Assistant Professor, Department of Defence and Strategic Studies, University of Madras; and Participants

A very good evening to you all.

At the outset I would like to thank Cmde Vasan and the NMF for inviting me to deliver the valedictory address on a very apt and contemporary topic: **Our Maritime Neighbours and the Regional Dynamics**.

The uniqueness of India's maritime neighbourhood is well established by its geography, demography and political divisions. India's relations with its neighbours have been largely dynamic, and the geostrategic advantage that India enjoys has always been viewed by others as being overarching one. This regional dynamism greatly influences our national interest and security perspective.

Before moving on to our core maritime issues, let me quickly address the broad security-challenges that persist in our immediate neighbourhood.

Sri Lanka, by virtue of its strategic location, is able to oversee major SLOCs and it is, quite naturally, attempting to exploit extant IOR geopolitical game-plays for its own development. Insofar as the India-Sri Lanka security challenges are concerned, issues of cross-border fishing, drug trafficking, and illegal migration, are major areas of concern.

Challenges for India in its engagement of the **Maldives** relate to that country's political upheavals, inherent climate-change perils, and the presence of radicalised elements.

With a recently-resolved IMBL, cooperation with **Bangladesh** *is on a positive track. However, security challenges by way of cross-border fishing, illegal migration, and the shadow of the ISIS, persist.*

Farther East, the issue of Rohingya migration from **Myanmar** *needs close monitoring, as does maritime poaching.*

Pakistan's inimical attitude towards India is always a disturbing challenge that adversely impacts India's own pursuit of her maritime interests. Other challenges within the maritime domain include an unresolved IMBL, State-sponsored terror, drug trafficking, smuggling, and increasing Chinese support for the capacity-building of Pakistan's maritime forces. All these are causes of worry for us. Staying with **China**, for a moment, while we remain acutely aware of the growing might of the Chinese military, we seem to have missed-out on the meteoric rise of the China Coast Guard. Established in 2013 with 16,000 personnel and 135 vessels, it aims to be the world's largest and most formidable Coast Guard in terms of both, tonnage and numbers. The expansion plans and operational ethos of the China Coast Guard requires close monitoring. Further, Chinese fishing vessels have been organised into a maritime militia with paramilitary roles in peacetime and conflict situations. Militia fishing boats are trained in intelligence-gathering, asserting territorial jurisdiction, and providing logistic-support to more conventional maritime forces. With its enhanced interoperability with the China Coast Guard, the exploitation of this irregular force by China needs to be recognised.

India's Maritime Interests

Having briefly scanned the neighbourhood for issues impinging on our interests, a quick appreciation of the EEZ of IOR littorals reveals a huge oceanic expanse that requires active Indian presence. Today, our economic growth and development are driven by increasing stakes in the EEZ. Ocean developments under the SAGARMALA initiative, Cruise-ship tourism for an estimated 1.5 lakhs tourists, burgeoning offshore activities under the new Hydrocarbon Exploration and Licensing Policy, and deep-sea fishing under the Blue Revolution, all entail inherent vulnerabilities and warrant a robust safety and security architecture.

Threat-Spectrum Analysis

Earlier on, the threats to Indian maritime interests were conventional, clear, distinguishable and identifiable. However, modern-day threats are 'Grey', with no clear dimensions.

Threats Envisaged

As we move towards realising our maritime vision, we need to be cognizant of non-traditional threats that may derail our ambitions. The growth of the marine wings of terror-groups fuelled by our inimical neighbour continues to challenge our maritime security. Likewise, the menace of transnational organised crime, which has traditionally posed a challenge to security, will continue to affect our national interests adversely. The issue of Privately Contracted Armed Security Personnel (PCASP) on board merchant ships, and the presence of Floating Armouries, both call for a great deal of caution. Moreover, the Indian Ocean Region, also known as the world's 'Hazard Belt', is always at risk of a climatic catastrophe, warranting large-scale HADR preparations and requirements. Further, our proximity to the Golden Crescent and the increasing fortification of land borders has increased maritime vulnerabilities when viewed against the backdrop of drug trafficking trends. Recent drug-seizures off the Gujarat coast and the established *gaanja* trafficking trends around the Palk Bay areas, could also be a source of funding for organised transnational crime. The Indian Coast Guard, by mandate, is expected to keep our waters free from the flow of drugs. It is imperative that our future outlook cater for regional maritime security dynamics, the nation's maritime vision, and the profusion of non-traditional threats.

In today's scenario, the Maritime-Threat Occurrence-Probability, when gauged with the above-mentioned perils, can be considered as being close to a crisis situation, requiring effective physical surveillance and a readiness to use force against anti-national elements so as to mitigate any given situation in our Area of Responsibility.

Ladies and Gentlemen, I would like to touch upon the ICG's own efforts as a microcosm of the larger government initiatives of engaging our maritime neighbours.

International Cooperation

The Indian Coast Guard has signed Memorandums of Understanding/ Cooperation with the maritime law enforcement agencies of several partner countries. Examples include the Bangladesh Coast Guard, the Japan Coast Guard, the Korean Coast Guard, the Royal Oman Police Coast Guard, the Sri Lanka Coast Guard and the Vietnam Coast Guard. High-level meetings and joint exercises are an annual feature under each of these MoUs. Significantly, a hotline for direct communication with Pakistan's Maritime Security Agency has also been established under an MoU.

Ship-visits constitute an important component of the ICG's outreach and its interaction with partner agencies. During these visits, cooperation and training in the areas of maritime search-and-rescue, marine pollution-response, and, maritime law-enforcement, have been subjects of particular focus.

The ICG places great importance on multilateral cooperation and has been at the forefront of all regional efforts aimed at capacity-building and capability-enhancement in the areas of maritime safety and security, through continuous engagement and cooperation with partner organisations in the region and beyond. These include the 'Regional Cooperation Agreement on Combating Piracy and Armed Robbery' (ReCAAP) against ships in Asia, to which India is a contracting party, and, the 'Heads of Asian Coast Guard Agencies Meetings' (HACGAM), where India is the Chair for the 'Working Group on Maritime Search and Rescue' and a member of the 'Working Group on Environment Protection'.

Search-and-Rescue (SAR)

Given the vastness of the Indian Search and Rescue Region — 4.6 million square kilometres — and the involvement of multiple stakeholders, regional collaboration in SAR efforts is an inescapable requirement. The Indian Coast Guard, through the National Maritime Search and Rescue Board, takes appropriate action for the continuous improvement of the SAR system. This calls for the finest SAR training and operational practices, the conduct of exercises, efficient on-ground coordination, and, enhanced integration with the global SAR system. With these aims, since 2003, a biennial national level Search and Rescue Exercise (SAREX) is conducted by the ICG. In addition to validating the National SAR Plan, this exercise serves to showcase India's Maritime SAR (M-SAR) capability and preparedness to international observers, thereby strengthening the regional cooperative mechanism by sharing best practices. Our concern for the safety of seafarers was typically demonstrated by the deployment of an ICG ship to extinguish a major fire onboard MV MSC Daniela 30 nm off Colombo, on 05 Apr 2017. In another incident on 11 April of the same year, upon a request from Maritime Rescue Coordination Centre, Karachi, ICG ships and aircraft were promptly deployed to search for seven Pakistan MSA personnel who had been reported as missing off the putative Indo-Pak International Maritime Boundary Line. By 14 April 2017, two PMSA personnel had been rescued and the bodies of the other five recovered.

Pollution Response

A robust maritime environment is a *sine qua non* for India's development, and towards this end, the ICG has, since 2009, been conducting a national level pollution-response exercise 'NATPOLREX'. Although the exercise is primarily meant to validate India's oil-spill response and preparedness, and for building multi-agency synergy, thanks to the presence of international observers, it is also a platform for sharing of latest developments and best practices being followed elsewhere. In a recent development, the ICG has signed an MoU for cooperation on the Response to Oil and Chemical Pollution in the South Asian Seas Region with the South Asian Cooperative Environment Programme (SACEP), an intergovernmental organisation headquartered in Sri Lanka.

The 'Regional Oil Spill Contingency Plan', developed by the organisation to facilitate international cooperation and mutual assistance in responding to any major oil-pollution incident in the seas around Bangladesh, India, Maldives, Pakistan and Sri Lanka, and to develop and maintain adequate capacity to deal with oil pollution emergencies, is likely to come into force shortly.

Capacity Building

Even though the ICG itself is facing a shortage of personnel and assets, it continues to contribute to capacity-building of the maritime safety and security agencies of India's maritime neighbours. Over the last two decades, India has gifted two Coast Guard Offshore Patrol Vessels (OPV) to Sri Lanka, two Interceptor Boats (IBs) to Mozambique, and one IB each to Mauritius and Seychelles. We also maintain a Coast Guard Advanced Light Helicopter (ALH) at Gan Island in the Maldives, which is exclusively engaged in SAR and MEDEVAC missions, and provides great succour to far-flung atolls of this archipelagic neighbour of India's. Other, more *impromptu* help is extended to our neighbours on a case-to-case basis, a typical one being the gifting of 1,000 litres of Oil Spill Dispersant to the Maldives, at very short notice, two years ago.

Regardless of the training stretch that we face, we conduct regular training programmes and ship-board attachments for the coast guards and navies of littoral States of India's maritime neighbourhood.

Having mentioned some of the more important initiatives, in order to place the larger canvas in perspective, I offer the following quote of our Hon'ble Prime Minister from his address during IFR 2016:

"The oceans and the world's waterways are global commons. *Vasudhaiva Kutumbakam* **– the concept of the whole world as a family – is perhaps witnessed on the oceans of the planet, that connects us all."**

Non-Hegemonism

India is an avowedly non-hegemonistic nation, which is more than can be said of some other nations. For instance, although the judgement of the tribunal of the Permanent Court of Arbitration (PCA), after the protracted Indo-Bangladesh IMBL dispute hearings under the UNCLOS, went largely against India's interests, our country accepted the ruling graciously. This was a mature reaffirmation of India's policy of settling maritime territorial claims amicably. But above all, it signalled to the world that India abides by a rules-based order and despite being a much larger and more powerful country, would not stoop to elbowing a smaller neighbour or disrespecting any outcome under the UNCLOS.

SAGARMALA

For India to reach out to her neighbours, our own economic foundations in the maritime domain need to first be strengthened. The SAGARMALA Project was approved by the Indian Government on 25 Mar 2016. Under this project, a National Perspective Plan (NPP) has been prepared for the comprehensive development of India's coastal infrastructure and the maritime sector as a whole. With four major components — port modernisation and the development of new Greenfield ports; enhanced port connectivity; port-linked industrialisation, and, coastal community development — the project is likely to have a transformative impact on India's EXIM trade and logistical competitiveness. The SAGARMALA project emanates from India's need to prioritise, and to target gaps in logistic- connectivity, infrastructure and efficiency, thereby laying down a strong foundation for the country's transition to a Blue Economy. Once in place, this will be a major facilitator for furthering relations on all fronts with our maritime neighbours.

India has already begun to lay the groundwork for a robust Blue Economy. In her inaugural address at the Indian Ocean Conference, on 31 Aug 2017, Mrs Sushma Swaraj, Hon'ble Minister of External Affairs, formally affirmed India's engagement of her neighbours through Blue Economy Initiatives. The recent relaxation of India's Cabotage Laws is another positive signal that the Government's focus on ease of doing business has not overlooked the maritime domain.

SAGAR

Given the scale and complexity of extant and future challenges within the maritime domain, maritime stability in the region cannot be the preserve of any single nation. It has to be a shared goal and responsibility of all littoral-States. In March 2015, during his visit to Mauritius, the Hon'ble Prime Minister of India put forth the concept of SAGAR, which is the Hindi word for 'Ocean', and is also an acronym for "Security And Growth for All in the Region". This is a clear, high-level articulation of India's vision for the Indian Ocean, where India is a key pivot, not only geographically, but also by virtue of its shared historical and cultural heritage with most of its maritime neighbours. The key elements of this initiative are enhancing capacities for safeguarding maritime territories and interests, deepening economic and security cooperation, promoting collective action to deal with natural disasters and maritime threats, working towards sustainable regional development through enhanced collaboration, and, engaging with our maritime neighbours with the aim of building greater trust and promoting respect for maritime rules, laws and the peaceful resolution of disputes. SAGAR, in effect, is an extension of the SAGARMALA Project, albeit in the foreign policy domain.

Maritime Domain Awareness (MDA)

After the tragic events of 26/11, India realised the need for 24×7 surveillance against seaborne threats. As a result, we have established a chain of static sensors at 46 locations on the Indian coastline, in order to enhance MDA. In Phase-II of the scheme, an additional 38 radars stations, along with integration of 13 Vessel Traffic Management System (VTMS) sites and 04 Mobile Surveillance Systems, are envisaged.

Other nations, too, are realising that events outside their national waters, especially those in a neighbouring country, can have grave repercussions for them, and that only a neighbouring nation can be a realistic first-responder in any crisis or catastrophe. There are three MDA networks in SE Asia. Two of these — ReCAAP ISC, of which India is a member, and, IMB PRC, Kuala Lumpur — are purely piracy/maritime-robbery-centric. The third, Singapore's 'Information Fusion Centre' (IFC) is the most broad-based and keeps tabs on eight types of maritime security incidents and vessel data. The MDA networks in the IOR are not so formally established and cater only to the piracy-prone and oil-rich Western Indian Ocean. The Djibouti Code of Conduct, though designed to mirror ReCAAP in some ways, is yet to mature fully.

Thus, India and her maritime neighbours fall in a sort of blind spot as far as formal multilateral MDA is concerned. Accordingly, India has taken the lead and installed six radars in Sri Lanka, eight in Mauritius and one in Seychelles. Radars were also planned to be installed in 26 atolls in the Maldives with 10 representing the first phase. However, this project is yet to get underway. India has also offered the radar system to Myanmar, Bangladesh and Thailand and offered to set up a pilot project in one of the Indonesian islands. These radars will be networked with the Indian Coastal Radar System (CRS), centrally coordinated by the Integrated Management and Analysis Centre (IMAC), to enhance regional MDA.

The public nature of the CSR development highlights India's openness about its enduring security interests in the Indian Ocean and its desire to share its capacity and capabilities with her neighbours in ensuring better MDA for the countering of seaborne threats. This is a collaborative exercise with partner countries, which addresses their own maritime security priorities, and, if taken to its logical conclusion and buttressed by other initiatives, could seal India's position as the most significant net provider of MDA in the waters of the Indian Ocean.

China's Influence

No security-centric discussion can be complete without acknowledging the elephant in the room — China. The 'String of Pearls' — which detailed China's dual-use ports and bases in Djibouti, Gwadar, Hambantota, Chittagong, Sittwe, Coco Islands, etc., and which would be eventually used by China to choke India — was a term that was much bandied about till a few years ago. This has now acquired overland linkages and metamorphosed into the Belt and Road Initiative (BRI) or One Belt One

Road (OBOR). Even though many experts dismiss the idea of BRI being a threat, China's intransigence in international disputes, the latest episode of which is playing out in the South China Sea, is something that should never be taken lightly. China, aware of its leverage, is challenging the established world order and aiming to create a structure favourable to its own interests. India cannot — mainly for want of material resources and capital — play the same game. Faced with this, we are at last realising the truth of what Polonius said to Laertes in Shakespeare's Hamlet – *"To thine own self be true, and it shall follow, as the night the day......"* we are now looking inwards in search of answers.

The creation of maritime and infrastructural assets, development of the hinterland, and the provision of last-mile-connectivity to all our VAs and VPs are benefits that are expected to accrue from the SAGARMALA Project. The project will not only lay a strong economic foundation but dual use of the facilities being set up will also stand us in extremely good stead in countering China, from a maritime-security perspective. As a bonus, it could even open up more accessible economic corridors for Nepal and Bhutan and keep Chinese influence at bay and, if the SAGAR vision achieves even half of what it promises, China's hopes of emasculating India within the IOR will never materialise.

Conclusion

India has always taken a moral and principled stand in all matters related to her maritime neighbours. However, till a few year ago its idealism was being construed as weakness—mere lip-service to high sounding ideals, but without much to show on the ground. Until recently, India was seen as being reluctant to take the lead, to assert itself and speak out. Now, however, India seems to be evolving a proactive three-pronged strategy — improving governance and formulating intelligent policies, building human and infrastructural capacities, and, deepening international cooperation.

The earlier pattern of *ad-hoc* and fragmented initiatives in response to perceived threats is transforming into a coherent roadmap. Unlike in the past, our initiatives are not merely reactions to a situation but a well-modulated recognition of the need for a comprehensive maritime plan to secure our strategic interests in the region. Our reaffirmation of positive engagement with our littoral neighbours is far more credible. It is based on mutual respect and consideration but underpinned by a strong economic and regional development agenda.

The country's 'Look East' policy of 1992 has become the far more proactive 'Act East' policy of 2015 and is designed to promote economic cooperation, forge cultural ties and develop strategic relationships with ASEAN countries at the bilateral, trilateral, minilateral, and multilateral levels. The Government has been making concreted efforts to reach out to our neighbours. And the SAGARMALA and SAGAR initiatives are prime examples of this holistic vision.

As Benjamin Disraeli famously said, *"Nations have neither permanent friends nor permanent enemies, only permanent interests"*. So, ensuring a non-hegemonic and inclusive approach to rules-based maritime governance is the *mantra*. We are determined to adopt an approach where the growth-aspirations and economic-imperatives of our neighbours are factored, and where there is realisation that symbiotic efforts at exploration and exploitation of the emerging Blue Economy is the only logical way ahead. And finally, for a 'peaceful periphery', new life must be infused into ongoing multilateral initiatives. It is the transparent, symbiotic, one-on-one bilateral or trilateral interfaces through which we engage our neighbours, which will yield the most significant results.

Thank You and *Jai Hind*

About the Contributors

Swarup S Bangara, Master Mariner. A distinguished and experienced officer of the merchant marine with over five decades of experience to his credit. He currently works as an independent maritime consultant for Sri Lanka, India, Bangladesh and East Africa. He is also the Director of the Tanzania Pacific Logistics Limited company, Tanzania, and a Director at the Bahari Oilfield Services FPZ Limited, Tanzania. He has spent 28 years at sea, and a further 24 years ashore in various senior management positions — as the Owner's Representative and Director of various Liner Shipping Companies and was involved in setting-up offices for major shipping lines in India, Sri Lanka and Bangladesh. During his seagoing service, he has served in India, Europe, and, East Asia. He retired as the Chairman of PIL India Pvt Ltd, a wholly owned subsidiary of Pacific International Lines PTE Ltd, Singapore, which owns and operates 120 container vessels. The Ministry of Shipping had earlier appointed him on the Board of Cochin Port Trust as a Trustee. During this period, Cochin Port Trust was involved in setting up of the International Container Transhipment Terminal (Vallarpadam Container Terminal). He also served as an advisor to the Ministry of Shipping and Education, in Seychelles.

Group Captain AV Chandrasekaran, IAF (Retd.). Gp Capt Chandrasekaran was commissioned in the Indian Air Force in June 1985 and has held various appointments in a career spanning 34 years. The officer is vastly experienced and was deployed on various duties of security, counter intelligence and infrastructure building. He was posted as Chief Administrative officer of a frontline fighter bases, Commanding officer of a counter Intelligence unit In the Jammu & Kashmir sector, was the Staff Officer Provost Training Command Air Force Bangalore, thereby responsible for the physical security of all the Air Force bases in the four southern states. He was also posted in the Andaman & Nicobar Islands to oversee the infrastructure being built to enhance the Indian Air Force's operational capability in the region. He has, in addition, served as an instructor in several prestigious training institutions of the Indian Air Force. The officer has been commended by both, the Chief of Air Staff, and the Air Officer Commanding-in-Chief, Central Command, for operational excellence. The officer retired on 31 July 2018. He has a Masters in Defence Studies from the University of Madras, and had won the coveted Ministry of Defence Gold Medal for being first in the overall order of merit. He also has an M Phil in Defence & Strategic Studies from the University of Madras and is pursuing his PhD in Strategic Studies from the University of Madras. He is a member of the guest faculty of the Department of Defence and Strategic Studies, University of Madras. Group Captain Chandrasekaran has been a Senior Fellow at the Centre for Air Power Studies and has authored a book titled "Insurgency and Counter Insurgency: A Dangerous War of Nerves".

Vice Admiral Pradeep Chauhan, AVSM & Bar, VSM, IN (Retd.), Director-General, National Maritime Foundation. An alumnus of the National Defence Academy, the Defence Services Staff College, the Naval War College, and the National Defence College, with BSc, MSc and MPhil degrees under his belt, Vice Admiral Pradeep Chauhan, AVSM & Bar, VSM, is currently the Director-General of the National Maritime Foundation, New Delhi. The admiral retired on 30 November 2013 after an illustrious four-decade-long career in the Executive Branch of the Indian Navy. His sea-going service incorporated for command tenures, culminating in his command of the aircraft carrier, the Viraat. As a Flag Officer, he was the Navy's first Assistant Chief of the Naval Staff (Foreign Cooperation & Intelligence) and conceptualised and executed the Indian Ocean Naval Symposium (IONS). As a Vice Admiral, he has been Chief of Staff of the Western Naval Command; and was, in his last naval appointment, the Commandant of the Indian Naval Academy (Ezhimala). He has been commended three times by the President of India for sustained distinguished service. Not one to rest on past laurels, he has remained active even after retirement and is a much sought-after thought-leader, leadership mentor, and a globally renowned maritime analyst. He is a visiting faculty at all Service-specific and tri-Service higher-command establishments in the country, as also the National Defence College. He is, in addition, a prolific writer with over 85 published professional articles and papers, and, a respected Adviser and Fellow of several important think-tanks.

Commodore Sushant Dam, VSM, IN, Director, Maritime Warfare Centre (Visakhapatnam) and Centre of Excellence (China Maritime Studies). An alumnus of the National Defence Academy, Cmde Dam was commissioned into the Indian Navy in 1987. As a Gunnery and Missile Warfare specialist, he has served aboard major indigenously-built frontline surface combatants — including the guided-missile frigate, INS Gomati, and the guided-missile destroyer, INS Delhi. The officer has commanded the Mine Countermeasures Vessel, INS Cuddalore, the guided-missile corvette INS Kirch, the Navy's premier shore-establishment for gunnery and missile warfare training, INS Dronacharya, and, the guided-missile destroyer INS Delhi. He has also served as the Fleet Gunnery Officer, and, later, as the Fleet Operations Officer of the Western Fleet. Cmde Dam has undergone his staff course at the Naval War College, Newport, USA, and the Higher Command Course at the Naval War College in India. Prior to taking-up his current assignment, he was appointed as the first Naval Attaché in the Embassy of India in Beijing. He also heads the Centre of Excellence (China Maritime Studies) and NMF-coordination at Visakhapatnam and actively participates in all China-related conferences and seminars. Cmde Sushant Dam was formally commended by the Chief of the Naval Staff in 1997, and by the President of India, from whom he received a Vishist Seva Medal in the year 2013.

Dr. Binoda Kumar Mishra, Director of the Centre for Studies in International Relations and Development (CSIRD). Dr Mishra holds a PhD from the School of International Studies, Jawaharlal Nehru University, New Delhi. Prior to this, he worked as a Fellow at the Maulana Abul Kalam Azad Institute of Asian Studies, Kolkata, and taught Political Science under Burdwan University, West Bengal. His current research-focus is the India-China relationship in the larger regional context. His research areas include traditional and non-traditional security issues, Indian foreign policy, development issues, and, diaspora studies. Dr Mishra was part of the Track II BCIM process and serves as the Secretary General of the only Sub-regional Civilian initiative between India and China, namely the Kolkata-to-Kunming (K2K) Forum. He also coordinates research on the Bay of Bengal Initiative for Multi-sectoral, Technical and Economic Cooperation (BIMSTEC). He has published widely on international relations and regional cooperation, both in India and abroad.

Major General G Murali, Indian Army (Retd.). An alumnus of the National Defence Academy, Maj Gen G Murali was commissioned in the Regiment of Artillery in 1977. His foundational military leadership was imbibed at the NDA, and was built-upon in his military career, which provided him with rich experience in a variety of operational situations and formal training and admirably equipped him for the command of troops, honing his authority and decision-making abilities in a carrier that spanned 38 years. Important experiences in his career inlude the induction of the Bofors guns into the Indian Artillery, the planning and execution of logistic operations of a Strike Corps in Op PARAKRAM, and heading the Information Warfare Team of the Northern Army. Maj Gen Murali has headed the planning, negotiating and finalising of Project Battle Field Surveillance System for artillery. He acquired a Masters and an MPhil degree in Defence and Strategic Studies from the Madras University. He retired as Deputy Commandant and Chief Instructor of the Officers Training Academy, Chennai. He is currently pursuing his doctoral research on Kautilya's Arthashastra.

Lt Gen S.L. Narasimhan, PVSM, AVSM, VSM, Indian Army (Retd.), Director-General, Centre for Contemporary China Studies. The General Officer is a retired Infantryman, who was commissioned in 1977. He has done his graduation in Mathematics, his post-Graduation in Defence Studies, and, holds a PhD in India-China Relations. Lt Gen Narasimhan has seen action in Operation PAWAN in 1987 in Sri Lanka and has vast experience in counter-insurgency operations, operations on the Line of Actual Control, and in high-altitude areas. He has been honoured by the President of India on four occasions for his outstanding contribution to the Indian Army. General Narasimhan has wide-ranging experience in various high-profile command, staff and instructional appointments in the Indian Army and has been an instructor in the Indian Military Training Team in Bhutan. He has been an avid China watcher for the last 18 years. Lt Gen Narasimhan served as the Defence Attaché in the Embassy of India in China for three years. He is a qualified Chinese language speaker. His expertise spans international relations and internal issues, economy and defence-related subjects of China. Gen Narasimhan has taken part in many Track-2 dialogues, both in India and abroad. He has authored numerous articles in various journals and magazines. He is, presently, a member of the National Security Advisory Board, India, and is also a Distinguished Fellow with the Centre for Air Power Studies, India.

S. Parmesh, PTM, TM, Inspector General, ICG. The Flag Officer is an alumnus of the Defence Services Staff College, Wellington, and the National Defence College, New Delhi. His professional career is studded with achievements and he has a proven track record of outstanding and meritorious performance in all appointments that he has tenanted. He has, over the last three decades, served in various capacities in ashore and afloat appointments of the Indian Coast Guard, with distinction. The IG specialised in Navigation & Direction and his sea commands have included all major vessels of the ICG, including the Advanced Offshore Patrol Vessel Samar and the Offshore Patrol Vessel Vishwast. His key staff assignments include Deputy Director-General (Operations & Coastal Security), Principal Director (Operations) at the Coast Guard Headquarters, New Delhi, and, Chief Staff Officer (Operations) at the Coast Guard Regional Headquarters (East), Chennai. He is a recipient of the President's Tatrakshak Medal (Distinguished Service), Tatrakshak Medal and was also awarded the Director General Coast Guard Commendation in 2012, and the FOC-in-C (East) Commendation in 2009.

Rahul Karan Reddy. Rahul is a former Research Officer at the Chennai Centre for China Studies. He completed his BA in International Relations from FLAME University, Pune. Foreign policy, security studies and domestic politics are his main areas of interest. His focus is on completing a post-graduate programme and working with a policy group that studies Asian geopolitics, and China, in particular. He would like to work on this issue and produce literature and research that has a problem-solving outlook.

B.S. Raghavan, IAS (Retd.), Patron, Chennai Centre for China Studies. Mr Raghavan is an extremely distinguished and accomplished civil servant. He joined the IAS (West Bengal cadre) in 1952 and has been the Commissioner of various Departments. He also served as the Chief Secretary of Tripura. He has been the Director (Political and Security Policy Planning) in the Union Home Ministry, and, the Secretary, National Integration Council during the period of the first four Prime Ministers. He is a former a US Congressional Fellow, former Policy Advisor to the UN (FAO), and has been the Chairman of three UN Committees. He has tenanted the offices of Chief Secretary, State Governments of West Bengal and Tripura, and, Secretary to the Union Ministry of Food and Agriculture, Government of India. He has also been the Chief Executive Officer of four major public sector enterprises. He is now a columnist and author, connected with social service and educational organisations.

C.V. Ranganathan, IFS (Retd.), Vice President, Chennai Centre for China Studies; Chairman, Asia Centre Bengaluru, and, former Ambassador of India. Having graduated with honours in Economics from the Madras University, Mr Ranganathan joined the Indian Foreign Service in 1959. Posted to Hong Kong to learn the Chinese language, he earned a diploma (with Honours) from Hong Kong University, in 1962. He has had several postings in the Ministry of External Affairs in Delhi, including as Joint Secretary in charge of Northern and East Asia Divisions. He has been India's High Commissioner of India to Hong Kong, Ambassador of India to Ethiopia, Deputy Chief-of-Mission (in the rank of Ambassador) in Moscow, Ambassador of India to China, and, Ambassador of India to France. He was also a Counsellor in the Permanent Mission of India to the UN for three years. He was the Convenor of the National Security Advisory Board in 2002 and 2003. An Emeritus Fellow of the Institute of Chinese Studies, he has co-authored a book, "India and China — the Way Ahead", along with former Ambassador VC Khanna; edited a book on the "18th Congress of the Communist Party of China" along with Dr Sanjeev Kumar under the auspices of the Indian Council of World Affairs; and another titled, "China and the Eurasian Region" also with Dr Sanjeev Kumar and with support from the Indian Council for World Affairs (ICWA).

Dr. Yugraj Singh Yadava. Director of the Bay of Bengal Programme Inter-Governmental Organisation (BOBP-IGO), Project Manager of the GEF/World Bank Project on 'Ocean Partnerships for Sustainable Fisheries and Biodiversity Conservation', operating in the Bay of Bengal Region. Dr Yadava is the former Fisheries Development Commissioner to the Government of India. In mid-2000, he joined the Food and Agriculture Organization (FAO) of the United Nations in its field programme, 'The Bay of Bengal Programme', and continued to stay with it after its conversion into an Intergovernmental Organisation. Dr Yadava has worked in several projects supported by UN Organizations (UNDP, IMO, WMO, UNESCO, UINTAR); international donor-agencies (Sida, GIZ); and, through bilateral arrangements with other Governments, (Centre for Disease Control, US; Ministry of Agriculture, Forestry and Fisheries, Government of Japan). Besides working in the BOBP-IGO member-countries (Bangladesh, India, Maldives, Sri Lanka), Dr Yadava has also worked in the Philippines, Indonesia, Thailand, and Vietnam, under a project funded by Japan to strengthen fisheries cooperatives in these countries. He has played a key role in the setting-up of the BOBP-IGO; the establishment of the FAO's Sub-Committee on Aquaculture, and, FAO's Voluntary Guidelines on Small-scale Fisheries, an international instrument guiding the development of small-scale fisheries across the world.

Editors.

Vice Admiral Pradeep Chauhan, AVSM & Bar, VSM, IN (Retd.), Director-General, National Maritime Foundation. (Bio-data already provided)

Commodore R. Seshadri Vasan, IN (Retd.), Regional Director, National Maritime Foundation, Tamil Nadu Chapter; and: Director, Chennai Centre for China Studies. An alumnus of the Defence Services Staff College, the Naval War College, and the International Visitor Leadership Programme, Commodore Seshadri Vasan has rendered distinguished service in the Navy and the Coast Guard, spanning over 34 years. His uniformed appointments include the sea-going command of warships, two major air stations, and, a maritime air squadron. He has participated both, in the 1971 India-Pakistan Conflict and in the IPKF operations. He has been an instructor at the Naval War College, India. Prior to his retirement, he was the Regional Commander of the Indian Coast Guard Region (East), overseeing EEZ patrols, search-and-rescue missions, anti-piracy operations, fisheries-protection, maritime border-control, marine pollution-prevention, and other maritime tasks in the Bay of Bengal. After his retirement he has enriched several think-tanks and is a regular speaker at many international and national conferences and seminars. He has a number of publications to his credit in a variety of journals, websites, edited books and the print-media. Think thanks in which he has worked include the Observer Research Foundation (ORF) where he steered the Maritime Security Programme, and the Centre for Asia Studies where he was the Head, Strategy and Security Studies. Currently, he is the Director of the Chennai Centre of China Studies; the Director of the Asian Bureau of Worldborderpol, and, the Regional Director of the National Maritime Foundation (Tamil Nadu Chapter). He is also a member of the visiting faculty at the Indian Maritime University, the Academy of Maritime Education and Training, the Great Lakes Institute of Management, and, the Hindustan Institute of Engineering Technology. He is also on the Board of Advisors at the Madras University, and the Stella Maris College.

Rishi Athreya. An alumnus of Flinders University, Adelaide and University of Leeds, wherein he acquired advanced degrees in International Relations and Development Studies, Rishi is a Public Sector and Political-Risk Consultant. He holds a Certificate in Consulting from the United Kingdom's Chartered Management Institute. He has worked in academic research within the public sector, as also international organisations, in the fields of consulting and risk analysis. He has served in the Governance Division of the Commonwealth Secretariat, where he worked on Public Sector Reform, and Democracy. He has rendered yeoman service in the areas of development assistance and technical cooperation. Mr Athreya is a widely published author and has written on various topics related to governance, security and diplomacy. He has also been the editor of several publications published by international organisations, thank-tanks and legislatures. His co-authors have included, amongst others, civil servants, officers of the defence services, and diplomats.